D0705743

How Insurance Works

Barry D. Smith
Eric A. Wiening

Second Edition • 1994

Insurance Institute of America
720 Providence Road
Malvern, Pennsylvania 19355-0716

Chapter 6 of this text includes copyrighted material
of Insurance Services Office, Inc., with its permission. Copyright Insurance Services Office, Inc., 1994.

Photographs by Kent Vann.

Second Edition • Second Printng • July 1997

Library of Congress Catalog Number 93-80121
International Standard Book Number 0-89462-080-0

Printed in the United States of America

In Appreciation

The first edition of this book was made possible through a gift from the son and daughter of the late Sydney B. Palley.

Sid Palley earned his CPCU designation in 1956 and devoted his entire career to furthering the professionalism of the insurance industry. He was particularly dedicated to encouraging young people to enter the insurance field and promoting their advancement through education.

The development of this book as a tribute to his memory would have given him great pleasure.

Foreword

The American Institute for Chartered Property Casualty Underwriters and the Insurance Institute of America are independent, nonprofit, educational organizations serving the needs of the property and liability insurance business. The Institutes develop a wide range of programs—curricula, study materials, and examinations—in response to the educational requirements of various elements of the business.

The American Institute confers the Chartered Property Casualty Underwriter (CPCU®) professional designation on those who meet the Institute's experience, ethics, and examination requirements.

The Insurance Institute of America offers associate designations and certificate programs in the following technical and managerial disciplines:

Accredited Adviser in Insurance (AAI®)
Associate in Claims (AIC)
Associate in Underwriting (AU)
Associate in Risk Management (ARM)
Associate in Loss Control Management (ALCM®)
Associate in Premium Auditing (APA®)
Associate in Management (AIM)
Associate in Research and Planning (ARP®)
Associate in Insurance Accounting and Finance (AIAF)
Associate in Automation Management (AAM®)
Associate in Marine Insurance Management (AMIM®)
Associate in Reinsurance (ARe)
Associate in Fidelity and Surety Bonding (AFSB)
Certificate in General Insurance
Certificate in Supervisory Management
Certificate in Introduction to Claims
Certificate in Introduction to Property and Liability Insurance
Certificate in Business Writing

The Institutes began publishing textbooks in 1976 to help students meet the national examination standards. Since that time, we have produced more than eighty individual textbook volumes. Despite the vast differences in the subjects and purposes of these volumes, they all have much in common. First, each book is specifically designed to increase knowledge and develop skills that can improve job performance and help students achieve the educational objectives of the course for which it is assigned. Second, all of the manuscripts of our texts are widely reviewed before publication, by both insurance business practitioners and members of the academic community. In addition, all of our texts and course guides reflect the work of Institute staff members. These writing or editing duties are seen as an integral part of their professional responsibilities, and no one earns a royalty based on the sale of our texts. We have proceeded in this way to avoid even the appearance of any conflict of interests. Finally, the revisions of our texts often incorporate improvements suggested by students and course leaders.

We welcome criticisms of and suggestions for improving our publications. It is only with such constructive comments that we can hope to improve the quality of our study materials. Please direct any comments you may have on this text to the Curriculum Department of the Institutes.

Norman A. Baglini, Ph.D., CPCU, CLU
President and Chief Executive Officer

Preface

This is no ordinary "introduction to insurance" textbook. Introductory insurance textbooks normally explain insurance principles and describe insurance policies. *How Insurance Works* tells the story of people—insurance people, the people who make property-liability insurance work. A large, complicated, automated business, insurance works only because so many people bring together a wide range of skills, experiences, talents, and responsibilities.

Like many other books, *How Insurance Works* can simply be read by itself. However, it was created as the key component of an Insurance Institute of America (IIA) course, Introduction to Property and Liability Insurance, better known as INTRO. Other components of the INTRO course include the *INTRO Course Guide* (a workbook) and the INTRO national exam. The national exam may be scheduled on any date. Those who pass the national exam are awarded a certificate of completion.

This book uses a story line involving insurance people at work. During the story, readers encounter many insurance principles that are then examined. But the story-line approach is not merely a gimmick to tie together a set of principles. The dynamic approach of this book helps the reader to understand the many human interactions that take place in insurance, involving several different people in even the most simple insurance transaction. The reader should gain a solid appreciation not only of many basic principles, but also of *how*—and even *why*—insurance works.

The first edition of this book (1984) was truly a pioneering effort that explored new frontiers. The authors (Barry D. Smith, primary author, and Eric A. Wiening, contributing author) began with a clear goal but only a faint vision as to how that goal might be met. The overall goal was to develop a self-standing, complete book that would provide a down-to-earth, practical understanding of property and liability insurance. Our plan was not to present theories about how insurance *should* work, but rather to describe accurately how insurance *does* work—and how insurance changes and evolves from day to day.

We had in mind two specific educational objectives that would be tested on the INTRO national exam: Students would understand the big picture of how property-liability insurance works, and they would understand how insurance jobs relate to one another. We also had several important additional goals: We intended to help each reader working in insurance understand how he or she fits into the big picture and how his or her work interrelates with the work of others. Above all, we wanted readers to share the positive experience that surrounds insurance work. The secret that insurance work can be exciting, dynamic, and rewarding is too well kept. Insurance work is rewarding in two ways—it leads to fulfilling careers, and it involves serving many important personal and business needs.

A major challenge resulted from the need to keep this book simple without sacrificing accuracy, and it was rewarding to meet that challenge with few compromises. We discovered that it is much easier to discuss complicated insurance concepts (with more exceptions than rules) at an advanced level than it is to explain them at a level appropriate for this book.

The first edition of this book was well received and widely used. Now, nearly ten years after it was introduced, well over 100,000 copies of the first edition are in print. Surprisingly, perhaps, nearly all the technical information remained accurate and timely over the years, but the 1984 text gradually began to show its age. Perhaps the most obvious sign of aging involved the once-stylish haircuts in the photographs. And so the time came to produce a second edition.

This revision has challenged us to make updates and improvements without impairing the unique qualities that made this text such a success. The look in this edition is substantially different, partly because of new publishing technology. The pictures involve '90s people with '90s haircuts, and a number of recent cartoons have been added. Many minor details have been updated to reflect the increasing use of automation in insurance. And we've introduced many editorial changes—and some substantive changes—to make the book even clearer. The most noteworthy changes involve the last two chapters, largely reflecting the shift to loss-cost rating and changes in the insurance environment. Nearly every paragraph has been improved in some way. Yet, for the most part, the substance of this course remains unchanged.

We are indebted to the following people who critically reviewed major portions of the manuscripts for this revision:

Michael M. Barth, Ph.D., CPCU, AU
Senior Research Associate
National Association of Insurance Commissioners (NAIC)

Catherine A. Brown, CPCU, AIM
Assistant Vice President and Director of Development and Education
Transamerica Insurance Group

Robert M. Burger, Ph.D., CPCU, AAI
Assistant Vice President
American Institute for CPCU

Robert J. Gibbons, Ph.D., CPCU, CLU
Vice President
American Institute for CPCU

Steven M. Horner, CPCU, CLU, AIM, ARM
Assistant Vice President
Harleysville Insurance Companies

Richard A. Litchford, III, CPCU
Claims Supervisor
Harleysville Mutual Insurance Companies

Bernard P. Mackowski, CPCU
Supervisor, Educational Services Section
Erie Insurance Group

James J. Markham, J.D., CPCU, AIC, AIAF
Vice President
American Institute for CPCU

Elan B. Morrison
Senior Fire Underwriter
State Farm Insurance Companies

Edwin S. Overman, Ph.D., CPCU
President Emeritus
American Institute for CPCU

Edward F. Oxner, CPCU, AIC
Senior Claims Representative
The Simkiss Agency, Inc.

George E. Rejda, Ph.D., CLU
V.J. Skutt Distinguished Professor of Insurance
University of Nebraska

Mark R. Wiening
Student
Henderson High School

We are also grateful to David G. Sterling, CPCU, CLU, ChFC, AIM, ARM, AU, ALCM, APA, AAI, ARP, AIC, CIC, Secretary, ITT Hartford, for arranging reviews by the following ITT Hartford employees in their areas of specialty:

Ray Denny, CPCU, AMIM
Marine Director

James W. Gray
Assistant Secretary, Personal Lines

Bruce D. Hale, CPCU
Staff Assistant to the Chairman

Marcia S. Kulak, CPCU, AIC, ARM, CIC
Senior Claims Supervisor
Hartford Environmental Facility

Douglas P. Mantz, CPCU
Account Executive, Commercial Risk Management

Douglas M. Morrill, CPCU, ARM
Director, Commercial Mass Marketing

J. Brian Murphy, CPCU, ARe
Director of Catastrophe Underwriting

Jeffrey G. Olmstead, CPCU
Associate Director, Property Line of Business

David J. Swanson, AIAF
Director, Business Development and Administration

At least one other book is also titled *How Insurance Works*—a book by R. R. Swatton, under the general editorship of Derek Walker-Smith, M.P., first published in London in 1948. In a foreword to that work, Mr. Walker-Smith included these thoughts: "This book is designed to bring understanding to the insured, as well as to provide for the apprentice or intending insurer an introduction to his calling....The practice of insurance grew out of the needs of seafaring merchants, hardly the least adventurous of mankind. Where there is no risk there need be no insurance. Where there is insurance, more risks can be taken. Insurance, therefore, is not only the guardian of security; it is also the friend of adventure." Like Mr. Walker-Smith, we invite modern insurance students to experience the adventure of insurance.

Barry D. Smith, Ph.D., CPCU, CLU, FLMI
Eric A. Wiening, CPCU, ARM, AU

Contents

Underwriting the Allied Manufacturing Submission ~ *Gathering the Necessary Information; Analyzing the Information; Identifying Underwriting Options; Evaluating the Options; Choosing the Best Option; Acting on the Decision*

The Home Office Underwriting Department ~ *Obtaining Final Approval; Line and Staff Underwriting Activities*

Underwriting the Personal Auto Application

What If the Underwriter Says No? ~ *Automobile Insurance Plans; FAIR Plans*

Summary

Chapter 4—How Is Insurance Service Provided? 49

Completing the Sale ~ *The Quote; The Insurance Proposal; Preparing To Present the Insurance Proposal; Presenting the Proposal; Concluding the Sale*

Policy Issue and Delivery ~ *The Insurance Company Issues the Policy; The Producer Delivers the Policy*

Billing ~ *Producer Billing; Direct Billing*

Policy Changes ~ *Changes Involving No Adjustment to the Premium; Changes Requiring a Premium Adjustment*

Loss Control Service

Policy Renewal ~ *Policy Renewal: The Underwriter's Perspective; Policy Renewal: The Producer's Perspective; Policy Renewal: The Insured's Perspective; The Renewal*

Premium Auditing

Summary

Chapter 5—How Are Claims Handled? 67

The Role of the Claims Adjuster

Notifying the Insurer ~ *The Producer's Responsibility; The Notification*

Types of Adjusters ~ *Insurance Company Claims Representatives; Independent Adjusters; Producers as Adjusters*

The Claim Is Assigned to an Adjuster

Verifying Coverage

Investigating the Accident

The Loss Reserve

The Investigation Continues

Summary

Chapter 6—What Is Found in an Insurance Policy? 87

Types of Insurance Policy Provisions ~ *Declarations; Insuring Agreement; Exclusions; Conditions; Definitions; Miscellaneous Provisions*

Arrangement of Policy Provisions

Using an Insurance Policy

Chapter 10—How Are Premiums Determined? 165

Chapter 11—Insurance in a Changing World 185

Glossary 203
Index 223

What Is Insurance?

Try to imagine how the modern world would strike Benjamin Franklin if he were to come back to life. Pretend you are among a group of tourists visiting Independence Hall and the Liberty Bell in "Old Philadelphia." Suddenly, Benjamin Franklin emerges from a nearby subway exit, squinting and shielding his eyes against the sunlight.

He looks around. He sees Independence Hall, a familiar sight to a signer of the Declaration of Independence. But the backdrop is bewildering: autos, skyscrapers reaching for the clouds, traffic signals, and the bridge named in Ben's honor visible in the distance, stretching across the Delaware River toward New Jersey.

Ben is stunned and speechless.

But once the initial shock passes and he regains his speech, Ben's curiosity takes over and he has many questions. Ben would probably first ask about things that concerned him in his lifetime. The man famous for his experiments with kite and key would be fascinated by the widespread use of electricity. The founder of the University of Pennsylvania would be full of questions about the state of public education and our colleges and universities. The former printer's apprentice and publisher of *Poor Richard's Almanack* would burst with interest in modern journalism—newspapers, magazines, TV, and radio. He would also want to know how the U.S. Constitution has held up.

And Ben would want to know about insurance. After all, he was active in establishing volunteer fire companies to protect lives and homes against losses caused by fires. He also has a modest place in the history of insurance in America as one of the founders of the first successful fire insurance company in the New World. The Philadelphia Contributionship for the Insurance of Houses from Loss by Fire was organized in 1752, and it is still operating today.

As a newcomer to today's world of insurance, Ben would have many questions. As a founding father of insurance in America, his first question would most likely be:

DID INSURANCE EVER CATCH ON?

The answer to this question is "yes." The insurance business in the United States today has more than 6,000 insurance companies holding more than $2 trillion in assets. More than 2 million people are employed in insurance agencies, companies, independent claims adjusting firms, and other organizations.

An **insurance company**, also known as an insurer, sells insurance policies that protect insureds against financial hardship caused by financial losses. As explained later in this chapter, insurers accept the risks of insureds, collect premiums, and pay losses.

Insurance people are no longer in the business of forming fire brigades to put out fires at members' homes, as they did in Franklin's day. But the idea of combining resources to protect against loss is still basic to the insurance business.

An **insured** is a person, business, or organization that is covered by an insurance policy.

An **insurance premium** is a periodic payment by the insured to the insurance company in exchange for insurance coverage.

Insurance companies are now financial institutions. They sell insurance policies to protect people against financial hardship caused by accidental losses. The insurance company is an **insurer.** A person, business, or organization that is covered, or "insured," by an insurance policy is referred to as an **insured.**

To purchase an insurance policy and become an insured, an insurance buyer pays a fee, called an **insurance premium**, to the insurance company. To keep the insurance policy in effect, the insured pays more premiums at periodic intervals.

The insurance company pools these premiums to form a fund from which those insureds who suffer losses—unfortunate victims of fires, auto accidents, tornadoes, and so on—can be reimbursed. Each insured pays a relatively small amount (the premium) into the pool. These relatively small premiums, added together, develop a sizable fund from which payments are made to compensate the insureds who have losses. In this way, for a reasonable cost, each insured can be sure that a loss will not cause undue financial hardship.

Insurance is a system by which a **risk** is **transferred** by a person, business, or organization to an insurance company, which reimburses the insured for covered losses and provides for **sharing** the costs of losses among all insureds.

WHAT IS INSURANCE?

Insurance is a system by which a risk is transferred by a person, business, or organization to an insurance company, which reimburses the insured for covered losses and provides for sharing the costs of losses among all insureds. Risk, transfer, and sharing are vital elements of insurance.

Risk

Risk can be defined as the possibility of financial loss.

Everyone is subject to many risks all the time; there is always the possibility of financial loss caused by death, a house fire, an auto accident, a lawsuit, and so on. Insurance helps reduce uncertainty about the possibility of financial losses.

> **Risk** is the possibility of financial loss.

Transfer

Through insurance, a risk (possibility of financial loss) is transferred from an insured to an insurance company. For instance, a homeowner faces the possibility of loss through fire damage to the home. By buying insurance, the homeowner transfers this risk to an insurance company.

> **Transfer and Sharing: An Example**
>
> Donald pays $1,000 to insure his car for one year. He wants insurance because he knows that an auto accident could cause him a large financial loss. Fortunately, Donald has no accidents.
>
> Jonathan also pays $1,000 to insure his car. During a rainstorm, his car skids into another car, and he is injured. Jonathan's auto insurance pays $2,250 to repair his car, $4,200 to repair the other car, and $5,000 for Jonathan's medical bills.
>
> Jonathan's insurance company can pay this loss because it has collected adequate premiums from Donald and many other insureds who did not have losses. Donald, Jonathan, and all of the other insureds were willing to pay a premium to transfer risks to the insurance company. In effect, all of the premiums went into a pool from which Jonathan's loss was paid; in this sense, Donald and others shared the cost of Jonathan's loss.

By transferring risks to insurance companies, insureds exchange the possibility of large losses with potentially devastating financial effects for smaller, certain, manageable costs (insurance premiums). Risks are transferred to insurance companies by use of insurance policies (sometimes called insurance contracts). The **insurance policy** is a contract that states the rights and duties of the insurance company (the insurer) and the insured.

> The **insurance policy** is a contract that states the rights and duties of the insurance company and the insured.

Sharing

In effect, insureds share the costs of one another's losses. They pay premiums to the insurance company, which pools the premiums into a large fund. Insureds who suffer losses are paid from this pool of money. The total cost of paying for losses that occur to relatively few insureds is spread among all members of the group. Sharing the cost among all insureds makes each insured's premium relatively small.

WHO BUYS INSURANCE?

This is another question Ben Franklin would probably ask if he should suddenly find himself in the modern world. The answer is "almost everyone." Most people have *property and liability insurance*. Most are covered by *health insurance* or some other plan. Most people are covered by *life insurance*. Nearly all workers and their dependents are protected by *Social Security,* and many are also entitled to benefits under *private retirement plans.*

Property and Liability Insurance

Every person who owns a home faces two major types of accidental financial loss. *Property losses* can be covered by property insurance, and *liability losses* can be covered by liability insurance.

A home could be destroyed partially or totally by a fire, tornado, explosion, or some other cause. The cost of repairing or replacing the home and its contents could easily amount to thousands of dollars. Damage to or destruction of a home and its contents is a property loss—the subject of property insurance. **Property insurance** covers accidental losses resulting from damage to property of the insured. If the loss is covered by the insurance policy, the payment is made directly to the insured.

Property insurance covers accidental losses resulting from damage to property of the insured. If the loss is covered by the insurance policy, the payment is made directly to the insured.

Also, a person could cause bodily injury to another person and be held legally responsible for the costs of that injury—for example, if a guest trips over a loose rug and falls down the stairway. One might also cause accidental damage to somebody else's property—for example, if a trash fire gets out of control and ignites a neighbor's garage. The costs of the injured guest's medical expenses and the costs of repairing or replacing the neighbor's garage are liability losses—the subject of liability insurance. **Liability insurance** covers accidental losses resulting from injury to the body or damage to the property of someone else for which the insured is legally responsible (legally liable). If the loss is covered by the insurance policy, the payment is made directly to the party who suffered the loss.

Liability insurance covers accidental losses resulting from injury to the body or damage to the property of someone else for which the insured is legally responsible (legally liable). If the loss is covered by the insurance policy, the payment is made directly to the party that suffered the loss

Likewise, a business—an auto manufacturer, for example—faces two major ways of suffering severe accidental financial loss:
- The manufacturer owns buildings, equipment, raw materials, and other assets necessary for the production of its products. The firm

needs to be protected against loss to this property by fire, earthquake, vandalism, and other causes. The costs of repairing or replacing a destroyed factory and its equipment could drive the manufacturer out of business. Rather than being constantly faced with the possibility of a large property loss, the manufacturer purchases *property insurance.* A loss can still occur, but the financial burden of it is transferred to the insurance company.

- If defects in the manufacturer's autos cause damage to someone else's property or bodily injury, the manufacturer could be held legally liable for the costs of such damage or injury. To avoid the possibility of paying legal liability claims, the manufacturer purchases *liability insurance.*

The United States insurance-buying public spends well over $200 billion annually in property and liability insurance premiums. This total is divided almost equally between (1) individuals and families, and (2) businesses and other organizations.

Health Insurance

Health insurance is like property and liability insurance in one way: The insured event (accident or sickness) might or might not occur. **Health insurance** provides two major types of benefits: payment of medical costs (hospital bills, doctors' fees, and so on) and disability income (monthly income to disabled workers during their disability).

> **Health insurance** provides two major types of benefits: payment of medical costs and disability income.

©Mell Lazarus. By permission of Mell Lazarus and Creators Syndicate.

Life Insurance

Even though death is certain, there is still a related risk: The date when a person will die cannot be predicted accurately. **Life insurance** is mainly designed to provide funds to survivors to ease the financial problems that result from a person's death. These problems include medical bills of the final illness, funeral expenses, loss of income (if the person who died was employed), child-care expenses, and college costs for the children of the person who died.

> **Life insurance** pays funds to ease the financial problems that arise from uncertainty regarding the timing of death.

Social Security

Social Security is a federal insurance program that provides four different benefit programs to individuals and families in the United States. Social Security is primarily funded by taxes that are paid by employees, employers, and the self-employed.

The best known Social Security benefit is the retirement program, which provides monthly income payments to people who have reached retirement age. A second program pays monthly benefits to the dependent survivors of workers who die before retirement. A third program provides a monthly income to workers who become disabled. The final program is Medicare, which provides health care benefits for people age sixty-five and older.

Social Security is a federal insurance program that provides (1) monthly income to retired people, (2) monthly income to the dependent survivors of workers who die before retirement, (3) monthly income to disabled workers, and (4) Medicare health care benefits to people age sixty-five and older.

Private Retirement Plans

Although life insurance involves the risk that a person might die earlier than expected, retirement involves the risk that a person might live longer than expected. Most people want to live a long time, but those who do face the risk that they might run out of money before they die.

Private **retirement plans**, including employer-sponsored pension plans and individual annuities, provide an income for people who retire. Plans that guarantee an income for life, no matter how long the person may live, are provided through life insurance companies.

Most employers provide their employees with retirement plans that guarantee an income for life. Many retirement plans are operated by life insurance companies. Life insurance companies also sell annuities, which guarantee a life income to the annuitant.

Private retirement plans supplement the retirement income provided by Social Security because most people are not able to retire comfortably on Social Security payments alone.

All states require employers to provide two other insurance benefits to their employees: workers compensation and unemployment insurance.

Reprinted by permission: Tribune Media Services.

Health insurance, life insurance, and retirement plans are often provided as employee benefits.

Workers compensation will be described in some detail in a later chapter; unemployment insurance provides temporary income after an employee is laid off from a job.

Health insurance, life insurance, and retirement plans are often provided as employee benefits with all or part of the cost paid by the employer. This is the last time we will discuss Social Security, retirement plans, life and health insurance, or unemployment insurance. The rest of this book will deal exclusively with property and liability insurance.

Ben Franklin was a frugal man. If he knew that over $200 billion is spent on property and liability insurance annually, he would probably wonder whether people were getting their money's worth. He might wonder whether society as a whole receives benefits in proportion to the amount of money spent on insurance. The next question he would likely ask is:

HOW DOES INSURANCE HELP SOCIETY?

Insurance helps society by reimbursing people and businesses for covered losses, encouraging accident prevention, providing funds for investment, enabling people to borrow money, and reducing anxiety.

Payment of Losses

The major benefit of insurance is the indemnification of insureds for their covered losses. An important role of insurance is to **indemnify** people, businesses, and organizations so that they can maintain their economic position and not be a burden to others. When a family's house is destroyed by fire and the loss is covered by insurance, the family is less dependent on relatives or public assistance for lodging. Likewise, when a business is covered for a large liability loss that would have otherwise driven the firm into bankruptcy, insurance contributes to society because the firm continues to provide jobs for its workers, products for its customers, and business for its suppliers.

> To **indemnify** is to restore the party that has had a loss to the same financial position as before the loss occurred.

Accident Prevention

Insurance exists to pay the losses that result from accidents. Insurance companies are naturally interested in lowering the costs of accidental losses. Insurance companies, or insurers, engage in a variety of accident prevention activities that lower accident costs by preventing accidents from happening. Insurers also work to reduce the effects of accidents that occur despite attempts to prevent them. Society benefits when losses are controlled—lives are saved, and property is preserved. Insurers and related organizations employ thousands of safety engineers, loss control representa-

ZIGGY copyright ZIGGY AND FRIENDS, INC. Dist. by UNIVERSAL PRESS SYNDICATE. Reprinted with permission. All rights reserved.

tives, and other specialists to help prevent auto accidents, fires, job injuries, injuries caused by defective products, explosions, and other accidental losses.

Investment in the Economy

Insurance provides funds to help businesses grow and create jobs. Premium funds that are not immediately needed are lent to businesses and people, providing them with the means to purchase buildings, equipment, and supplies. Compared to less-developed countries, the United States enjoys a higher standard of living, partly because these funds are available from insurance companies.

Support for Credit

Most banks require property insurance on a home before they will lend money to help the buyer pay for the home. Likewise, a business applying for a loan to purchase inventory might be required to show that the inventory is insured before the loan is granted. These examples illustrate the importance of insurance to the use of credit in our economy.

Reduction in Anxiety

Anxiety is reduced if the insured knows insurance will provide indemnification when a loss occurs. Even if a loss never occurs, insurance reduces worry.

WHAT DO INSURANCE COMPANIES DO WITH THE PREMIUMS THEY COLLECT?

At this point, Ben Franklin has a better understanding of the types of insurance available and the importance of insurance in society. Recalling the insurance business of his day, he asks, "What do insurance companies do with all the money they receive?"

Insurance companies basically do three things with the premium dollars they receive from insureds. First, they pool the money to pay for claims. Second, insurance companies must pay for the expenses involved in selling and providing insurance protection. Third, insurance companies invest money not needed right away. The earnings from these investments help keep down the cost of insurance to policyholders.

"I always arrive right after disaster strikes because I'm...Insurance Man!"

©1981. Reprinted courtesy of Bunny Hoest and Parade Magazine.

Pay Claims

When a loss occurs, a claim is filed with the insurance company. A **claims adjuster** is the person responsible for paying or otherwise settling claims.

In general, fairly straightforward claims paid directly to the insured (property insurance) can usually be settled promptly; payments made to a third party (liability insurance) are sometimes delayed for several months or even years if the claim is going through the courts. About 80 percent of the premium income collected by insurance companies is used to pay claims and the expenses of handling them.

Pay Expenses

A portion of the insurance premium is used to cover the costs of the operations necessary to sell, issue, and service insurance policies. For the policy to take effect, the policy must be sold and an application for insurance submitted to the insurance company's underwriter, who might request additional information or conduct an inspection of the applicant's premises. If the underwriter decides to issue the requested insurance, the premium must be calculated and the policy issued.

Selling, underwriting, inspecting properties, issuing policies, and adjusting claims—these and related activities will be described in other chapters. For now, it is enough to realize that the costs associated with all these activities require about 20 percent of the premium income of insurance companies.

Generate Profits and Contingency Allowances

Because losses cannot be predicted with complete accuracy, it is necessary for insurers to build a fund for unexpected losses.

Money that is left over, after paying claims and expenses, serves to build a fund for contingencies (by increasing the insurer's assets) and also to pay dividends to the insurance company's stockholders or policyholders.

Profits and contingency allowances do not necessarily come directly from premiums. Insurers make many investments, as noted earlier, and these investments also generate earnings. When investment income is considered, it is possible for insurers to generate a profit and increase their assets even when premiums are less than claims costs and expenses. We will deal with this subject in more detail in a later chapter.

WHERE DO WE GO FROM HERE?

This chapter has presented a brief overview of the property and liability insurance business. By answering questions that Ben Franklin might ask about the business if he were to come back to life today, this chapter has acquainted you with some of the fundamental terms and concepts you will need in order to understand how insurance operates.

We have seen how large the insurance business has become when compared with its humble beginnings in Franklin's day. We have defined insurance, we have looked at the basic types of insurance that people buy, and we have seen how insurance benefits society. Finally, we have described how insurance companies use the premiums they collect from their insureds.

In the following chapters, we will begin to see how insurance coverage is put into effect. We will follow the insurance policy life cycle from the initial sale of a policy through to the payment of a claim. Most important, in seeing how this occurs, we will see how the people in different insurance jobs make insurance work.

How Is Insurance Sold? 2

Insurance works because many people throughout the insurance business can depend on one another to do their jobs well. This chapter and the next three chapters will look at the people who are involved during the "life cycle" of an insurance policy. This should help you develop a basic understanding of the connections among different insurance people in different jobs. Understanding these connections will help you see how insurance works.

SELLING INSURANCE

The *insurance policy life cycle* involves all activities necessary:

- to get the insurance coverage started,
- to pay all covered claims,
- to provide services during the policy period, and
- to renew the policy when coverage expires.

In this chapter we will study part of the first step, getting the insurance coverage started. The first insurance people we will look at have jobs that relate to selling insurance.

Selling insurance coverage is far different from selling a car. A car is "tangible"—something you can touch. A person shopping for a car can look under the hood, kick the tires, get behind the wheel, and even test drive it. When you buy insurance, the only thing you can touch is a "policy"—a few pieces

Producer

In this book, we use the term **producer** to mean anyone who sells insurance. Other terms often used for these people include **insurance agent**, **insurance broker**, and **sales representative**. For all of these people, the job involves "producing" insurance business—selling insurance.

Producers work in many different types of marketing systems. Some producers sell for only one insurance company and might be employees of that company, while others sell insurance for many different insurers and work as independent businesspersons. The different marketing systems are described at the end of the chapter.

of paper. The insurance buyer really purchases something "intangible"—something that cannot be touched and consists only of promises written on the pieces of paper. These promises provide protection and security, which are also intangible. The person who sells insurance is called an insurance **producer**. What does he or she do to convince people to purchase and pay for a promise of protection and security? How can a person successfully sell something intangible?

Being a successful insurance producer involves a number of factors. Some of the most important are described below.

Thorough Technical Knowledge

Producers must be ready and able to provide clear and complete explanations of the protection each policy provides. That requires producers to have thorough technical knowledge of insurance coverages.

"Now then—suppose somebody were to hit you with a great big rock. . . ."

Reprinted by permission of Rex F. May (Baloo).

The insurance producer uses technical knowledge to answer "what-if" questions.

Many insurance policies are complex and difficult to understand. When selling insurance, the producer uses technical knowledge to tailor insurance protection to specific needs and to answer the "what-if" questions that are posed by customers. Consumers want an insurance producer who can answer their questions satisfactorily.

Technical knowledge is also important when an accident happens. The producer might be the first person contacted after an accident. If the producer seems uninformed about the insurance coverage involved, that apparent lack of knowledge might cause the client to look elsewhere for future insurance protection. Also, if the insurance was mishandled, the client might sue the producer or the insurer. Thorough technical knowledge of insurance coverage is necessary to sell insurance to clients, to keep clients satisfied, and to avoid serious problems.

Sound Customer Service Skills

Products rarely sell themselves, especially if they are expensive. Even though a car might be necessary transportation, selling a car requires sales skills. An automobile salesperson tries to convince drivers that the car will meet their needs.

Insurance is necessary for most people and businesses. In fact, it is almost impossible to do without insurance in many situations:

- When a home is purchased with the help of a mortgage loan, the lender usually requires the borrower to carry homeowners insurance.

- Most states require proof of auto insurance coverage before a car can be registered.

- Every state requires most employers to carry workers compensation insurance.

When insurance is a necessity, the producer does not need to convince a prospect to buy insurance. The key is to convince a prospect to buy *from that producer.*

Insurance is not always required. A producer can help a **prospect** decide whether certain types of insurance should be purchased. A producer can also help **clients** by pointing out what other insurance is available.

Even when insurance is necessary, a consumer does not usually have the expertise to identify all insurance needs. Sales activities often begin with identifying the specific insurance needs of the prospect. The first step in uncovering insurance needs is the identification of **loss exposures**. The producer has expertise in identifying the loss exposures faced by the consumer.

Identifying loss exposures is usually more complex for businesses than for individual insurance buyers. For individuals, the process of identifying property loss exposures might be as simple as taking an inventory of owned property and recognizing that the property might become damaged in an accident, with resulting financial loss. A business with manufacturing plants in fifteen states must use a much more involved identification process. Inspections of the business operation and detailed **survey questionnaires** are often used by producers to help identify their business clients' loss exposures.

Once a prospect's loss exposures are identified, the producer can help select insurance policies that will cover the exposures. Although expo-

> A **prospect** is a person, business, or organization to which a producer hopes to sell insurance. After the sale is completed, the person, business, or organization is referred to as a **customer, client, policyholder,** or **account**.

> **Loss exposures**, or simply **exposures**, are situations that could lead to an accidental loss.

> **Survey questionnaire**
> Often called a **survey**, this form lists a large number of loss exposures often found in businesses. The producer and the insurance buyer use the survey form as a list of possibilities. The business being surveyed is evaluated according to the list to find the actual exposures of the business.
> For example, the survey questionnaire might ask whether the business has any "valuable papers." Examples of valuable papers are blueprints or architects' drawings. A skilled producer knows the question is in the survey because special insurance coverages are available for certain kinds of valuable papers. The producer might ask additional questions to determine whether any of the special coverages are needed.

sure identification and coverage selection are important, they are not the only services producers can provide. A prospect becomes a customer and remains a customer only if other needs are properly met as well.

Customers can have many needs during the course of their business relationship. The producer must be available to answer questions, resolve billing problems, and handle changing insurance requirements, such as changes in covered cars or insured drivers.

Some customer needs are met by people other than the producer who makes the initial sale. In fact, in many situations, the producer does nothing but sell. Once a sale is made, most other matters (such as handling claims) are the responsibility of other people, whose jobs we will examine later.

Good Public Image

Successful insurance producers need more than product knowledge and an interest in serving their customers' needs. It is also important for a producer to maintain a good public image.

A good public image is created in part by treating members of the public in a courteous manner. Discourteous treatment by the producer—or by any member of the production staff—is likely to lose a customer.

Taking the time to provide complete, accurate information serves an important need and enhances the producer's public image. Consumers often have inaccurate information about insurance. Producers and their staff must be able to aid consumers by providing accurate information.

Producers also find that participating in civic events and charitable activities helps their image. This can also lead to new insurance prospects among the people the producer meets during these activities.

A Producer's Profile: Paul Proctor, CPCU, AAI

Paul Proctor has been a producer for fifteen years. During that time, he has concentrated most of his efforts on the sale of property and liability insurance, although he also sells some life and health insurance. Paul is a member of the Lions Club and is on the Board of Directors of the local Chamber of Commerce. He has served on the city council and the school board. These activities have enhanced Paul's public image as an insurance producer and have helped to provide a steady stream of new prospects for insurance. Paul's insurance business also receives some publicity whenever the local newspaper mentions his name in connection with his civic activities.

Paul believes technical knowledge is important to success in the insurance business, and he continually stresses this fact to the people who work for him. All his employees complete INTRO—the Introduction to Property and Liability Insurance course of the Insurance Institute of America (IIA). Several members of his staff have also taken other IIA courses. Both Paul and his staff attend seminars and workshops to keep their knowledge current. He subscribes to several insurance magazines and encourages people in his office to read them regularly. Paul recently completed the IIA's educational

Paul Proctor has been a producer for fifteen years.

program for insurance producers and became an "Accredited Adviser in Insurance," which entitles him to use the initials "AAI" after his name. Several years ago, after five years of study, Paul completed the Chartered Property Casualty Underwriter (CPCU®) program of the American Institute for Chartered Property Casualty Underwriters. The CPCU designation shows that Paul has completed this challenging educational program and has agreed to abide by a code of professional ethics. Paul is an active member of the local chapter of the CPCU Society—an association of insurance professionals who have earned the CPCU designation.

Paul tries hard to meet all the needs of his customers. His office is open on evenings and Saturday mornings for the convenience of clients who cannot come in during normal working hours. Paul's staff is trained to be friendly and courteous and to treat customers the way they themselves would want to be treated. Customers always receive a careful analysis of their insurance needs, which often leads to a recommendation that they buy additional insurance protection. The files of existing clients are regularly reviewed to see whether changes in their exposure or changes in the insurance that is now available could improve their protection.

THE INITIAL CONTACT

We will now see what Paul Proctor, a producer, does to sell insurance to Allied Manufacturing, the largest business in his city. We will see how Paul makes his initial contact with Allied and how Allied decides to consider buying insurance from Paul. Chapter 3 will show how other people become involved during the life cycle of the policy sold to Allied.

Connie Sue Rapp is Paul Proctor's customer service representative.

The People Involved

Three principal people are involved in this chapter. Paul Proctor is an insurance producer. As you know, a producer's major responsibility is to produce insurance sales—in other words, to sell insurance.

Connie Sue Rapp is Paul Proctor's **customer service representative**. While Paul is busy selling insurance, Connie Sue's primary role is to provide whatever service is necessary for customers. We will see her at work throughout the next several chapters.

In every business, someone is responsible for buying insurance to protect the business. At Allied Manufacturing, this is one responsibility of Rick Manning, the **risk manager**.

To begin, Paul Proctor meets with Rick Manning in the Allied Manufacturing Company offices. Paul wants to produce some additional insurance business. He hopes to convince Rick that Allied Manufacturing should purchase its auto insurance through him. This meeting takes place sometime before Allied Manufacturing becomes one of Paul's customers.

Customer Service Representative

As a **customer service representative**, Connie Sue supports the sales efforts of Paul Proctor, the producer. In some offices, these responsibilities are divided among several people with different titles. The particular title used for this position is not important. What is important is understanding the tasks that somebody needs to do to make insurance work.

Many titles are assigned to people who basically perform the same activities as Connie Sue. Some titles are:
- **agency underwriter**
- **marketing specialist**
- **insurance placer**
- **account analyst**
- **administrative assistant**
- **office manager**

Allied Manufacturing Company

Allied Manufacturing Company is the largest business in Plainfield, where Paul Proctor's office is located. Allied

Risk Manager

As a **risk manager** for Allied Manufacturing, Rick Manning is responsible for preserving the business firm's assets against accidental losses of various kinds. Many methods can be used to handle the possibility of a severe financial loss. One of the most widely used methods is buying insurance protection. Other useful methods emphasize safety.

Large firms might have a **risk management department** with several people, while medium-sized companies often have one person who performs this function. Smaller companies cannot usually afford to have a full-time risk manager handling this job, so risk management tasks like managing the insurance program are handled by someone such as the treasurer.

makes farm implement parts that it distributes in an eight-state area. It owns a large fleet of trucks used to deliver parts. Company representatives use a fleet of cars to make sales calls on parts dealers.

Paul knows Rick Manning through the Plainfield Lions Club, since they both are members. When Paul previously tried to sell insurance to Allied, Rick insisted that he was satisfied with the coverage and service he was receiving from a different insurance company. However, since the producer who was serving Allied Manufacturing has just retired, Paul believes that now might be a good time to try again. Another producer has taken over for the one who retired, but she has not yet established a good working relationship with Rick.

Paul considers Allied Manufacturing to be a good prospect for insurance. In this case, Paul decides to approach Rick Manning about insuring Allied's fleet of trucks and cars. (Both trucks and cars are called "autos" in insurance policies.) If he can make the auto insurance sale, Paul expects it will be only a matter of time before he is given an opportunity to handle all of Allied's insurance.

The Interview

Paul Proctor has made an appointment with Rick Manning. Paul's objective is to get Rick's permission to "quote" on Allied's auto insurance. To quote on the insurance, Paul must obtain at least enough information to complete an **application** for insur-

Paul Proctor interviews Rick Manning.

Application

The **application** form, often called an **app**, is used to gather information that will be used by underwriters. All apps ask for the name and address of the applicant and the date when coverage would begin. The rest of the application form contains questions specifically relating to the type and amount of insurance being requested. For example, among other things, an auto insurance app would ask for specific information on each vehicle to be insured—the make, model, body type, year, vehicle identification number (VIN), and who the drivers will be. The app also asks what specific coverages and limits are desired.

Applications for other types of insurance ask different questions. For example, an application for homeowners insurance asks for the type of occupancy (single-family dwelling, apartment, or condominium), whether it is of wood or brick construction, and the distance to the nearest fire hydrant.

All questions in the app must be answered before it is sent to the underwriter. Otherwise, the underwriter would have to contact Paul to obtain the missing information, and Paul might have to get it from Rick. This would slow down the process and create unnecessary work. It might also affect Rick's reputation for technical competence.

An **underwriter** evaluates requests for insurance. Underwriters determine which applicants for insurance are accepted and which are rejected. If an application is accepted, the underwriter also determines how much coverage the insurer is willing to provide and at what price. Underwriting is the topic of Chapter 3.

ance. The application form, often called an **app**, is used to gather information that is used by an **underwriter** to evaluate a request for insurance and, if appropriate, to determine how much to charge for the coverage.

As a part of exposure identification, Paul asks the questions that are necessary to identify the exposures connected with Allied's cars and trucks. For a complicated operation involving many vehicles, Paul might see a need for some special coverages that would not be provided unless they are specifically mentioned on the app. By carefully identifying Allied's loss exposures, Paul is preparing to recommend proper insurance coverage.

Because Allied Manufacturing has many cars and trucks, Rick has a computer printout of all vehicles Allied owns, and he offers Paul a copy. This saves Paul the trouble of having to write down all the vehicle information.

As Paul tries to get the information he needs for the application, Rick raises a question:

RICK: We've had a $500 **deductible** on all our vehicles. Perhaps we should consider changing to a $1,000 deductible. How much premium do you think this might save us?

Deductible

A **deductible** is a portion of an insured loss that is not paid by insurance. For example, if there is a $100 deductible on an auto insurance policy and there is an accident involving $500 of covered collision damage to the auto, the insurance company would pay $400. The policyholder would have to pay $100 of his or her own money, in addition to the amount paid by insurance, to get the car completely restored. For minor damage involving repair costs of $100 or less, the insurance company would pay nothing.

As deductibles get higher, premiums get lower. With higher deductibles, fewer claims are paid (because small claims are within the deductible amount), and fewer dollars are paid on large claims. But lower premiums are not the only reason for deductibles.

Allied Manufacturing is considering a $1,000 deductible instead of its present $500 deductible. The insurance premium will no doubt be lower with the $1,000 deductible, but the dollar loss Allied will have to bear for each accident will be higher. Rick Manning will need to compare the cost of insurance with both deductibles to determine which seems like the best overall value. He will not know in advance exactly how many accidents Allied's vehicles will have next year, but he can make some sound estimates based on past accident records.

PAUL: I'm not sure, Rick, but I'll get two **quotes** from the underwriter—one with a $500 deductible and the other with a $1,000 deductible. That way we can compare.

A **quote**, or **quotation**, is a statement regarding the premium that will be charged for certain coverage.

During the interview, Rick Manning mentions a driver safety program for Allied's drivers. He gives Paul a brochure describing how the program works. Allied's drivers complete the program before they are permitted to drive for Allied. They also take a refresher course every two years. Rick also gives Paul a copy of his present insurance policy and a current computer printout from the insurance company showing all of the auto insurance claims that Allied had during the past several years.

As the interview closes, Paul explains that he will put the information together and send it to the IIA Insurance Company underwriter as soon as possible. However, before Paul leaves, Rick raises another question:

RICK: By the way, the insurance on my family's Buick expires at the end of this month. Do you suppose you could give me a quote on that, too?

PAUL: Sure, Rick. Let me get the information now, and I'll have Connie Sue, my customer service representative, call you tomorrow morning. She has the information at her desk and can give you quotes right over the phone for whatever **auto insurance coverages** and **limits** you want to consider.

Auto Insurance Coverages

There are different types of auto insurance coverage. Two important coverages are described below.

- **Physical damage coverage**, also known as "damage to your auto" coverage, insures against loss resulting from damage to an auto owned or operated by the insured, and it also provides coverage if the car is stolen. Auto physical damage coverage is property insurance.
- **Liability coverage** will apply if an insured person or business is responsible for hurting someone else or damaging someone else's auto or other property as a result of an auto accident. Auto liability coverage is liability insurance.

The Submission

When Paul returns to his office, he gives his notes to Connie Sue Rapp, the customer service representative in his office. Paul has not actually filled in all the blanks on the application form. The vehicle descriptions are in Allied's computer printout. The rest of the important information is found in his notes taken at his interview with Rick Manning. Connie Sue needs to put together all these

Limits

Also called **limits of insurance, limits of liability,** or **policy limits, limits** indicate in an application how much insurance is requested. Once the policy is issued, the limits in the policy set the maximum dollar amount the insurance company will pay. Auto liability insurance always has policy limits in a stated dollar amount.

Since cars and trucks are regularly sold, their value is determined based on the current market price for similar used cars. Therefore, it is not usually necessary to state a dollar limit in the policy for physical damage coverage.

details to prepare a complete application. She might also need to provide the .underwriter with some information in addition to a completed application form.

Connie Sue's first step is to check whether she has everything she needs. If not, she will ask Paul if he has the information. If Paul needs something else, he will make a call to Rick Manning. A prompt follow-up will show Allied that Paul is acting quickly on his promise to get a quote. Calling a week later for missing basic information might make Paul seem slow and inefficient.

Connie Sue's goal is to prepare a **submission** for the IIA Insurance Company underwriter. Besides the app, another important item included in the submission, especially on a large one like Allied's, is a cover letter.

The package of materials that will go to the underwriter is called a **submission**. The app is usually the most important part of the submission.

Paul Proctor writes a cover letter that briefly describes Allied Manufacturing, explains his relationship with Rick Manning, and explains why he thinks he will be able to convince Allied to purchase auto insurance from IIA Insurance Company if he gets a competitive quote. In the letter, Paul also states that he thinks he can sell Allied other kinds of insurance if he can just "get his foot in the door." The purpose of the cover letter is to give the underwriter a picture of the prospect and the type of working relationship the insurance company can expect to have with Allied. Paul would like the underwriter to look favorably at the submission and respond with a quote that will help him complete the sale.

In addition to a cover letter and app, Connie Sue includes a few other pieces of information with the Allied submission. She attaches the computer listing of vehicles rather than copying all the information onto the application form. Connie Sue also encloses the brochure describing Allied's driver safety program. (Remember, Rick Manning gave Paul the brochure during their interview.) Connie Sue thinks this information shows that Allied has safety-conscious management, and that should make a good impression on the underwriter. The final item in the Allied submission is a copy of the computer printout listing Allied's insured auto losses during the past three years.

Connie Sue adds an important note at the front of the submission packet stating the date when she needs the quote. With that, she sends the submission to the IIA Insurance Company's commercial insurance underwriter. However, she is not quite finished. Connie Sue writes herself a reminder to call Rick in the morning and quote on his personal car insurance.

Personal Insurance, Commercial Insurance

Insurance coverages that are purchased by individuals and families covering nonbusiness exposures are called **personal insurance**. Most people own one or more personal insurance policies—auto insurance, homeowners insurance, motorcycle coverage, boat insurance, snowmobile insurance, jewelry insurance, and so forth.

Insurance coverages sold to businesses or to institutions—such as schools, hospitals, and governments—are called **commercial insurance**. Typical commercial coverages are building and contents insurance, workers compensation insurance, commercial liability insurance, business auto insurance, and crime insurance.

The Personal Insurance Application

We have seen that a commercial insurance submission often requires information that can best be obtained in an interview with the prospect. This information is then submitted to an underwriter for evaluation. Unless the underwriter requests additional information, little more will be done by the producer until the quote is received.

The procedures for **personal insurance** are usually much simpler than the procedures for **commercial insurance**. Often the entire process can be handled by telephone.

Paul Proctor has already obtained the basic information Connie Sue needs to develop a quote on Rick Manning's Buick. Using the IIA Insurance Company **rating manual** stored in her computer, she needs only a few minutes to determine the premium based on the coverages and limits that Rick is carrying. When she calls Rick with the quote, Connie Sue suggests that Rick Manning might want to increase the liability coverage limits on his auto policy. She also quotes a premium for higher limits. He thanks her for the suggestion and tells her to use the higher limits.

Since Connie Sue has passed the state examination and is a licensed insurance agent, she could legally **bind coverage** (put coverage in force immediately). However, that is not necessary in this case because Rick's current policy is still in force. Rick asks Connie Sue to have an IIA Insurance Company policy issued that will be effective on the date when his present auto insurance expires.

Up to this point, Connie Sue has not filled out a complete application on the personal auto insurance—she has received only enough information to calculate and quote the premium. Now that Rick has accepted the quote, Connie Sue asks the additional questions that are necessary to complete the entire application.

Once Rick Manning's auto application is sent to the IIA Insurance Company personal insurance underwriting department, there is little reason to doubt that a policy on his Buick will be issued within the next week. The Allied Manufacturing business auto policy submission has been completed and sent to Carla Underwood, the IIA Insurance Company commercial insurance underwriter. In the next chapter we will see how Carla handles the submission. For now, we will take a closer look at the different marketing systems that are used to produce insurance business for insurance companies.

Rating Manual

A **rating manual** is a book or computer program used in determining premiums. Personal insurance premiums are usually quoted from a rating manual by producers or their assistants.

Commercial insurance rating manuals are more complicated. It is usually more difficult to determine a final premium for a commercial lines applicant. This is one reason an underwriter is often asked to prepare a quote for commercial insurance.

Some commercial premiums are not determined by the use of a rating manual. Instead, personal judgment of the underwriter is used. In many cases, although the manual provides a guide or starting point, the insurance company underwriter will also consider other factors in arriving at a final premium. As we will see in Chapter 3, some judgment is used with the Allied submission.

Bind Coverage, Binder

An insurance agent is usually authorized by the insurance company to **bind coverage**. A **binder** is a statement that coverage is in force. Its purpose is to provide temporary coverage until an actual insurance policy can be issued.

A binder need not be in writing. If Connie Sue tells a customer over the phone that insurance coverage is bound, that customer has coverage just as though the customer were holding a written insurance policy. So that there can be no dispute over what coverage is provided, producers issue a written binder as soon as possible after orally binding coverage. The written binder will be replaced with an insurance policy as soon as the application is accepted by an underwriter and the policy is issued.

INSURANCE MARKETING SYSTEMS

Paul Proctor works as a producer for IIA Insurance Company. IIA Insurance Company provides insurance policies and bears the risks of the people who buy IIA insurance. Paul acts as a matchmaker by bringing buyers to the insurance company and bringing insurance to insurance buyers.

IIA is not the name of a real insurance company. For purposes of this book, Paul and IIA might be a part of almost any of the insurance marketing systems described below.

Insurance companies use different arrangements to market insurance. The idea of using different marketing systems is not unique to insurance. Before examining insurance marketing systems more closely, let us briefly examine the problem of marketing a different product, like furniture. A furniture manufacturer might make excellent furniture, but it will go out of business unless it develops a system for marketing its furniture. Several approaches are possible:

- A furniture manufacturer might sell its furniture to retail customers through independent furniture stores that also carry other manufacturers' furniture. Such stores buy furniture wholesale and sell it for retail prices. Each store hires employees, including sales representatives, who might receive a percentage commission for each item they sell.

- A furniture manufacturer might make arrangements with independent businessowners who agree to sell only that manufacturer's products. The store owner will buy furniture wholesale and sell it at retail prices, possibly hiring commissioned or salaried employees to help with customer sales and service.

- A furniture manufacturer might open its own company-owned stores, operated by commissioned or salaried employees.

- A furniture manufacturer might sell its products directly to the public, with customer service representatives accepting telephone or mail orders. This system might involve low selling costs because it requires none of the usual sales representatives. However, advertising costs or the costs of printing and distributing a catalog might be high.

- A furniture manufacturer might also accept orders from dealers who do not normally carry its products.

Furniture is obviously different from insurance. One difference is that furniture is tangible, but insurance is intangible. Another difference is that a couch, for example, is paid for once (or in installments) and lasts for many years. Most insurance policies have a limited life and must be renewed when they expire. Repeat business is usually much more important for insurance producers than for furniture sellers.

Most insurance marketing systems involve an insurance producer like Paul Proctor and customer service representatives like Connie Sue Rapp. This section will briefly explain the most common insurance marketing systems and the terms used in connection with each.

Independent Agency System

An independent agency might be loosely compared with a privately owned furniture store that sells several brands of furniture at one or more locations.

An **independent agent** is a businessperson who contracts with several unrelated insurance companies to represent them by selling and servicing all these companies' insurance policies. The insurance companies pay the independent agent a commission for each policy that is sold. Independent agents earn a commission that typically averages from 10 to 15 percent of the premium. The commission rate usually applies for either a new customer's policy or a renewal of an existing customer's policy. The commission percentage might be higher or lower and usually changes with different kinds of policies. The rate of commission is defined in a contract between the agency and the insurer.

An independent agent's business organization is known as an **independent agency.** Although some independent agents operate a one-person business, a large agency might employ a number of insurance producers, customer service representatives, and other specialists.

An independent agent decides which insurance company to recommend to a particular client. If Paul Proctor is an independent agent, he might represent several insurance companies who could insure Allied Manufacturing, and he would have to choose the one that is best equipped to meet Allied's needs. In our case, Paul chose to send the Allied submission to IIA Insurance Company. As an independent agent, Paul could also decide to send a submission to another insurance company he represents so he would get quotes from two or more insurers. And even if IIA issues an insurance policy covering Allied, Paul might recommend changing the insurance next year to another insurance company he represents. According to his contract with IIA Insurance Company, Paul "owns the expirations." This means that Allied is Paul's customer, not the insurance company's customer. IIA does not have the right to sell insurance to Allied—or to renew Allied's coverage when it expires—without Paul's involvement. Paul also has the right to sell his expirations to another independent agent. For example, he might sell his insurance agency, and the new buyer would want to keep the agency's customers. (Of course, a customer could always decide he or she does not like the new owner, and a customer has the right to choose a different insurance representative.)

The largest insurance company using independent agents is Aetna Life and Casualty Company. Most Aetna agents also represent other companies.

> An **independent agent** sells insurance for several unrelated insurance companies. The producer decides which of several insurance companies to recommend for a particular client. The independent agent's business organization is called an **independent agency.**

Jones sure thinks a lot of his prospect list.

Reprinted with permission of Insurance Information Institute.

Exclusive Agency System

An exclusive agency might be loosely compared with a privately owned furniture store that sells only one brand of furniture, usually at a single location. An **exclusive agent** is not an employee of the insurance company, but an independent contractor who has a contract to sell insurance for that company. According to the usual contract, an exclusive agent may not sell

> An **exclusive agent** has a contract to sell insurance exclusively for one insurance company (or several related companies).

insurance for other insurance companies. If Paul Proctor is an exclusive agent for IIA Insurance Company, he has agreed to sell insurance for only IIA. When Allied's policy expires, Paul will naturally encourage Rick Manning to renew it with IIA.

Like independent agents, exclusive agents are usually paid by commissions. Often, for exclusive agents, the commission percentage on new business is higher than the commission percentage on renewals. An exclusive agent may own the expirations of his or her customers, but only while the exclusive agent's contract with the insurance company is in force. If this contract terminates, the customers "belong to" the insurance company. The agent cannot sell the expirations to another producer.

The largest insurance company that uses exclusive agents is State Farm. (Actually, "State Farm" is a group of related companies such as State Farm Fire and Casualty Company and State Farm Mutual Automobile Insurance Company.) A State Farm agent sells only State Farm insurance.

Direct Writing System

A **direct writer** might be loosely compared with a company-owned furniture store that sells only that company's brand of furniture. A direct writer is like an exclusive agent in one way—both sell insurance for only one insurance company (or group). The difference is that a direct writer's sales representative is an insurance company employee rather than an independent contractor. A direct writer might receive a salary, a commission, or a combination of the two. A direct writer's sales representative might stop working for the company or be transferred to another job, but the insurance company will continue to own the business produced by that representative. In other words, the insurance company owns the expirations.

If IIA is a direct writing insurance company, Paul Proctor will sell insurance only for IIA. Liberty Mutual Insurance Company is one large insurance company that sells through producers who are employees.

A **direct writer** is an employee who sells insurance for one insurance company. The term **direct writer** is also used to refer to an insurance company that sells insurance directly to insurance buyers through employees.

Direct Response Marketing System

An insurance company using direct response marketing might be loosely compared with a furniture manufacturer that sells furniture directly to the public by telephone or mail. In the past, direct response marketing was often called *direct mail.* Today, however, a large part of the business is done by telephone.

Instead of producers calling on potential customers, insurance companies using the **direct response marketing system** rely heavily on television, radio, and newspaper advertising and word-of-mouth recommendations to encourage prospects to make the first contact. The largest insurance company using this marketing system is United Services Automobile Association, better known by its initials, USAA. Since producers are not used in direct response marketing systems, Paul Proctor and the IIA Insurance Company are obviously not involved in this marketing system.

> The **direct response marketing system** has no local producers making face-to-face sales but handles sales by mail or telephone.

Brokers

In contrast to the insurance producers just described, all of whom represent insurance companies, insurance **brokers** represent insurance buyers. Many brokers work for large, country-wide or international brokerage firms with offices in many locations. The largest international insurance brokerage firm is Marsh & McLennan.

> **Brokers** are representatives of insurance buyers. They resemble agents except for the fact that, in the legal sense, they represent the party seeking insurance.

Like other producers, brokers identify insurance prospects and work to identify their insurance needs. Brokers work on behalf of the insurance buyers to find an insurance company that will meet those needs. Many insurance companies sell insurance through both brokers and other kinds of producers described earlier.

Because brokers place insurance with many different companies, they closely resemble independent agents. Like independent agents, brokers are normally compensated by a commission, and they generally own the expirations. In a legal sense, a broker represents the insurance buyer, not the insurance company. In practice, there is often little difference between brokers and independent agents.

Which is the best insurance marketing system? All of these systems attract many customers. Most people think the system with which they are involved is the best. All serve an important role in making it possible for insurance buyers to purchase insurance coverage. They all help to make insurance work.

"You know, it's a real jungle out there, Fred!"

Reprinted with the permission of Bituminous Casualty Corporation

What Is Underwriting? 3

Insurance works for people who have insurance, but not everyone who applies for insurance is accepted. Some have to shop around before they find an insurance company willing to sell them insurance. **Underwriters** are the people who decide which applicants for insurance are accepted and which are rejected. Underwriters also decide how much coverage their insurance company is willing to provide and at what price.

You can see that underwriters make some very important decisions. But why do they have to be selective? Why not just sell insurance to anybody who wants it and is willing to pay for it? And if underwriters have to be selective, how do they decide who is acceptable and who is not? These are some of the questions that will be addressed in this chapter.

GOALS OF UNDERWRITING

Before we examine the process used in underwriting the Allied Manufacturing application and Rick Manning's personal auto application, we will examine some of the things underwriters try to accomplish. You will see that underwriters try to protect the insurance company against adverse selection and that they try to consider all reasonable options that might be available. You will also see that an insurance company's underwriting results can be evaluated by examining several ratios.

Protecting Against Adverse Selection

People choose to buy insurance because it covers risks that they face. People have more incentive to buy a particular kind of insurance when their risk is high. There is less reason to buy insurance when the risk is low. In other words, the people who are most likely to buy insurance are those who are most likely to have losses.

Adverse selection is the increasing likelihood that consumers will purchase insurance when the premium is low relative to the risk. Under those circumstances, insurance seems like a good buy. Insurers, on the other hand, are increasingly interested in selling insurance when the risk is low relative to the premium.

"You'd think an underwriter would know what 'risk' is!"

Reprinted with the permission of Bituminous Casualty Corporation.

Adverse selection occurs when the people who buy insurance are mainly those who are likely to have a loss in the near future. Adverse selection always exists to some degree. After all, people do not usually buy insurance unless they think they need it. But when there is too much adverse selection, insurance cannot continue to work.

People in flood-prone areas are most likely to buy flood insurance, and they would certainly be willing to pay more for flood insurance than people who live on hilltops. And businesses in high-crime areas are more interested in crime insurance than those in low-crime areas.

Risk, transfer, and sharing cannot operate when most of the people who buy insurance expect an early loss. Remember, risk is the possibility of financial loss. Instead of a being a possibility, loss in some cases is almost certain. When a loss is almost certain, the insurance company must charge a premium that might be as high as the expected loss. Nobody would buy insurance at that price, so there could be no sharing of losses.

One important goal of underwriting is to protect the insurance company against adverse selection. Underwriters guard against adverse selection by rejecting applications from those prospects who seem likely to have losses that would be too costly in relation to the premium they would pay.

Underwriters know that, among a large group of insureds, some insureds will have losses. Indeed, some insureds will have several losses. The underwriter's task is to try to assure that the group's collective losses are in balance with the premium income derived from the group.

One way to accomplish this is to keep out of the group those applicants that appear to present significantly higher-than-average loss potential relative to the premium that would be charged. To do this, it is necessary for underwriters to screen each application and reject those that would lead to adverse selection. An auto insurance underwriter, for example, should normally reject applications from drivers who have received several tickets for driving while intoxicated. An insurance company that did no such screening would be likely to have a relatively large number of drunk drivers. As a result of such adverse selection—providing coverage on a number of drivers with serious drinking problems and an above average loss probability—losses would be unacceptably high in relation to the premium paid by insureds.

Considering All Reasonable Options

Like all decision-makers, an underwriter has three basic responses. When deciding whether to accept a submission, an underwriter may respond yes, no, or maybe.

☐ **YES**   The underwriter accepts the application and is willing to provide the coverage requested by the applicant.

☐ **NO**   The underwriter rejects the application and refuses to provide the applicant with any insurance coverage.

☐ **MAYBE**   The underwriter will accept the application subject to modification (that is, with some strings attached).

The modifications an underwriter might suggest will be discussed later in this chapter in connection with the Allied Manufacturing submission. First, we will examine how ratios are used to measure the results of an insurance company's collective underwriting decisions.

Ratios—Tools for Measuring Underwriting Results

To be financially successful, all insurance companies must be able to pay losses, meet expenses, and generate some additional funds for profits and contingencies. Stock insurance companies share their profits with stockholders; mutual insurance companies share their profits with policyholders. To determine whether an insurance company is financially successful, you need to examine some of the ratios that are used in measuring insurance company performance—the loss ratio, the expense ratio, and the combined loss and expense ratio.

Stock and Mutual Insurance Companies

Stock insurance companies are owned by stockholders who have invested in the company by purchasing shares of stock. Their reason for making this investment is to earn a return on the investment. Stockholders, also called shareholders, hope that the value of the stock will increase so that it can be sold at a higher price. They also receive a share of the profits earned by the insurance company's underwriting and investment activities. Insurance company profits distributed to stockholders are referred to as dividends.

Mutual insurance companies are owned by their policyholders. Profits earned by a mutual insurance company might be returned to policyholders. Mutual insurance company profits distributed to policyholders are also referred to as **dividends**.

Neither stock insurance companies nor mutual insurance companies guarantee that a dividend will be paid to stockholders or policyholders because neither type of insurer can guarantee that it will earn a profit.

Not all earnings over an above loss and expense costs are paid out in dividends. It is necessary for stock and mutual insurance companies to hold on to some of the profits to increase their capital—which provides an additional source of funds to handle a series of large, unexpected losses.

Loss Ratio.   The loss ratio is the percent of premiums that goes to pay clam. The loss ratio is a simple fraction multiplied by 100 to put it in the form of a percentage, as shown below:

> The **loss ratio** is the percent of premiums that goes to pay claims.

$$\frac{\text{losses (dollars)}}{\text{premiums (dollars)}} \times 100 = \text{loss ratio (in percent)}$$

Expense Ratio.   The **expense ratio** is the percent of premiums that goes to pay the insurance company's operating expenses.

> The **expense ratio** is the percent of premiums that goes to pay the insurance company's operating expenses.

$$\frac{\text{expense (dollars)}}{\text{premiums (dollars)}} \times 100 = \text{expense ratio (in percent)}$$

Combined Loss and Expense Ratio.   The **combined loss and expense ratio** is simply the sum of the loss ratio and the expense ratio.

> The **combined loss and expense ratio** is the sum of the loss ratio and the expense ratio. Sometimes it is referred to as the **combined ratio**.

$$\text{loss ratio} + \text{expense ratio} = \text{combined ratio}$$

When the combined ratio is exactly 100 percent, every premium dollar has been used to make loss payments and cover operating costs, with nothing left for profit and contingencies. When the combined ratio is greater than 100 percent, an **underwriting loss** occurs; more dollars are being paid out than are being taken in as premiums. When the combined ratio is less than 100 percent, an **underwriting gain,** also called an **underwriting profit,** occurs because all premium dollars taken in are not being used for claims and expenses. Some amount is available for profits and contingencies.

> An **underwriting loss** occurs when the combined ratio is greater than 100 percent.

> An **underwriting gain**, also called an **underwriting profit**, occurs when the combined loss and expense ratio is less than 100 percent.

It is relatively easy to see how to calculate these ratios for a period in the past. For example, assume that during the past year ABC Insurance Company collected $1,000,000 in fire insurance premiums and $720,000 was paid for fire claims. The loss ratio for ABC Insurance Company's fire insurance in this particular year was 72 percent. This is calculated by substituting the numbers into the loss ratio equation:

$$\frac{\$720,000}{\$1,000,000} \times 100 = 72\% \text{ loss ratio}$$

During the past year ABC Insurance Company's operating expenses—such as wages, salaries, and building rental costs—totaled $230,000. The expense ratio for last year was 23 percent, calculated by substituting the numbers in to the expense ratio equation:

$$\frac{\$230,000}{\$1,000,000} \times 100 = 23\% \text{ expense ratio}$$

ABC's combined loss and expense ratio was 95 percent, calculated as follows:

72% + 23% = 95% combined loss and expense ratio

Since the 95 percent combined ratio is *less* than 100 percent, ABC Insurance Company's fire insurance business earned an **underwriting profit** last year.

Projecting loss ratios, expense ratios, and combined ratios for the future is much more difficult than calculating ratios for a period in the past. Nobody knows what events could take place—such as natural disasters, riots, severe windstorms, hot spells, cold spells, or even a streak of bad luck involving a few large losses. When losses happen, not all claims are settled immediately. Therefore, the dollar value of claims can be uncertain even when the amount of premiums is known. Although insurance companies plan carefully, these factors make it difficult to project ratios accurately into the future. Even if an underwriting profit is expected, some unanticipated disaster could lead to an underwriting loss.

As mentioned, to be financially successful an insurance company must be able to pay losses, meet expenses, and generate some additional funds for **profits and contingencies**. It would seem, then, that the goal of an insurance company would be to earn an underwriting profit. However, this overlooks the fact that insurance companies also have substantial amounts of money invested and that the investments also generate funds. Despite an underwriting loss, an insurance company might be able to earn a profit for stockholders or policyholders because of the investment income the insurance company receives. An insurance company that is operating at a modest underwriting loss can still be financially successful.

Profits and Contingencies

Profits are income that exceeds expenses. All or part of an insurer's profits may be paid to stockholders or policyholders as dividends.

Contingencies involve unpredictable or extraordinary events that might draw upon an insurance company's assets. Hurricane Andrew, the largest property catastrophe in insurance history, is an example of an extraordinary event.

Insurers generally try to retain a portion of their profits to build a surplus that provides a cushion for contingencies. Technically, all retained earnings are profits, but increasing an insurer's retained earnings increases its ability to respond to unforeseen or extraordinary events.

We used 72 percent as a loss ratio in this example. Insurance companies typically have loss ratios around 80 percent for property-liability insurance, but the ratios might be higher or lower. Different insurance companies have different loss ratios for the same type of insurance. And the same insurance company can be content with different loss ratios for different kinds of insurance because expenses are not the same with all kinds of insurance.

Experienced home office underwriters, known as *staff underwriters*, are responsible for setting up guidelines to help *line underwriters* make decisions that help insurance companies to achieve satisfactory ratios. The guidelines are available in an *underwriting guide*.

HOW IS UNDERWRITING DONE?

The underwriting process involves several steps:

- Gathering the necessary information
- Analyzing the information
- Identifying the options
- Evaluating the options
- Choosing the best option
- Acting on the decision

As we return to the Allied Manufacturing Company case, we will see how Carla Underwood goes through these steps in order to arrive at an appropriate underwriting decision.

Carla Underwood is an underwriter in a branch office of IIA Insurance Company.

A **commercial underwriter** analyzes insurance requests from businesses and other organizations.

UNDERWRITING THE ALLIED MANUFACTURING SUBMISSION

Carla Underwood is an underwriter in a branch office of IIA Insurance Company. As a **commercial underwriter**, she analyzes requests for insurance from businesses and other organizations that have asked IIA to consider providing their insurance.

Lance Conrad is a **loss control representative** for IIA. Although he has a desk in the same branch office as Carla, he spends most of his time outside the office conducting inspections for **loss control reports.**

The loss control report provides underwriters with important information on the applicant. It often gives significant information that does not appear on the application itself.

As we trace what happens with the Allied Manufacturing Company submission, we will see what a commercial lines underwriter, with the help of other people does when handling a submission.

The submission addressed to Carla Underwood arrives at the mail room of the IIA Insurance Company

Home Office, Branch Office, and Regional Office

A typical insurance company is headquartered in a location called the **home office,** but has smaller offices—called **branch offices** or regional offices—located throughout the states where it does business. Most of the important functions dealing with insureds might be handled in a local branch or regional office.

One of the key functions often handled in branch or regional offices is underwriting. Other activities usually found in a branch office include issuing insurance policies, investigating and paying claims, and conducting loss control inspections. Travel time and expense are reduced when claims and loss control representatives work from offices that are close to the insurance company's customers.

Some insurance companies give the branch or regional office virtually total control over activities within the territory covered by the office. Other insurance companies involve home office people in the decisions that involve large amounts of insurance, large claims, or large premiums.

Loss Control Representative, Loss Control Survey

Insurance companies employ **loss control representatives** (sometimes called **safety engineers**) to perform **loss control surveys** (also called **inspections**) and write **loss control reports** that describe their findings.

 The loss control report provides a firsthand picture of the applicant for the underwriter. A loss control report describes the operations and hazards of the applicant's business as they relate to the type of insurance the applicant is requesting. The report also describes safety programs and other measures to control the hazards. The report not only describes strengths and weaknesses, but also makes recommendations for improvement.

The content of the loss control report varies according to the type of insurance. For auto insurance, one important kind of information in the report relates to vehicle maintenance. Well-maintained vehicles mean fewer accidents, so the loss control representative evaluates maintenance practices and then reports the results of that evaluation. The loss control report also describes any special safety program that the loss control representative has discovered.

The chances of having an auto accident increase as the amount of driving increases. For example, trucks that are used on 500-mile trips usually present a greater risk than a fleet of trucks used for short trips in one area. Even though basic vehicle information appears in the app, underwriters find it helpful to have the additional insights a loss control representative gains by looking at the trucks and talking with fleet managers and mechanics.

In many areas, vandalism or theft problems are likely unless precautions are taken to prevent losses. For this reason, it is common to lock all vehicles inside buildings or well-lighted, fenced parking lots. The loss control representative's report will describe the building or lot where the vehicles are parked when not in use ("where they are garaged," in insurance terminology).

Finally, the loss control representative will usually discuss recent auto accidents with the fleet operator and will summarize them in the report. The loss control representative and the underwriter are both interested in recognizing similar losses that indicate a pattern. Perhaps more miles have been driven and more vehicles have been used during the past year. A corresponding increase in the number of accidents can be expected. However, an increase in the number of accidents could also be the result of problems, such as a reduction in the quality of drivers or a slackening in the vehicle maintenance program.

These are the types of things that the loss control representative must investigate to provide the underwriter with a clear picture of the applicant. While a policy is in force, additional loss control surveys can serve a dual purpose of maintaining or improving safety and of keeping underwriters informed.

Loss control surveys are more common for commercial insurance than for personal insurance.

ranch office. A mail clerk, Mel Clark, receives the envelope in the mail room and sees that it is addressed to Carla Underwood. Unless an envelope is marked "Personal" or "Confidential," it is standard procedure for Mel to open it. This is done for three reasons. First, it is most efficient for envelopes to be opened by a machine in the mail room. Second, it is Mel's job to confirm that the material is indeed intended for Carla Underwood. Despite the name on the envelope, it could be that Carla was recently transferred to another department and the mail is really intended for the person now in her old job. Mel must be able to look at a piece of mail and decide who should get it. A third reason for opening the mail—and perhaps the most important—is to determine whether a **file** should be attached to the incoming mail before it is taken to someone's desk.

A **file** includes most of the information concerning a particular prospect, applicant, or policyholder. A file is often contained in a file folder, but it is becoming more common for paper files to be replaced by records stored in a computer.

A file for a commercial account usually includes the information page (or "declarations") of all policies (but not the entire policy), loss control reports, claim reports, and all correspondence. In most cases, the underwriter needs the file to take action on any specific account, so time is saved by "pulling the file" when the mail is received.

No file probably exists for a new application like Allied's, but Mel should still check for one in the filing department. It might be that a different producer has previously quoted on Allied's insurance or that IIA already writes some of Allied's insurance. If nobody checked for a file, Carla might be underwriting without some important information that would affect her decision.

In this case, no old file on Allied is found, so Mel labels a new file folder with Allied's name. Mel puts the submission into the file and delivers it to Carla Underwood, along with Carla's other mail.

Gathering the Necessary Information

The submission materials provide the first information used by the underwriter. Carla cannot visit every business operation that is being considered. This means that the submission must paint a clear picture of the business seeking insurance. Carla starts to get the picture by reading the application.

The Application.   As we saw in Chapter 2, an application provides much of the information an underwriter needs to evaluate a request for insurance. In an auto insurance application, important pieces of information include a description of each vehicle to be covered, where the vehicles are parked when they are not being used, what specific coverages are requested, and what dollar limits of coverage are wanted.

A **motor vehicle report**, also known as a **motor vehicle record** or **MVR**, lists the moving violations (such as speeding tickets) and serious accidents that a driver has had in the past several years.

Once Carla examines the application and other submission materials, she decides to do two things. First, she orders a **motor vehicle report** (**MVR**) from the state department of motor vehicles (or other state agency) for each driver listed on the application. The MVR lists the moving violations (such as speeding tickets) and serious accidents that a driver has had in the past several years. Carla also immediately orders a loss control report.

The Loss Control Report.   When an application for insurance or a large business like Allied is underwritten, the underwriter usually orders a loss control survey.

Lance Conrad, a loss control representative employed by IIA, conducts the loss control survey for Allied Manufacturing. In some cases an insurance company will pay an independent outside organization, rather than an employee, to conduct a loss control survey.

...nce Conrad conducts the loss control survey on Allied Manufacturing.

Loss Control Surveys from Independent Outside Organizations

Many individuals and companies provide loss control services and other services to various insurance companies for a fee. Two large national organizations that conduct loss control surveys for insurance companies are **Equifax Commercial Specialists** and **ISO Commercial Risk Services**.

An independent outside organization can provide basically the same information as a loss control representative employed by the insurer. A small insurance company with a few widespread commercial accounts might find it costs less to purchase this service when it is needed than to have an in-house loss control department. An insurance company with its own loss control department might use an independent service because it would be costly for an employee to travel to the applicant's location, because some special expertise is necessary, or simply because its own employees are too busy to conduct the survey in time.

Lance's survey reveals vehicles that seem to be in good condition, indicating good maintenance. The maintenance facility appears to be well equipped, with an adequate number of mechanics working in reasonably clean conditions. Service records are kept for each vehicle.

He also discovers that Allied has used a well-proven driver safety program for all drivers. He sees evidence in Allied's accident records that this program has helped reduce on-the-road accidents since its introduction three years ago.

Lance prepares a loss control report for Carla that contains all the necessary information, along with his evaluation that Allied presents a desirable prospect for insurance. He also takes a few photographs of Allied's vehicles and maintenance facilities, which will help the underwriter get a better overall "picture" of what Lance describes in his written report.

Financial Reports.   Underwriters are interested in the financial condition of insurance applicants for two important reasons. First, if a business faces financial problems, maintenance programs might suffer cutbacks, and might have more claims.

Second, underwriters want to make certain that the applicant is able to pay the insurance premiums. It makes no sense to waste time with an applicant who would be unable to make the required premium payments.

One of the best sources of financial information is a **Dun & Bradstreet Report.** "D&Bs," as these reports are called, are one source of current, unbiased information on thousands of firms throughout the country.

Carla orders a D&B on Allied Manufacturing.

Dun & Bradstreet

D&B is the world's largest credit reporting organization. Its business is gathering and maintaining information on businesses and supplying information to interested parties, including underwriters. A "D&B" reports on the history of the company and the background of its owners and managers, describes its operations, outlines its paying record, analyzes its financial condition, and assigns a credit rating.

Analyzing the Information

After Carla receives the necessary information—the submission, the MVRs on drivers, the loss control report, and the D&B—one of her duties is to compare the information from her various sources. When Carla does this, she discovers that some information seems to contradict other information. In comparing the computer list of vehicles (a part of the submission) with the loss control report, she finds that three trucks Lance has mentioned in his report are not included on the computer list. By itself, this is not a serious problem with a company as large as Allied. Vehicles are often added to a large fleet. The problem lies in the type of vehicle Lance saw—three trucks with overnight sleeping berths. The application indicates that Allied delivers to three nearby states and that none of the delivery points is more than 150 miles from the Allied Manufacturing plant. Carla Underwood had assumed that Allied does no "long-haul" trucking. (Underwriters consider long-haul trucking more hazardous than shorter trips because of driver fatigue, speed, and other factors.) Now Carla wonders whether her assumption was correct because the inspection report indicates that sleeping berth trucks are now in use.

When underwriters get conflicting information, part of their job is to resolve the differences and determine which information is correct. Carla calls Connie Sue Rapp to see whether she knows the reason for the discrepancy. Connie Sue does not know, so she offers to call Rick Manning at Allied to see what she can find out about the three trucks.

Rick clears up the discrepancy. He explains that Allied recently decided to lease three trucks for a few months. The only trucks available for lease were trucks with sleeping berths. Even though Allied is using long-haul-type trucks, their radius of operations has not changed from the 150 miles cited in the application.

When Connie Sue gives this information to Carla, it clears up Carla's only concern with the application. She knows IIA Insurance Company is interested in insuring good short-haul truck fleets. The loss control report is favorable. And the D&B indicates that Allied Manufacturing is in sound financial condition. Moreover, Paul Proctor's cover letter (which accompanies the submission) suggests that he has a good chance of handling more of Allied's insurance if the price for the auto insurance is favorable.

The IIA Insurance company **underwriting guide** is one important tool Carla will use as she decides

Food for Thought

What if Allied had been using its trucks for long hauls, but Carla never discovered it? This could have had some unfortunate results. IIA Insurance Company might have insured an operation that was much more hazardous than it expected. The premium Carla quoted might have been too low to reflect the true hazards. Claims might have exceeded the claims that Carla would have predicted. If the policy Carla eventually issued excluded coverage for trips outside a 200-mile radius, but trucks were actually traveling from coast to coast, Allied might not have been covered for a big loss.

This example shows how an applicant, a producer's customer service representative, a loss control representative, and an underwriter work together to gather accurate information for use in underwriting a submission. With the correct information, IIA Insurance Company can provide a fair, accurate quote on coverage that will meet Allied's needs.

An **underwriting guide** is a book or computer database that communicates staff underwriters' guidelines to the line underwriters who must follow them. Also called an **underwriting manual, underwriting guidelines, or a manual of underwriting policy**, it details the underwriting practices of the insurance company and provides specific guidance about how underwriters should analyze all of the various types of applicants they might encounter.

Underwriting authority Is the limit on decisions an underwriter can make without receiving approval from someone at a higher level. If an application exceeds an underwriter's underwriting authority, an underwriting decision to accept the application must ultimately be made by a superior with higher underwriting authority.

whether Allied Manufacturing Company is the type of client that IIA desires. For example, the IIA Insurance Company underwriting guide states that the company is not interested, in most cases, in insuring long-haul truck fleets.

It is also important for Carla to remember the limits of her **underwriting authority**, which are spelled out in the underwriting guide or in her job description. For a commercial underwriter with Carla's experience, the guide or job description might specify that Carla can underwrite, on her own authority (without a supervisor's specific approval), any short-haul trucking account with limits up to $500,000 per accident, as long as the manual premium is not more than $75,000 per year. When the premium involved or the amount of insurance requested exceeds Carla's "underwriting authority," she must have her decision approved by the branch manager, Beth McDonald. If the premium or coverage for a particular applicant exceeds Beth's authority, she, in turn, must have her decision approved in the underwriting department at the home office.

An underwriting trainee or junior underwriter might have less authority than Carla. In any case, the limits of authority are clearly described in the underwriting guide or underwriter's job description.

Identifying Underwriting Options

Carla has a range of choices with Allied Manufacturing. The alternatives Carla considers for Allied are described in the following paragraphs.

The **manual premium** for a policy is the premium determined from the rating manual, not including discounts or surcharges.

Two options are clear to Carla. She could reject the application. Carla disregards that alternative because she believes that Allied Manufacturing is an applicant that IIA Insurance Company would like to have as a customer. A second obvious alternative is to quote on the coverages Allied has requested at the premium determined from the rating manual—the **manual premium**. Other options exist, however, and Carla should consider them before making her quote.

Loss Control Program. One of Carla's options is to offer coverage on the condition that the applicant adopt some loss control measure or measures. Lance Conrad has been very impressed with the driver safety program that Allied already uses and has also been satisfied with vehicle maintenance. Although his loss control report contains a few minor recommendations to improve safety at Allied (such as changing the fire extinguishers on some trucks), Lance Conrad did not see the need for a completely revamped safety program.

Carla Underwood will pass along Lance's recommendation if Allied accepts her quote. But since the recommendations are minor, she decides that a quote subject to compliance with loss control recommendations is not appropriate for Allied Manufacturing.

Modifying Coverage.   Another alternative available to Carla is to offer coverage different from that requested in the application. This option usually involves a restriction of coverage—giving the applicant less insurance than what was requested.

One type of coverage restriction might involve excluding coverage in certain locations. Most auto insurance policies provide coverage throughout the U.S. and Canada. Carla might exclude coverage for Allied trucks operating beyond 150 or 200 miles from Allied's manufacturing plant, which would include the normal radius of operations, since her premium quotation will be based on the information that the vehicles are used within a 150-mile radius. However, she decides that such an exclusion would be unnecessary in this case.

Modifying the Price.   Carla has some flexibility regarding the final price to quote on Allied Manufacturing. As a preliminary step to making this final decision, she had already taken the application materials to Rachel Rollings, a **rater** in the underwriting department. Carla gave her the task of developing the manual premium. Allied has a large fleet, so computing the premium took Rachel quite a bit of time. Of course, it is important that Rachel calculate the premium carefully because her calculations help determine the premium that IIA Insurance Company quotes to Allied Manufacturing.

When Rachel completed her work a few days ago, she informed Carla that the annual premium for Allied Manufacturing's business auto policy would be $150,000, based on the manual rates in the rating manual.

A **rater** (or **rating clerk**) handles the important job of calculating insurance premiums with the aid of a calculator and a rating manual. Although most of the math is usually done by a computer, a rater must make sure the right numbers and codes are entered in the right places. Mathematical ability helps a rater prevent and correct errors.

Carla has a difficult pricing decision to make. She wants to see IIA insure Allied Manufacturing Company because it appears to be very desirable from an underwriting standpoint. However, she knows that other insurance companies have also been asked to quote and that her quote must be competitive with others that Allied receives. From her experience with similar cases in the past several months, she knows that the competition is likely to offer Allied a 10 to 15 percent discount.

Evaluating the Options

Carla knows that Allied has had relatively few losses in the last three years and believes their driver safety program and vehicle maintenance are largely responsible. This information, along with a good financial report, good driver MVRs, and other information, leads her to believe that Allied fleet is a much better than average fleet of trucks and cars. She sees no need in this case to offer a quote with any strings attached.

Choosing the Best Option

With all these factors in mind, supplemented by her years of underwriting experience and judgment, Carla decides to offer a 20 percent discount to Allied. Based on a $150,000 manual premium, the 20 percent discount equals $30,000, so the quote that she feels comfortable with is $150,000 less the $30,000 discount, or $120,000. This quote is based on physical damage insurance with a $500 deductible; if Allied selects a $1,000 deductible, Carla decides to lower the premium to $117,000—a $3,000 premium reduction for the higher deductible.

Acting on the Decision

Carla knows that her underwriting authority is limited to cases smaller than Allied. This means that she will have to obtain the consent of her superiors to make a quote on Allied's auto insurance.

Beth McDonald, the manager of the IIA Insurance Company branch office, discusses the Allied Manufacturing case with Carla and agrees that she has made an appropriate decision. But Beth cannot give final approval on a case this large—her own authority is limited to cases in which the manual premium is $125,000 or less. Beth approves Carla's suggestion that the file be submitted to the home office underwriting department for approval.

Carla Underwood discusses the Allied Manufacturing case with Beth McDonald.

THE HOME OFFICE UNDERWRITING DEPARTMENT

At this point, we will turn our attention to the role performed by the underwriting department at the home office of IIA.

Obtaining Final Approval

Beth McDonald contacts the IIA Insurance Company home office to request final approval of the Allied Manufacturing quote. Howard Upchurch is the home office underwriter assigned to this case.

Howard's job is to decide whether this account is one that IIA wants at the price suggested by Carla Underwood. Howard must also determine whether the pricing is consistent with quotes being offered elsewhere. He can look objectively at the facts and figures and compare similar cases. Howard can make these judgments because he sees many large account submissions from different branch office underwriters.

If Howard agrees to write the Allied Manufacturing auto policy, he must also make sure that **reinsurance** will be in effect for the Allied policy. After studying the entire file, Howard gives his final approval and sends Carla a message to that effect.

Reinsurance, Reinsurer

Reinsurance is an agreement with another insurer with which a risk is shared. An insurance company buys reinsurance for the same reasons that individuals and businesses purchase insurance—to reduce uncertainty by transferring some risks and sharing losses. Using reinsurance, one insurance company can transfer ("cede") some of the risk to another insurance company, and it will pay a portion of the premium to the **reinsurer** who shares the risk.

Almost every insurance company purchases reinsurance. However, policyholders are seldom aware of the transaction. In fact, they have little need to think about reinsurance since they will look to their own insurance company to pay any claims. Their insurance company will directly pay any claims under a reinsured policy. However, the insurer will share the cost of "reinsured" losses with the reinsurer.

Carla still has to present her quote to Paul Proctor, and Paul needs to have it accepted by Rick Manning at Allied, before the insurance sale is completed. We will see how these events unfold in Chapter 4. Meanwhile, let's take a closer look a the home office underwriting department and some other home office departments. Giving final approval on large accounts is only one of many functions performed there.

Line and Staff Underwriting Activities

Underwriting activities can be classified into two categories; both involve making decisions and acting on them.

- **Line underwriting activities** involve decisions on individual applicants or insureds—such as the decision to quote on the allied Manufacturing submission or, at renewal time, a decision to keep coverage in force. (Both Carla Underwood and Howard Upchurch perform line underwriting activities, although Howard has more **underwriting authority** than Carla.)

- **Staff underwriting activities** involve decisions on an insurance company's entire set of accounts. Staff underwriters look at the big picture to determine what kinds of insurance their insurance company should sell, to whom it should sell, and at what price it should sell. These decisions by staff underwriters are written in **underwriting guides,** which help line underwriters like Carla Underwood and Howard Upchurch in making their day-to-day line underwriting decisions.

Line underwriters are directly on the firing line, so to speak. They analyze every submission and decide how it will be handled. Line underwriters at different levels have different amounts of authority.

Staff underwriters do not have much to do with the daily decisions involving specific applicants or accounts. Working together with other people in the insurance company home office, they help to determine what overall goals the company should set. Next, they decide what steps should be taken to meet the goals. Then they develop an underwriting guide to explain to line underwriters exactly what kinds of business the home office underwriters are willing to write and how to evaluate it.

Staff underwriters periodically review the work of line underwriters to be sure they are following the guidelines. The process for doing this is known as an **audit**. If the underwriting guide is being followed and the company is still missing its goals, then the underwriting guide might need revisions. However, if the underwriting guide is not being followed, it is hard to determine whether the written guidelines would produce satisfactory underwriting results. Audits help staff underwriters determine whether the company results can be attributed to the underwriting guidelines.

During an **audit**, members of the home office staff underwriting department examine files to see whether the underwriting guidelines are being followed.

Developing an underwriting guide involves many decisions. It is difficult to describe underwriting practices that staff underwriters believe will meet the insurance company's goals. Some of the information used in making these decisions relates to:

- regulation,
- price competition,
- competition from new insurance products,
- a need for new insurance products, and
- feedback from the field.

Regulation. Insurance companies must comply with all legal requirements, and many insurance regulations affect underwriting and pricing decisions. These regulations often vary from state to state. For example insurers may not be permitted to deny property insurance on a sound building just because it is located in an area where most buildings are unsound. Or they may not be able to raise their auto insurance premiums without the state's approval.

When developing underwriting guidelines, the staff underwriting department needs to remain aware of all regulations that might apply. Insurance regulation is discussed again in Chapter 11.

Price Competition.   Carefully studying the competition is an important function that the staff underwriting department often shares with the home office marketing department. At what levels are competitors pricing their policies? Even though rates in the insurance company's rating manual might be based on sound statistical grounds, conditions in the marketplace often play a role in determining a quote.

Competition From New Insurance Products.   Are new insurance products—new types of policies, for example—coming into the market? If one insurance company introduces a new policy or service that is very popular with consumers, other insurers must be aware of it to compete effectively. An example involves the "businessowners" package policies that were introduced some years ago. These policies combine many important coverages for small businesses into a single policy that is easy to quote and sell. After one large insurance company introduced such a policy and it was accepted by the buying public, many insurance companies made a similar product available.

A Need for New Insurance Products.   New insurance products are often needed when a new type of loss exposure appears. One example of this type of situation might involve insurance on solar-heated or earth-sheltered homes. How should an insurer cover electric-powered cars? How should line underwriters deal with them? What guidelines should be prepared to help them make appropriate decisions?

Feedback From the Field.   Staff underwriters must listen to their insurance company's producers, to policyholders, and to the public to determine what changes in policies, procedures, or pricing might

From the Wall Street Journal—Permission, Cartoon Features Syndicate.

New insurance products are developed in response to consumer demand.

be needed to better serve their needs or desires. The underwriting staff must then properly communicate and implement these changes to make certain that the recommendations result in the outcomes that were planned.

Most staff underwriting activities involve interacting with other department in the insurance company home office. For example, the home office marketing department—and possibly the training department—has to prepare producers to sell any new product. The home office loss control department might have to design new report forms to gather the information that will be needed by underwriters. The home office claims department needs to arrange to handle claims arising out of any new product. And in most automated insurance offices, even minor changes must be coordinated through the data processing department or other departments responsible for information and systems management.

UNDERWRITING THE PERSONAL AUTO APPLICATION

Some insurance companies would handle Rick Manning's personal auto application just like Allied Manufacturing's business auto application. An application form would be mailed to the insurance company, an underwriter would order an MVR, and the application and MVR would be compared with the underwriting guide. Finally, the application would be rated.

"The computer handles all our applications."

HERMAN copyright Jim Unger. Reprinted with permission of UNIVERSAL PRESS SYNDICATE. Reprinted with permission. All rights reserved.

IIA Insurance Company uses an automated system to handle most personal insurance applications. Instead of mailing Rick Manning's personal auto application to IIA Insurance Company, Connie Sue Rapp entered the information into a computer terminal in Paul Proctor's office. This terminal is linked to the computer in the IIA Insurance Company office. A complicated computer program, connected with the state office that maintains motor vehicle records, checks the MVRs on all drivers listed. It then examines other information to be sure the application meets all underwriting guidelines. If not, the application is referred to an underwriter for closer examination. Rick Manning's application meets all IIA Insurance Company requirements, so the computer approves and rates the policy. Finally, the policy is printed on a printer in Paul Proctor's office, and Connie Sue Rapp mails it to Rick Manning.

One difference between commercial auto insurance and personal auto insurance is that it is easier to automate the personal policy. With personal insurance, any discounts or surcharges are usually included in the manual premium. Commercial insurance is more complicated, and more underwriting judgment might be involved. In many offices, computers also play an extensive role in commercial insurance underwriting.

WHAT IF THE UNDERWRITER SAYS NO?

IIA Insurance Company will, in fact, become Allied Manufacturing's auto insurer. But we should consider the other possibility: What if IIA Insurance Company decides to reject Allied's application? Such a decision might be made if some underwriting information about Allied Manufacturing was unfavorable. If Allied were engaged in long-haul trucking, it might not be an account IIA would choose to write. Or it might be that the loss control report would have revealed that the vehicles were poorly maintained—perhaps that many trucks were running on bald tires. Carla or her superiors might also have rejected the application if IIA could not provide the necessary loss control or claims service on an account of that type or was unable to obtain the necessary reinsurance.

If IIA rejected the application, another insurer might still find the application desirable. Different insurance companies have different underwriting practices. This is one of the reasons Rick Manning has invited more than one producer to quote on the policy.

The problem of being unable to find an insurer is not confined to commercial insurance. Some drivers have difficulty getting personal auto insurance if they have been responsible for several accidents or have received several traffic tickets within a short period of time.

To improve the availability of insurance, state governments and the federal government have created plans to insure people or businesses who are unable to obtain insurance in the so-called **voluntary market**.

Voluntary Market, Residual Market

In the usual case, underwriters for an insurance company voluntarily decide whether to accept or reject an insurance application. Business accepted in this way is considered to be part of the **voluntary market**. Applicants that are rejected by underwriters in the voluntary market may find insurance available through one of the **residual market** programs described here.

These plans have become known as **residual markets**, or **shared markets**. Although many residual markets exist, the largest and best known are state **automobile insurance plans** and the so-called **FAIR plans** for property owners.

Automobile insurance plans are residual market programs providing auto insurance to people who cannot obtain coverage in the voluntary market.

Automobile Insurance Plans

In automobile insurance plans, also called assigned risk plans, people unable to obtain auto insurance in the voluntary market apply for coverage in the state auto insurance plan. The specifics vary by state, but people can generally apply through any licensed insurance agent or broker. The state auto insurance plan cannot reject applications—except, possibly, for some very serious reasons. In most cases, the insurance coverage is not actually provided by the state, but is instead "assigned" to an insurance company that must accept the assigned applicant. Each insurance company that sells auto insurance in the state receives "assigned" applications in proportion to the amount of auto insurance it voluntarily writes in that state.

"Honestly, George, you've just dispelled everything I was told about underwriters."

Reprinted with the permission of Bituminous Casualty Corporation.

Drivers who cannot get auto insurance in the voluntary market are generally those who have the most accidents. It is considered desirable to enable all drivers to buy insurance to reduce the number of uninsured drivers on the road. Apportioning applications in these plans is a reasonably fair method of insuring this pool of drivers.

Every state has some kind of a residual market for auto insurance. However, the specific operation of the plans varies considerably.

FAIR Plans

Another residual market available in many states is designed for individuals or businesses who have been unable to obtain property insurance on their personal or business property in the voluntary market. "Fair Access to Insurance Requirements," or "FAIR," plans are set up on a state-by-state basis and include insurers in the state that, in the voluntary market, regularly write the kind of property insurance sold through the plan.

The applicant can apply to the FAIR plan. Some underwriting selection does take place, and the FAIR plan might require that certain loss control measure be implemented before accepting a building for coverage. For example, physical defects such as bare electric wires would probably have to be corrected.

SUMMARY

This chapter described underwriting decision making. We have seen that underwriters make two important decisions—whether the applicant should be approved and, if approved, on what basis coverage should be granted. Underwriters strive to avoid adverse selection. The results of all insurance company underwriting decisions are measured by its loss ratio and other related ratios.

Line underwriters use various tools in making underwriting decisions—the materials submitted by producers, loss control reports, financial information (such as a Dun & Bradstreet Report), and the insurer's underwriting guide. In making decisions, the underwriter has a wide range of options available—including accepting the application as submitted, accepting it subject to modification, or rejecting it.

Selecting the proper price is important. In some cases, a manual premium must be used. In other cases, the manual premium might be modified by the underwriter to fit the conditions of the case. This often means anticipating competition from quotes that are given by other underwriters.

When line underwriters make day-to-day decisions on individual accounts, they do so based on guidelines from staff underwriters. Staff underwriters use various types of information to decide what direction an insurance company should take in its underwriting activities. The underwriting guidelines they prepare reflect these decisions.

We have also seen how people in other jobs help underwriters make the best decisions. People in the mail room and file department get the necessary information to underwriters. Raters help by computing accurate insurance premiums. Managers (such as the branch manager in our story) guide underwriters toward making appropriate decisions and support their work.

Lastly, we saw that residual market systems are often available to provide insurance for those who are rejected by underwriters in the voluntary market.

How Is Insurance Service Provided? 4

I nsurance service is provided by many people working together. We have seen how Paul Proctor and Connie Sue Rapp, in the producer's office, worked together to prepare a submission on Allied Manufacturing. We have seen how Carla Underwood and many others in the IIA Insurance Company offices worked together to analyze the Allied submission and prepare a quote. Other people play important roles that are not so obvious. In this chapter, we will observe the final steps necessary to get insurance coverage started. We will also see what service is provided after coverage is in effect as we observe some of the things that IIA Insurance Company and Paul Proctor do during the policy year. And we will see what happens near the end of the policy life cycle as various people work together to renew the policy so that the cycle can run again for another year.

Paying covered claims is the most important service that is provided, when necessary, during a policy's life cycle. Claims handling will be discussed in Chapter 5.

COMPLETING THE SALE

Before insurance coverage can begin, Paul Proctor must convince Rick Manning that Allied's insurance needs will be best served by choosing the IIA policy that Paul Proctor is proposing. If Rick agrees, policy coverage may begin on whatever date is agreeable to all parties. Since Allied already has auto insurance coverage on its fleet of vehicles, the new policy's effective date will probably be the date when the old policy expires.

It would be possible to **cancel** the existing policy before it **expires** and replace it with the IIA policy. However, most policyholders change insurance companies only at the expiration of an existing policy.

The Quote

Because Carla Underwood has agreed to write the Allied Manufacturing insurance and has obtained approval from both Beth McDonald, the branch manager, and from the home office, she is now ready to make a commitment to Connie Sue Rapp and Paul Proctor. The quote from Carla Underwood includes the premium, the type of coverage (a business auto policy), and any limitations or restrictions on coverage (such as the deductibles).

Carla could telephone Connie Sue Rapp with her quote, and she might do so if things were rushed. But a written record is best to avoid any later misunderstanding. In this case, Carla Underwood enters the quote, including all necessary details, into the computer terminal on her desk. Carla can then transmit the quote to Connie Sue by computer link or fax, or she can print a copy and mail it to Paul Proctor's office.

The policy is not issued yet. IIA will not go to the expense of issuing a policy until it is certain that the prospect, Allied Manufacturing, is going to choose IIA. Remember that the current insurer and other insurance companies are also quoting on this policy. Rick Manning might not buy Allied's insurance from IIA. He might buy the insurance from a different producer and insurer. Therefore, it would make little sense for IIA to issue a policy at this point.

Once Connie Sue Rapp receives the quote, she examines it to be sure no mistakes have been made and turns it over to Paul Proctor. With Connie Sue's help, Paul must now put together an insurance proposal.

Expiration, Cancellation, Nonrenewal

Most insurance policies provide coverage for a specified **term** or **policy period**, often one year. At the end of that term the policy **expires**. At the **expiration date**, or "**x-date**," coverage ceases unless the policy is renewed.

Sometimes either an insurer or a policyholder decides to stop coverage during the policy term before the policy expires. Stopping coverage during the policy period is called **cancellation**.

A *policyholder* can cancel most policies at any time. State laws often prohibit an *insurer* from canceling a policy once it has been in force for a certain amount of time. When cancellation is permissible, the insurer is required to notify the policyholder in advance of the cancellation date so that the policyholder has time to find another insurer.

When an *insurer* decides not to renew a policy at the end of a policy period, this is not a cancellation, but is called **nonrenewal.**

The Insurance Proposal

An **insurance proposal** is often used in commercial insurance sales presentations. The proposal is usually a booklet that highlights important features of the coverage

---

An **insurance proposal** is a booklet that highlights the important features of the proposed coverage and related services and states the premium

and related services and states the premium. A proposal is particularly useful when a prospect, such as Rick Manning at Allied Manufacturing, is getting quotes from several producers. The written proposal will help Rick compare the alternatives. A neatly printed, clearly written proposal will also help show Rick Manning that Paul does a thorough, professional job.

For Allied Manufacturing, Paul's proposal outlines the coverage limits and the premium that IIA is quoting, provides a description of the vehicles to be covered, describes IIA's expertise in providing loss control and claims service for large auto fleets, and details any **premium financing** method that IIA might offer to its clients.

Premium financing may allow the insured to pay part of the premium when coverage takes effect and pay the rest during the policy period. Any premium financing that is available is an important feature of the insurance proposal and can be an important sales tool.

Although only one proposal is developed for the IIA quote, two options are included. IIA has quoted a $120,000 premium but is offering a $3,000 discount if Allied Manufacturing decides to increase its physical damage deductible from $500 to $1,000. Rick Manning requested both quotes. Carla Underwood has obliged, and both are found in the proposal. The two quotes provide identical coverage except for the difference in deductibles.

Preparing To Present the Insurance Proposal

Paul makes an appointment to present the proposal to Rick Manning. At this presentation, he plans to give Rick a detailed written description—the proposal—of the coverage and services that he and IIA Insurance Company offer to provide as well as the price. Paul plans to go through the written proposal with Rick. He will emphasize the strongest points of his proposal and explain how well it meets the needs of Allied Manufacturing. If Rick has questions, Paul hopes to answer them correctly and confidently, showing Rick that he is a capable and knowledgeable insurance professional. He does this, of course, because he hopes to convince Rick to buy insurance from IIA Insurance Company through Paul.

Paul has developed technical expertise over the years. He has not relied on experience alone, but he has also taken a number of insurance education courses, has attended many seminars, and regularly reads insurance periodicals. This technical expertise helps Paul to make effective sales presentations because he is well-equipped to handle confidently many types of questions.

Producers must be well-prepared when making a sales presentation. Before meeting with Rick Manning, Paul reviews the entire Allied file, studies the proposal, and considers the coverage of the business auto policy he will recommend. He spends some time evaluating the deductible alternatives so that he is prepared to offer a recommendation, if asked. And he tries to anticipate the points that will be most important to Rick as he makes the decision so that Paul can be sure to mention them during the presentation.

A risk manager is usually interested not only in the insurance coverage and pricing, but also in the insurance company and producer that provide insurance services. Paul must convince Rick that IIA Insurance Company can handle an account as large as Allied Manufacturing. He decides to stress IIA's strong financial standing, its excellent reputation for prompt, effective claims service, the fact that IIA claims adjusters are located throughout the region where Allied's trucks and cars operate, and the fleet loss control services that IIA can provide.

Last but not least, Rick must be persuaded that Paul Proctor can provide the necessary services as well as, or better than, any other producer. Because Rick and Paul have been working in the same city for many years, Paul thinks his own business reputation is already well established. He decides not to spend too much time on this point.

Presenting the Proposal

Rick Manning has scheduled the insurance presentation so that other Allied Manufacturing managers can also be present. Because of his careful preparation, Paul finds that the presentation goes smoothly. Rick and the other managers ask questions that seem to show they are interested in what he has to offer. A few of the questions will require more information from IIA; Paul tells the group that he will discuss them with the underwriter and give Rick the answers as soon as possible.

Paul Proctor presents the proposal to Rick Manning and other Allied Manufacturing managers.

The presentation ends when Paul has finished reviewing the proposal and has fielded all questions. Knowing that Allied is also receiving other proposals, Paul does not expect an immediate decision. Before he leaves, Paul finds out when Allied will be making its decision so that he knows when to expect a definite answer.

Concluding the Sale

Ten days later, Paul learns that his hard work has paid off. Rick Manning calls and tells Paul to have the policy issued with the $1,000 deductible, effective as of the date Allied's current policy expires.

Paul and Connie Sue are delighted with the results of their hard work and attention to details. They have gained a new account that will add substantially to their office's annual commissions. Of course, Paul and Connie Sue and their co-workers have also picked up additional work. They will spend many hours over the coming year servicing the Allied account.

POLICY ISSUE AND DELIVERY

With the approval of her superiors, Carla Underwood has been able to quote on a business auto policy for Allied. Paul Proctor has been able to present the quote in the form of a proposal and has been able to answer detailed questions about the coverage IIA is willing to provide. All this has been possible even though a written insurance policy for Allied Manufacturing has not yet been prepared. Everybody has been talking about a policy that nobody has seen. Now we will observe what goes into actually preparing the policy and delivering it to the policyholder.

The Insurance Company Issues the Policy

When Carla Underwood learns that the Allied quote has been accepted, she turns the file over to Paula Irwin. Paula is the supervisor in the IIA Insurance Company's policy issue department. The Allied Manufacturing policy will be prepared in her department, and it will eventually be delivered to Allied by Paul Proctor.

Policy issue involves several steps:

- The policy declarations must be computer printed or typed,
- The policy declarations must be combined with the appropriate pre-printed forms and endorsements,
- The assembled policy must be checked for accuracy, and
- Copies must be distributed to the policyholder and other parties.

In some insurance companies, for some types of coverage, a typist prepares insurance policy declarations by filling in the blanks on a pre-printed form. IIA Insurance Company's policy issue operation is computerized, so Allied Manufacturing's business auto policy declarations will be printed out by a computer in Paula Irwin's department.

When Carla Underwood learns that the Allied quote has been accepted, she turns the file over to Paula Irwin, supervisor of the policy issue department.

The process begins when a data entry technician in Paula's department enters the necessary information into the IIA computer. The file Carla assembled in the process of preparing her quote contains the information needed by the data entry technician. The declarations page is printed by a high-speed computer printer, and the policy information is stored in IIA's computer, which will also receive and store information related to premiums and losses for this policy.

Various forms and endorsements need to be added to Allied's policy declarations to complete the written contract between IIA Insurance Company and Allied Manufacturing. The numbers of these forms are printed in the declarations. A policy issue clerk is responsible for taking the necessary pre-printed forms from IIA's shelves and filing cabinets and attaching these papers to Allied's policy. The clerk must be careful to check all form numbers to be sure the proper **forms** and **endorsements** are used.

Forms and Endorsements

A **form**, often several pages long, contains standard pre-printed wording that makes up the bulk of the insurance contract. **Endorsements** can be used to amend the coverage in the otherwise complete policy. For example, a form might contain a clause stating that a $500 deductible applies; an endorsement might amend this to provide a $1,000 deductible in exchange for a reduced premium.

The declarations and form(s), together with any applicable endorsements, make up a complete insurance contract, or policy.

Not all policies contain endorsements. Endorsements may be attached to a new policy if the coverage is a little different from that shown in the standard pre-printed form. Endorsements may also be added during the course of a policy life cycle.

In some offices, forms and endorsements are stored in a computer, and they are printed on a laser printer, together with the declarations, when a policy is issued. Policy printing may occur in the home office, in a regional or branch office, or even in the producer's office. An automated system reduces the labor and expense involved in assembling each policy, but it requires considerable expense to set up and maintain.

Once the policy has been assembled, it is checked to be sure there are no errors. Paula Irwin then sends it to Mel Clark in the mailroom. Mel will insert one copy of the policy declarations into the Allied Manufacturing file and will mail the complete policy—together with an extra declarations page—to Paul Proctor.

The Producer Delivers the Policy

When Connie Sue Rapp opens the mail a few days later, she finds the Allied policy. After examining it to see whether it is complete, she places it on Paul's desk. The extra copy of the policy declarations will go into the Allied Manufacturing file in her office. There is no need to clutter the files for each policyholder with a copy of the standard pre-printed forms and endorsements.

Under normal circumstances, Connie Sue would check the policy herself without involving Paul. In this case, Connie Sue knows that Paul wants to go over the Allied policy personally.

Paul carefully double-checks the policy to be sure it contains the coverage he has promised and to assure himself that it contains no embarrassing spelling errors or mistakes in calculating the premium. If he should find any errors, he would ask IIA to correct them before he delivers the policy. Finding no problems, Paul calls Rick Manning and makes an appointment to deliver the policy.

Paul delivers most commercial insurance policies in person for three reasons. First, because commercial insurance is often complicated, he likes to go over the policy with the insured.

Second, policy delivery provides one more face-to-face meeting with the client. Now Paul can not only present the client with the completed policy—the first tangible evidence of his labors—but he can also use the meeting to pursue the possibility of other insurance sales. Paul would like to convince Rick Manning that he should be given a chance to quote on Allied's other insurance needs. This attempt to handle all of a client's insurance is known as **account selling.** Account selling is an important way for Rick to gain sales without having to make new contacts.

> **Account selling** is trying to handle all of a client's insurance needs, rather than providing for only a portion of those needs. Account selling is an important way for producers to gain sales without having to find new clients. When one producer handles all of a client's insurance, this also reduces the number of contacts a client has with other producers and lessens the chances that a customer will be lost to competition.

A third reason for delivering the policy concerns premium payment. Paul Proctor wants to make it clear that the premium is due as soon as the policy goes into effect. He wants to pick up a check or receive a clear promise as to when it will be sent.

When he delivers the policy, Paul goes over the coverage with Rick, states his willingness to work with Allied on its other insurance needs, and receives Rick's promise that Allied's accounting department will issue a check within a day or two in full payment of the premium.

BILLING

Because of his time spent at Allied Manufacturing, Paul Proctor actually made two sales—the business auto insurance on Allied's fleet of cars and trucks and the personal auto insurance coverage for Rick Manning's family car. Since the billing is handled differently for each, this gives us a chance to compare two billing approaches.

Producer Billing (Agency Billing)

A bill for the insured is prepared in the producer's office showing the insurance premium that is due. The insured pays the premium directly to the producer's office.

Meanwhile, the insurance company bills the producer for premiums due on all policies the producer has sold. The producer collects premiums from insureds and remits them to the insurance company after deducting the producer's commission.

Producer Billing

Allied's business auto policy will be **producer billed**. Paul Proctor's office will send Allied a bill for its insurance premiums, and Allied will make the payment to Paul Proctor. Proctor's office, in turn, will pay the premium to IIA Insurance Company after deducting a commission. The billing process involves a number of people.

When Paul Proctor receives word from Rick Manning that Allied Manufacturing has chosen the Proctor Agency and IIA to provide its auto insurance, Paul immediately notifies Carla Underwood at IIA Insurance and Bobbie Kemp, the bookkeeper in Proctor's office. Carla Underwood will make sure that the policy is issued, and Bobbie Kemp will be responsible for billing Allied Manufacturing.

Rick Manning told Paul Proctor that he preferred the $1,000 deductible plan, so a $3,000 discount from the $120,000 premium quote is applicable. This reduces the premium to $117,000. No special premium financing plan is being used, so Bobbie Kemp is instructed to bill Allied Manufacturing for $117,000.

Though Allied will make a single payment, Paul Proctor's contract with IIA provides that a part of the premium, in this case 10 percent, goes to Proctor's office as a commission for making the sale and servicing the account. Because part of the premium remains with the producer and part is sent to the company, the $117,000 billing to Allied appears as two transactions on Bobbie Kemp's books. Ten percent of the total, or $11,700, represents commission income to the producer's office. The remainder, $105,300, is an "account payable" to IIA Insurance Company.

From the insurance company's perspective, the $117,000 premium results in only a $105,300 "account receivable," to be received from Paul Proctor. The insurance company does not handle the 10 percent commission; Proctor's office keeps it.

Here is how it works. Every month, IIA Insurance Company bills Paul Proctor for the premiums due, after deducting the commissions, on current accounts. A current account could be "new business," like Allied, or a renewal of "old business"—policies previously sold and being extended for additional periods of time. Both "old business" and "new business" are included in the insurance company's billing statement, which is called an **account current**. Paul is required to submit a check to IIA soon after his office receives the account current.

> An **account current** is the billing statement an insurance company sends to its producer.

Bobbie Kemp, the bookkeeper in Paul Proctor's office, reconciles IIA's account current with her own records to make sure that neither she nor the bookkeeper at IIA has made any errors.

However, before Paul signs a check, Bobbie Kemp, his bookkeeper, "reconciles" IIA's account current with her own records to make sure neither she nor the bookkeeper at IIA has made any errors. If discrepancies are found, she might need to discuss them with a premium accounting specialist in IIA's accounting department. Since Paul's office and the IIA office handle many transactions every month, mistakes sometimes happen. When the records disagree, it sometimes requires a great deal of work to locate the error and correct everyone's records. The process is important, of course, because Paul Proctor does not want to pay premiums on business he has not produced. And IIA wants to collect all premiums to which it is entitled.

Direct Billing

Rick Manning's personal auto policy will be **direct billed.** A statement, showing the premium due, is generated by a computer and is mailed di-

Direct Billing

When a policy is **direct billed**, the insurance company sends bills directly to the policyholder, and the policyholder makes payments directly to the insurance company. The producer is not involved in billings or collections, except when a problem develops.

The insurance company pays commissions or other compensation for producing new business and servicing renewal business directly to the producer in a monthly check for all business produced or renewed during a one-month period.

rectly from the insurance company to Rick Manning. Paul Proctor's office is sent a copy of the billing. IIA Insurance Company receives the check from Rick Manning in payment of the premium. At that point, the payment will be recorded in IIA's computer. At the end of the month, IIA's computer will prepare a check for Paul Proctor paying his commission on direct-billed premiums collected that month by IIA. The check is accompanied by a list of all policyholders who have paid premiums and the amounts paid by each. Bobbie Kemp, Proctor's bookkeeper, reconciles this list against her own records and resolves any discrepancies.

POLICY CHANGES

Even after an insurance policy has been issued and billed, and after premiums have been paid, the need for service continues. Various circumstances might require that a change be made to an existing insurance policy. Some policy changes require only a modification of the policy itself and no change in the premium. Other changes, however, require an increase in the premium, or a premium refund, and necessarily involve the bookkeeping or accounting department.

Changes Involving No Adjustment to the Premium

About two months after the auto policy for Allied Manufacturing has gone into effect, Rick Manning calls Connie Sue Rapp:

RICK: Connie Sue, I've got a question for you. Allied just purchased a garage outside the Plainfield city limits and we're going to start keeping our trucks there. This new location gives us a lot more room. I wonder if this needs to be reported to the insurance company.

CONNIE SUE: We'll pass the information along to IIA. The new garage won't affect your premium for now, but the new location should be shown on your policy.

After Connie Sue gets the address, she writes a short note to Carla Underwood, stating that a new garaging address is being used by Allied. Carla notes this information in Allied's file, approves the change, and asks Lance Conrad, the loss control representative, to inspect the new garage the next time he is in the area.

Penny Charter in the policy change department at IIA receives the notification of this policy change from Carla. Using a computer terminal at her desk, she types the policy number for Allied Manufacturing. The declarations for Allied's auto policy appear on her screen. Penny changes the garage location in the appropriate field on the declarations and signals to the computer that no other changes are necessary. The computer prints a declarations page showing the new address. Two copies of the new page are sent to Paul Proctor's office. Paul will send one copy to Allied.

Changes Requiring a Premium Adjustment

Premium adjustments are necessary when policy changes are made that affect the premium. This section shows one such change, involving Rick Manning's personal auto insurance.

Midway through the policy year, Rick and his wife, Ruth, decide to buy a new car for their daughter as a graduation gift. He calls Connie Sue about adding the new auto to his policy:

RICK: Connie Sue, I have an addition for my personal auto policy. My daughter Jill is graduating, and Ruth and I decided to buy a car as a graduation gift. We'll need to add it to our insurance. I know it will increase my premium, but I wondered if you would give me some idea how much more the insurance is going to cost.

Connie Sue gets all of the important information concerning Jill and the car, checks the rates, and tells Rick what the additional premium will be.

Rick promises to call Connie Sue with more details soon after the Mannings pick up the car. The information will then be fed into the IIA Insurance Company computer, and a new declarations page will be printed. The computer will also generate a premium notice showing the additional premium for the coverage on the car. IIA will mail both the declarations and the bill directly to Rick Manning. The bill will be reflected in Proctor's records from IIA once the policy change premium is paid by Rick Manning.

LOSS CONTROL SERVICE

Both IIA Insurance company and Allied Manufacturing are interested in making sure that Allied's trucks and cars continue to operate safely. If the number of auto accidents is low, and if the accidents that occur are not severe, IIA will not be spending large sums of money to pay claims under Allied's policy.

Allied does not want serious claims either. As long as its claims experience is good, insurance companies will probably continue to charge Allied a relatively low premium for its insurance; if there is a trend towards more serious accidents, insurers are likely to look much less favorably at Allied in the future. Moreover, accidents are expensive and disruptive, even when they are covered by insurance. A great deal of time and effort is involved in handling accident reports, repairing damaged trucks, and aiding the insurance company in settling claims. These problems do not come up when accidents are prevented. Allied is also concerned for its drivers and wants to prevent injury to its employees if at all possible.

The goal of IIA Insurance Company's loss control service is to help prevent serious accidents. IIA's loss control representatives aid IIA's policyholders in minimizing accidental losses.

Halfway through the policy year, Lance Conrad, IIA's loss control representative, visits Allied Manufacturing to provide loss control service. As long as IIA continues to insure Allied's autos, Lance will make similar visits at approximately six-month intervals—and more often, if some special need arises.

While visiting Allied, Lance meets with Rick Manning, the risk manager, and reviews the recent accidents involving Allied vehicles. He looks for ways in which the accidents could have been prevented and tries to identify measures that could prevent similar accidents in the future. He notices that a few recent accidents occurred when an Allied truck was backing up and suggests that better mirrors be installed and that safe backing procedures be discussed at the next drivers' meeting.

After reviewing the records, Lance asks to look at some of the vehicles. Most of Allied's cars and trucks are on the road, but a few are in the garage and maintenance area. Lance is pleased to see that all trucks now have fire extinguishers of the type he recommended during his last inspection. He asks whether the drivers have been instructed in their use and is informed that the extinguishers were discussed in a recent drivers' meeting, shortly after the new ones were purchased.

Lance notices keys in the trucks parked in the garage and asks whether this is standard procedure. Informed that it is, he suggests that keys be removed from the trucks overnight.

After carefully examining the new garage building, Lance observes that the building presents no unusual fire hazards. However, he notes that the locks on the doors are not very secure and recommends that they be replaced with bars across the entire door.

Lance discusses his recommendations with Rick Manning, who thanks him for the useful suggestions. Lance's observations and recommendations will also be contained in a report to the IIA underwriter, Carla Underwood, and will be verified by a written copy to Rick Manning.

This brief example shows how insurance company loss control representatives work together with commercial policyholders to encourage safety and prevent losses from occurring. Measuring the work of loss control representatives is difficult because safety results in an absence of accidents. However, loss control representatives provide important services that help to make insurance work.

POLICY RENEWAL

Most commercial insurance policies are written for a one-year period. Personal policy periods tend to be either six months (auto policies) or one year (homeowners policies) long. Some matters must be taken care of near the expiration date of the policy.

We will look at policy renewal from three different perspectives—those of the underwriter, the producer, and the risk manager. Usually, all three parties cooperate to renew the policy for another policy term.

Policy Renewal: The Underwriter's Perspective

Policy renewal refers to continuing the policy in force for another period after the expiration of its term. Most insurance companies have a **diary system** in their computer that automatically brings up a reminder of the coming expiration either sixty or ninety days before the policy expires. This gives the underwriter plenty of time to handle the renewal process.

> A **diary system**, or **diary**, calls a file to somebody's attention on a specified date. The date might be stated when the diary for a particular file is set up, or an automatic system might call up all files, say, sixty days before expiration of a policy. A diary often involves a computer-generated report.

Underwriting a policy for renewal resembles underwriting a policy when it is "new business." When the Allied Manufacturing policy comes up for renewal, Carla Underwood again analyzes the information she studied when the account was first presented to her as well as any information (such as claims reports) that has since been added to the file. Her concern is primarily with events or changes that might have occurred since her last evaluation. She is now more familiar with Allied, so underwriting at renewal is much easier than underwriting a new account. Carla asks herself, "What has happened since last year that might change my opinion of this account?" In particular, Carla wants to make certain that the business operations have not deteriorated.

Although it is unlikely that there has been a major shift, some important change could have occurred. For example, Allied might now be marketing its products in a different territory. Remember that Carla was concerned when she found that Allied had three sleeping berth rigs in its fleet of trucks until she discovered that Allied was not engaged in long-haul operations. If Allied has now begun selling its products in areas farther from the manufacturing site, it would, at least, affect the renewal premium she charges to Allied Manufacturing. The change could also mean that the account is no longer acceptable to IIA.

To aid Carla in determining whether any changes have occurred, a renewal questionnaire can be used. A **renewal questionnaire** is like a simplified application form. It asks questions about possible changes during the past coverage period. Once Rick Manning at Allied completes the questionnaire, Carla will have more information to help her decide how the account looks now compared to the previous year.

> A **renewal questionnaire** asks questions about changes during the past coverage period.

Policy renewal is a time when the most recent loss experience of the insured is carefully studied. Allied's loss experience had been excellent before IIA wrote the insurance, but Carla wants to make certain that this record has continued. She is also interested in the types of losses that have occurred. Maybe she can identify an important trend. She knows that Allied purchased a new garage for its trucks. Has this change had any effect on

"MARGARET SAYS SHE KEEPS A DIARY, BUT I'VE NEVER SEEN ONE SINGLE COW!"

Reprinted by permission of Hank Ketcham.

A diary system calls a file to someone's attention on a specified date.

losses? Have there been fewer vandalism losses because of a more secure structure? Or have vandalism losses increased because the new garage is located away from the plant or is not so well protected? It is important for Carla to carefully review the loss experience so that important underwriting or rating factors are not overlooked. Carla reviews the reports prepared by Lance Conrad on his loss control visits. The reports continue to suggest that Allied is interested in maintaining its safety record.

Carla also needs to know whether Allied had any significant change in its financial status. Carla must make certain that the company is still financially strong. Carla can usually resolve her financial concerns by a look at the company's current Dun & Bradstreet Report.

If Carla decides to renew the policy, most of the same rating, policy issue, and billing procedures will be the same as last year's. Carla realizes that Allied might be obtaining quotes from other insurance companies, so the pricing situation is just as competitive at renewal as it was with the original submission. Although she must make the pricing decision, subject to approval by her superiors, she asks Paul Proctor for his recommendation. The producer's pricing recommendation will be carefully considered, along with other information.

Policy Renewal: The Producer's Perspective

Producers also set up a diary system to signal when an insurance policy comes up for renewal. In many offices, a computer is programmed to do this. The program is designed to give the producer plenty of time to act on every account before the policy expires. It also gives the producer a chance to verify that the underwriter is working on the renewal.

Paul Proctor's office does not have a computerized diary, but Connie Sue Rapp has a color-coded filing system in which every account file is assigned a color based on the month of policy expiration. Connie Sue knows which policies expire every month and can make certain that a policy is not allowed to expire without attention from the producer.

The expiration point is important because the client might look elsewhere for next year's coverage. This is particularly true with a policy that is being renewed for the first time. After just one year, the client and the agency personnel are still getting to know each other, and a long-term business relationship has not yet been established.

For most commercial accounts, the renewal process begins with a meeting. Paul Proctor makes an appointment to visit Rick Manning and discuss the renewal. As Paul prepares for his meeting with Rick, he has four important points in mind.

Paul Proctor prepares for his meeting with Rick Manning.

First, Paul knows that Rick might decide to look to another producer if he is not completely happy with Paul. Because of this, Paul wants to be well prepared so that Rick has complete confidence in Paul's ability to continue servicing the account. Throughout the year Paul has kept in touch with Rick, and he expects no surprises now.

Second, Paul wants to discuss any insurance-related problems that he or Rick has had during the past year. If any serious problems had come up, Rick probably would have made them known to Paul. Still, there is a chance that something is troubling Rick. The meeting provides an excellent opportunity to discuss problems and possible solutions.

Paul also wants to verify whether a continuation of the current insurance program will in fact meet Allied's needs. Does Rick still believe that the higher deductible is worth the premium savings? Is there any question about adequacy of limits? Have any changes in operations or laws affecting vehicles or drivers affected coverage needs? It is just as important to renew the policy carefully as it was to set up the account properly in the first place. Any coverage changes that Paul and Rick believe are necessary will be passed on to Carla Underwood.

Renewal is also an excellent time to make additional sales. If Rick is satisfied with the service that the Proctor Agency has provided for the insurance on Allied's fleet of vehicles, now is a good time for Paul to inquire about providing coverage for some or all of Allied's insurance needs.

After the meeting with Rick Manning, Paul will submit any coverage changes to Carla Underwood. If he has convinced Rick Manning to allow him to quote on some of Allied's other insurance needs, Paul and Connie Sue will begin preparing a new submission packet for them.

When the policy is renewed, Bobbie Kemp, the bookkeeper, again performs her billing and premium collection functions. It is also necessary to make certain that the diary system is once again set so that the policy will be automatically identified for renewal processing at the correct time next year.

Policy Renewal: The Insured's Perspective

Rick Manning has been in charge of insurance for Allied Manufacturing for many years and can easily compare the service that he is now receiving with what he had before. (Because Allied had used another producer for its fleet coverage for several years before the switch to Proctor, it is natural for Rick to make a comparison.)

If Rick is satisfied with Proctor and with IIA, he would probably have little reason to look elsewhere for coverage. Remember that Rick gave Paul the opportunity to quote on this account only because Allied's previous producer retired. Most insureds wish to develop a long-lasting relationship with the producer and the insurance company as long as everything is going smoothly.

Rick must decide how he stands well before the renewal date arrives. If he is not completely satisfied with Paul Proctor or IIA, he will have to decide which other producers and insurance companies to try. He needs to give others plenty of time to prepare quotes if necessary.

Rick Manning would not need to look far to find someone to quote on his insurance. Allied receives many inquiries from other insurance producers who consider it a prospect. But since each quote takes a fair amount of time and effort by Rick and others at Allied, he will probably reject most other offers to quote as long as he is content with Paul Proctor and IIA Insurance Company.

Rick Manning prepares to review his operations with Paul Proctor before renewal.

Rick must also be prepared to review his operations with Paul before the renewal.

The Renewal

As it turns out, the annual review goes smoothly. Rick Manning is pleased with both Proctor and IIA Insurance Company. He decides to renew the business auto policy with Paul Proctor, and he also agrees to allow Paul to quote on Allied's other insurance coverages when they expire. Carla Under-wood is happy to renew the policy at the price recommended by Paul Proctor and her superiors approve this decision.

Renewal for the Allied Manufacturing policy is accomplished with no problems, and another policy cycle begins. But before the old cycle is completely over, the premium auditing process must take place.

PREMIUM AUDITING

For many commercial insurance policies, the premium paid at the beginning of the policy period is a "provisional premium" based on an estimate of the extent of operations to be insured. At the end of the policy period (usually one year), the policyholder's records are examined, or audited, by a **premium auditor** to determine the audited premium. The premium auditor examines the insured's records to see how extensive the insured's operations were. If more extensive than estimated, an additional premium will be due; if less extensive, the insured will receive a partial refund.

Perry Andrews is the IIA Insurance Company premium auditor assigned to Allied Manufacturing's audit. Allied's insurance policy states that all vehicles used during the policy period are automatically insured, regardless of how many are added or deleted during the year. The audited premium will reflect these additions or deletions. Perry's job is to calculate the final premium based on the actual changes in vehicles and when they took place during the year. To do this, he meets with Rick Manning and goes over Allied's fleet records for the policy period. Perry must examine the dates the vehicles were added or sold and determine proportional adjustments to the premium based on these changes. If there were no changes, Perry Andrews' audit at the end of the year would indicate that no adjustment is necessary.

> A **premium auditor** examines policyholders' records at the end of the policy period to determine the audited premium.

If Allied's sales were strong and increased during the year, additional trucks might have been purchased or leased. Perry's audit would then show that the audited premium exceeds the provisional premium because of the larger number of vehicles actually used during the year. Allied would be charged this difference after the audit.

If Allied's sales had decreased, the opposite might have occurred. Allied Manufacturing could have found that part of its fleet was idle and might have decided to sell some vehicles. With a decrease in the size of the fleet, Perry's audit would indicate that a refund is due to Allied Manufacturing because the audited premium is less than the provisional premium.

Food For Thought

Rick Manning has to decide whether to renew Allied's policy through Paul Proctor's agency or to give other producers the right to bid often for the account. Rick also has one other option—**self-insurance**, also called **retention**.

Many large corporations now choose this alternative because of two important cost savings obtained through self-insurance. First, the insurance company's administrative costs, such as the producer's commission, underwriting expenses, policy issue costs, and general overhead, are eliminated. Of course, this benefit is offset to some extent because the corporation itself must spend money on administering the plan and paying claims.

The second advantage is the investment return. The corporation keeps the dollars that would have been paid in premiums until they are actually paid out for losses. Investment income generated by the funds in the meantime is kept by the corporation. When insurance premiums are paid to the insurance company, the insured receives no direct investment return.

It is necessary to perform a careful analysis to determine whether self-insurance is a better alternative than purchasing insurance. For most, purchasing insurance coverage is still a necessity—at least for some exposures. Even when self-insurance is used, it is often combined with "excess" insurance to protect the firm against losses that exceed a set self-insured amount.

During his audit, Perry makes a few vehicle changes and determines that Allied owes IIA Insurance Company an additional premium of $1,200. This is billed to Allied through Paul Proctor.

SUMMARY

In this chapter we saw how Paul Proctor presented an insurance proposal to Rick Manning and that Rick chose the IIA policy to cover Allied's fleet of trucks and autos. We saw the processes involved in issuing, delivering, and billing the policy. And we looked at the services provided while an insurance policy is in force.

During the year, a change in Allied Manufacturing's operations (the new garage) caused a modification to the insurance policy that involved no change in premium. We saw how that was handled. We also saw how a policy change is handled when Rick adds a car to his personal auto policy, requiring additional premium. And we saw how IIA's loss control service helps to meet Allied's needs.

We also looked at policy renewal from three different perspectives—those of the underwriter, the producer, and the insured.

Finally, since many commercial insurance policies are audited at the end of the policy period to determine the final premium, we examined the important role of premium auditors—who are among the many people who help make insurance work.

How Are Claims Handled?

5

ick Manning and his wife, Ruth, have decided to buy a new five-speed Dodge two-door for use by their daughter, Jill, as a graduation gift. They contacted Connie Sue Rapp, as we saw in Chapter 4, to make sure they would have coverage for the new car on their IIA Insurance Company personal auto policy. Our story resumes as Ruth Manning picks up the car, which is to be a surprise gift at Jill's graduation party the next evening. Harry Anderson, the owner of Anderson Dodge, handles the sale himself.

Ruth gets into the car and drives away. Thinking a big bow on the hood of the car would add a nice touch, she decides to stop at the Schuman Stationery Store and buy some ribbon. She sees a parking space and begins to park. But when she tries to stop, her foot follows the brake pedal all the way to the floor—there are no brakes! The car jumps the curb and crashes into the plate glass window of the stationery store. The flying glass seriously injures Susan Cleamons, a store customer who is near the window at the time of the accident. Ruth's leg is very sore after the accident, and she is taken to the hospital for X-rays and observation.

Ruth has no complications and is released from the hospital the next day, in time to attend Jill's graduation ceremony. The car, which did not fare so well, is in the body shop.

A **claim** is a demand by a person or business seeking to recover for a loss.

A claim can be made against an individual. For example, the stationery store might make a claim against Ruth, asking that she pay for the damage to the store.

A claim can be made against an insurance company when an insured asks the insurance company to pay for a loss that might be covered by an insurance policy.

A **claims adjuster** is the person directly responsible for investigating and settling claims that might be covered by insurance.

In this chapter you will see how the **claims** resulting from this accident are handled. The person directly responsible for investigating and settling insurance claims is known as a **claims adjuster**.

THE ROLE OF THE CLAIMS ADJUSTER

The claims adjuster might be one of the few insurance people an insurance buyer meets—besides the producer, of course. The reputation of any insurance company is strongly influenced by the behavior and competence of its claims adjusters.

Policyholders pay money to the insurance company for protection against losses. When accidents occur, claimants expect to be compensated fairly and promptly for the resulting losses as they have been promised by the insurance company.

A claims adjuster's job is to handle claims quickly and fairly. This means that the adjuster should contact **claimants** promptly in order to pay covered claims as soon as possible.

Claimant

A **claimant** is anyone who presents a claim.

For a liability insurance loss, the claimant is a person or business that has suffered a loss and seeks to collect for that loss from an insured. The insurance company is involved because it has promised in a liability insurance policy to pay covered losses on behalf of the insured.

For a property insurance loss, the claimant is the insured that wants the insurance company to pay for repairing or replacing his or her damaged property.

The adjuster must also protect the interest of the insurance company by making sure that claims that are not covered are not paid and that covered claims are paid only to the extent promised by the insurance company. Striking the proper balance between the interest of the insurance company and the interest of claimants is not always easy. Few occupations challenge one's understanding of human behavior more than the job of claims adjuster. The adjuster must be knowledgeable about insurance coverage and claims adjustment procedures and must also be able to provide assistance and peace of mind to people who have suffered a loss and are injured, distraught, or under a great deal of stress.

With the insurance policy as a guide, the adjuster investigates the facts surrounding each claim and tries to answer two fundamental questions:

- **First, is the claim resulting from the accident covered by the insurance policy?**

"Whom shall I say is blowing his cool?"

Reprinted courtesy of Bituminous Casualty Corporation.

If the answer to this question is yes, the adjuster moves on to the second question:

- **How much will be paid, according to the policy?**

The insurance policy can be summarized in one word—promise. It is a promise to pay for certain types of losses if an insured event occurs. The policy attempts to be precise in describing the circumstances under which the insurance company's promise applies. In other words, the policy tries to state clearly the situations for which it provides "coverage."

The policy also specifies how to establish the amount to be paid following covered losses.

- **Policy limits** state the maximum amount that may be paid. In effect, they place an upper boundary on how much the insurer may pay under a certain insurance policy.

- Property insurance policies contain a **valuation clause** that clarifies the method that will be used to place a value on damaged property.

- **Deductibles** can reduce the amount to be paid. No payment is made for losses that are entirely below the deductible, and the deductible amount is subtracted from claims that exceed the deductible.

> The **valuation clause** in a property insurance policy states the method that is used to place a value on damaged property.

In short, a claims adjuster's job is to treat all parties fairly. If the facts indicate that the insurance company's promise to pay does not apply to a certain event, fair treatment means that no payment should be made and that the insured should be told as soon as possible that the claim is not covered. Payment should be made promptly to claimants who have covered claims, in accordance with the terms of the insurance policy.

Earlier, you read the story of Ruth Manning's accident. As this chapter continues, you will see how a claims adjuster and other people play a role in the claims resulting from Ruth's accident.

NOTIFYING THE INSURER

Whenever an accident occurs, the insured has an important duty—to notify the insurer as soon as possible. Timely notification is vital to the insurance company, so this duty is stated in the insurance policy. Investigation of the claim can best take place when the evidence is fresh and when the memory of witnesses is clear. Notification to the insurer "as soon as possible" (or words to that effect) is required by most insurance policies. It is usually easy to meet this requirement.

Claims Clerk, Claim File

A **claims clerk** in the insurance company claims department has the job of taking claims reports over the telephone. **Claims clerks** also do many other important things to help in the process of adjusting claims—such as placing tape-recorded statements, along with other information, in the proper claim files.

A **claim file** is simply a folder or computer entry that is created ("opened") when a claim is made. A paper claim file is sometimes kept separate from other customer files that contain general correspondence and coverage and billing information. Into the claim file folder are placed all pieces of information that pertain specifically to the claim, such as a completed claim form and bills showing repair costs.

The insured rarely gives notice directly to the claims adjuster who will handle the claim. Sometimes the notice is received by a **claims clerk** in the insurance company claims department who has the job of taking claim reports over the telephone and opening claim files. The producer might never become involved in handling a claim that is reported directly to the insurance company claims department.

Often, the first notice of a claim is given to the producer—or someone in the producer's office—in a telephone call or personal visit. Notice to an agent or agency satisfies the requirement that an insured notify "the insurance company" of an accident since an insurance agent is legally a representative of the insurance company.

The Producer's Responsibility

What does a producer do after learning of an accident? Normally, the producer (or someone on the producer's staff) gets the facts and quickly analyzes the situation. At this point, the producer tries to determine whether the insurance company should be told of the accident. The producer has to decide into which of three categories the event falls:

1. The loss is not covered.
2. The amount of damage is within the deductible.
3. The loss is (or might be) covered.

A claims clerk in the insurance company claim department takes the report.

The Loss Is Not Covered.   It might be clear to the producer that the event is definitely not covered by the insurance policy. For example, a customer notifies the producer that his or her auto has been damaged in a collision with a telephone pole, but the producer finds that the insured had chosen not to insure against physical damage to the car resulting from collision. There is little reason to proceed with a claim report, assuming that no other damage or injury occurred (such as property damage to the telephone pole, for which the insured might be responsible).

The producer will inform the client that a claim like this is not covered. The producer takes this action only when it is absolutely clear that the claim is not covered. If there is any uncertainty, the insurance company should receive a report on the accident.

The Amount of Damage Is Within the Deductible.   The producer might believe that the accident is covered by the insurance policy, but that the amount of physical damage falls below the deductible. For example, assume that a client with an auto policy is involved in a minor accident. It appears that it will cost about $200 to replace a damaged molding, and the auto policy has collision coverage with a $500 deductible. There is no reason to waste time processing a claim for less than the deductible because the insurer has no obligation to make any payment unless the deductible is exceeded. In cases like this, the producer informs the client and either makes a note of the claim in the insured's file or "opens" (creates) a claim file for the accident.

A producer who is aware of a claim usually creates a claim file in the production office. Even when producers or their staff do not adjust the claim, they try to follow the progress of the investigation and to keep the policyholder informed of important developments.

Why even make a note when it appears that nothing is payable under the policy? Immediately after an accident, it is not always clear what repairs will cost. The loss might eventually exceed the deductible. By noting the claim or setting up a file, the producer is recording the fact that the insured has satisfied the requirement to give the insurer prompt notice that an accident has happened. If the repairs turn out to be more costly than originally assumed, or if additional claims arise in the future from the same accident (such as a claim from the telephone company for damage to the telephone pole or wires), the event can be easily identified, and a claim will then be filed by the producer with the insurance company claim department.

The Loss Is (or May Be) Covered.   For claims in this category, the producer knows that coverage is provided by the insurance policy. Or if the producer is not certain of coverage—perhaps because the facts surrounding the accident are not entirely clear—the producer may refer the claim to the claims department for reevaluation. In either case, the producer sets up a claim file and immediately informs the insurance company claims department that an accident has occurred.

Medical Payments Coverage

The **medical payments coverage** of an auto insurance policy covers the medical expenses of a covered person who is injured in an auto accident. Medical payments coverage usually applies to each covered person in some modest amount, such as $1,000 or $5,000. The coverage applies no matter who was at fault in the accident.

In some states with "no-fault" auto insurance, a driver's injuries would be covered by "**personal injury protection**"— the usual name for a no-fault coverage—rather than by medical payments coverage.

Ruth Manning's accident falls into this category. The accident caused significant physical damage to the Dodge—well in excess of the $500 deductible. Ruth will have medical expenses because of her injuries, and these will be covered by the **medical payments coverage** of her policy. Moreover, it appears that Ruth might be legally responsible for the damage to the stationery store and for the injuries to the customer. Let's see how the notification process takes place.

The Notification

On the morning after the accident, Rick Manning calls Paul Proctor's office to report it. Connie Sue Rapp answers the telephone.

RICK: Connie Sue, I'm afraid I have some bad news for you this morning. My wife, Ruth, was in a serious auto accident yesterday.

CONNIE SUE: How did it happen?

RICK: You remember I just called you last week about that new car for our daughter, Jill, and....

Connie Sue takes the information about the accident from Rick Manning and completes an **accident report form**. Although Ruth's injuries, the property damage to the Dodge, and the property damage to the store are important, Connie Sue realizes that the most important part of the insurance claim relates to the injured customer. At this time, she does not know how badly the customer was hurt, but with any accident involving bodily injury there is a possibility of the injury being serious and creating a very large liability claim. It is especially important that a claims adjuster get right to work on such a case.

As the conversation ends, Connie Sue indicates that she will immediately notify the IIA Insurance Company. She tells Rick that he may, if he wishes, get a couple of **estimates** of the cost to repair the collision damage to the Dodge and that he will hear from a claims adjuster soon.

TYPES OF ADJUSTERS

After Connie Sue Rapp informs the IIA claims department about the accident, someone must be assigned to handle it. In this case, Craig Sartin, the IIA claims supervisor, must decide among one of three different types of claims adjusters.

Insurance Company Claims Representatives

Most claims are handled by full-time employees of the insurance company. Although most insurance

Estimates, Drive-In Claims Service, Physical Damage Appraiser, Material Damage Appraiser

When damage is minor, an insurance company sometimes requests that the insured obtain two or three written **estimates** from body shops to establish what it will cost to repair a damaged car. The estimates help to determine the amount that the insurance company will pay.

Many insurers have streamlined this system in recent years by providing **drive-in claims service** in areas where they have many insured cars. If the car is still driveable, the owner takes it to a designated claims center. The car is inspected by a **physical damage appraiser**, sometimes called a **material damage appraiser**, who is able to estimate the repair cost based on auto parts prices and labor costs. A draft (check) is issued for the amount of the estimate—minus any deductible that applies. The insured is usually permitted to select the body shop that will perform the repairs.

6/27

"Find out how much to fix it. Take it to three different toy stores."

HERMAN copyright Jim Unger. Reprinted with permission of UNIVERSAL PRESS SYNDICATE. All rights reserved.

The vehicle owner sometimes gets estimates to establish the cost of auto repairs.

ACORD. AUTOMOBILE LOSS NOTICE

DATE (MM/DD/YY) 6/1/x4

PRODUCER	**PHONE (A/C, No, Ext):** 215-555-2100	COMPANY		MISCELLANEOUS INFO (Site & location code)

Paul Proctor
Plainfield OI 58740

COMPANY: IIA

POLICY NUMBER PA-68-0097-45		REFERENCE NUMBER	CAT #

CODE: 39542	SUB CODE:	**EFFECTIVE DATE** 3/1/x4	**EXPIRATION DATE** 9/1/x4	**DATE OF ACCIDENT AND TIME** 6/1/x4	x AM / PM	**PREVIOUSLY REPORTED** YES / x NO

AGENCY CUSTOMER ID:

INSURED   CONTACT   CONTACT INSURED

NAME AND ADDRESS	NAME AND ADDRESS	WHERE TO CONTACT
Rick Manning 837 Fourth Avenue Plainfield, OI 58740	Ruth Manning 837 Fourth Avenue Plainfield, OI 58740	Home
		WHEN TO CONTACT Anytime

RESIDENCE PHONE (A/C, No) 215-555-7535	BUSINESS PHONE (A/C, No, Ext) 215-555-1944	RESIDENCE PHONE (A/C, No) 215-555-7535	BUSINESS PHONE (A/C, No, Ext) ----

LOSS

LOCATION OF ACCIDENT (Include city & state) 478 N. Main St. Plainfield OI	AUTHORITY CONTACTED: Plainfield Police	VIOLATIONS/CITATIONS None
	REPORT #: X40601-1	

DESCRIPTION OF ACCIDENT (Use reverse side, if necessary): New car just picked up from dealer. Brakes failed while parking. Car crashed through storefront.

POLICY INFORMATION

BODILY INJURY (Per Person)	BODILY INJURY (Per Accident)	PROPERTY DAMAGE	SINGLE LIMIT	MEDICAL PAYMENT	OTC DEDUCTIBLE	OTHER COVERAGE & DEDUCTIBLES (UM, no-fault, towing, etc)
			300,000	5,000	100	UM 50,000

LOSS PAYEE None	COLLISION DED 500

INSURED VEHICLE

VEH #	YEAR	MAKE: Dodge	BODY TYPE: 2 dr		PLATE NUMBER	STATE
2	19x4	MODEL: Shadow	V.I.N. 1743753486		2K4110	OI

OWNER'S NAME & ADDRESS Rick Manning	RESIDENCE PHONE (A/C, No): 215-555-7535
	BUSINESS PHONE (A/C, No, Ext): 215-555-1944
DRIVER'S NAME & ADDRESS Ruth Manning (Check if same as owner)	RESIDENCE PHONE (A/C, No): 215-555-7535
	BUSINESS PHONE (A/C, No, Ext):

RELATION TO INSURED (Employee, family, etc.) Spouse	DATE OF BIRTH 1/26/44	DRIVER'S LICENSE NUMBER 897-5602-235	STATE	PURPOSE OF USE Pleasure	USED WITH PERMISSION? x YES / NO

DESCRIBE DAMAGE Airbag Front end, fender	ESTIMATE AMOUNT 4,000	WHERE CAN VEHICLE BE SEEN? Plainfield body shop	WHEN CAN VEH BE SEEN? Daily 9-5	OTHER INSURANCE ON VEHICLE No

PROPERTY DAMAGED

DESCRIBE PROPERTY (If auto, year, make, model, plate #) Stationery store building	OTHER VEH/PROP INS? YES / NO	COMPANY OR AGENCY NAME: Unknown POLICY #:

OWNER'S NAME & ADDRESS Schuman Stationery Store	RESIDENCE PHONE (A/C, No):
	BUSINESS PHONE (A/C, No, Ext): 215-555-6442
OTHER DRIVER'S NAME & ADDRESS (Check if same as owner)	RESIDENCE PHONE (A/C, No):
	BUSINESS PHONE (A/C, No, Ext):

DESCRIBE DAMAGE Windows and brickwork	ESTIMATE AMOUNT 10,000	WHERE CAN DAMAGE BE SEEN? 478 N. Main St. Plainfield OI

INJURED

NAME & ADDRESS	PHONE (A/C, No)	PED	INS VEH	OTH VEH	AGE	EXTENT OF INJURY
Ruth Manning 837 Fourth Ave. Plainfield	215-555-7535		x		45	Leg injury
Susan Cleamons APA Accountants Plainfield	215-555-3800	x			23	Glass cuts to face

WITNESSES OR PASSENGERS

NAME & ADDRESS	PHONE (A/C, No)	INS VEH	OTH VEH	OTHER (Specify)
Unknown				

REMARKS (Include adjuster assigned): Assigned to Clarence Atwood

REPORTED BY Rick Manning	REPORTED TO Connie Sue Rapp	SIGNATURE OF PRODUCER OR INSURED *Paul Proctor*

ACORD 2 (1/93)   **NOTE: IMPORTANT STATE INFORMATION ON REVERSE SIDE**   © ACORD CORPORATION 1993

companies have some adjusters in the home office, these people cannot travel throughout the country investigating routine claims because of the heavy expense it would involve. It is important to have adjusters close to the "action" because the adjuster must often do a good deal of work at or near the scene of an accident.

Because of this, most insurance company adjusters work from a branch or regional office. If the branch or region covers a large territory, the insurance company might also set up separate claims offices in areas too far away to be served easily by adjusters from the branch office.

> Most claims are adjusted by full-time employees of the insurance company.

Independent Adjusters

As you might suspect, it can be expensive to set up many claims offices in widespread geographic areas—especially in areas where a particular insurance company does not do much business. In some places, it is not practical for an insurance company to set up a remote claims office. Instead, the insurance company might use employee adjusters only in those areas where the company has heavy concentrations of policyholders (such as around large cities) and use **independent adjusters** everywhere else. Independent adjusters provide claims services to insurance companies for a fee.

> **Independent adjusters** are independent contractors who provide claims services to various insurance companies. Independent adjusters charge insurance companies a fee for each claim that they handle.

Independent adjusters are also used when employees are too busy to handle all the claims. For example, when a tornado strikes an area, there might not be enough insurance company claims representatives to handle all the claims as quickly as the insurance company would like. When this happens, independent adjusters are used.

Often, independent adjusters are used when special skills are needed. Certain independent adjusters are experts in highly specialized fields, such as investigating aircraft accidents.

Some insurance companies use independent adjusters for all field claim activity. These companies employ claims personnel in the home and branch offices to assign claims and monitor their progress, but all field work is done by independents.

Independent adjusters earn a fee for their work. Although some independent adjusters are self-employed, most work with an adjusting firm. Some adjusting firms have one small office with a few adjusters, and others are national companies with hundreds of offices and thousands of adjusters. The two largest independent adjusting firms are Crawford & Company and GAB Business Services. Several other independent adjusting companies also have claims adjusters in many areas.

Producers as Adjusters

In some cases, the producer acts as the claims adjuster. Some producers are given **draft authority** up to a certain amount, such as $2,500, so that

Draft Authority

A producer with **draft authority** is permitted to handle small claims and issue **drafts**—which are similar to checks written on the insurance company's checking account—to pay certain types of covered claims that are within the dollar limit of the draft authority.

Inside Adjusters, Telephone Adjusters

Inside adjusters, also called **telephone adjusters,** are generally used when the claim is clearly covered and there is no question about the circumstances of the accident or whether the claim is valid. Suppose, for example, that a home is burglarized and a television is stolen. Police have investigated the incident and filed a written report, and the claimant has provided a receipt that shows the date of purchase and the purchase price of the missing TV.

A claims adjuster would not accomplish much by visiting the policyholder, talking about the burglary, and looking at the empty table where the TV used to be. The entire claim can be easily handled over the telephone and through the mail.

small claims can be handled entirely in the production office. The producer is allowed to issue a draft directly to the policyholder who has a covered claim. A brief claim report is sent to the insurance company, and, unless complications arise, the claim is closed.

THE CLAIM IS ASSIGNED TO AN ADJUSTER

After taking the accident report information over the telephone, the IIA claims clerk gives it to Craig Sartin—the claims supervisor. After reading the report, he assigns claims adjuster Clarence Atwood to the Manning case. Clarence, an employee of IIA Insurance Company, spends most of his time away from the office providing claims service. Craig does not assign this claim to an **inside adjuster** because it requires some outside investigation.

Clarence receives his assignment late in the afternoon, several hours after the claim was reported by Rick Manning.

VERIFYING COVERAGE

Coverage verification—making sure that the claim is covered by an insurance policy that is in effect—is the first step in Clarence Atwood's handling of a claim. For the Ruth Manning accident, coverage verification is not difficult. The claim was promptly reported. The auto policy covers losses caused by accidents of this type. Unless it can be shown that Ruth intentionally smashed into the stationery store, the damage to Ruth's car and any resulting liability for damage and injury to others are covered.

INVESTIGATING THE ACCIDENT

The next thing Clarence Atwood must do is to investigate the accident. This important step has one important goal—GET THE FACTS. Clarence must try to develop a clear understanding of how, when, where, and why the accident occurred. In some situations, this is a simple task. In other cases, however, it is difficult to establish all the facts surrounding the event. Auto accidents involving several cars, for which each driver might have a different version of the facts, can be especially tough.

When Connie Sue Rapp took the accident report from Rick Manning, she entered it into an **accident report form**. When she called the IIA claims office, a claims clerk entered the information into a blank copy of the same accident report form that appeared on her computer screen. This report provides Clarence with the first information about the claim.

The claims adjuster seeks two types of information in every investigation—physical evidence and oral evidence.

Physical evidence is any tangible thing that is relevant in determining the facts concerning the accident. Most physical evidence is found at the scene of the accident. In this investigation, physical evidence will be found at the stationery store (where Clarence will check the damage to the building). Physical evidence will also be found at the auto repair shop, where the Dodge can be examined. The injuries to Ruth and Susan can also be important physical evidence.

Oral evidence involves statements from people—often people who were at the scene of the accident. Oral evidence helps to clarify the events surrounding the accident. Unfortunately, witnesses often provide conflicting reports on what happened. When this happens, the adjuster has the challenging task of determining what actually occurred.

The next morning, as Clarence drives down Main Street in Plainfield, the boarded-up windows make the stationery store easy to find. He is surprised to see that both front windows are boarded up, even though it is obvious from the damage that the car crashed into the left window and not the one on the right. Before entering the store, he pauses to examine the damaged bricks and window frame. He is happy to see that the store is open for business. As he enters the store, he sees that a cash register and check-out counter are located directly behind each of the two broken windows. With the check-out counters so close to the windows, it is fortunate that only one person was hurt by flying glass.

Clarence finds a store clerk, identifies himself, and asks if the owner of the store is available. He is told that Stan Schuman is in his office near the back of the store. Clarence goes directly to the office and introduces himself.

STAN: Well, it's ironic that you should show up right now. I've just talked with Smithson Glass Company. They plan to stop by this afternoon to fix one of the front windows. The can't fix the window on the side that got hit by the car because the building damage will have to be repaired first, but they'll slip in a new pane on the other side. It certainly was an unfortunate accident. I'm a good friend of Rick and Ruth Manning. I sure hope Ruth wasn't badly injured.

Accident Report Form

An **accident report form** is used to record key information about the accident.

The same **accident report form** is used in the producer'a office and in the claims office. This makes it easy to transmit accident reports over the telephone because information is already in the right order. In fact, Connie Sue does not have to read the various questions or headings on the form, but can simply read the answers in order.

Physical evidence is any tangible thing that is relevant in determining the facts concerning the accident.

Oral evidence involves statements from people—often people who were at the scene of the accident. Oral evidence helps to clarify the events surrounding the accident.

CLARENCE: It certainly was an unusual accident. By the way, how did that other window break? Did the impact knock it out?

STAN: It must have. Both windows shattered simultaneously. In fact, the only serious injury occurred on that side of the store. One of my regular customers, Susan Cleamons—she's a young accountant—was looking at the ledger paper next to that window. The flying glass cut her pretty badly, especially on her face, I'm sad to say. I hear she's still in the hospital.

CLARENCE: Was anybody else injured?

STAN: No, we were really lucky. There were no other customers at the front of the store just then and both cashiers were away from the registers, helping customers. And since the car stopped just short of the checkout counter, nothing inside the store was damaged.

CLARENCE: That was lucky. How's your business been since the accident? Has the damage caused any slowdown?

STAN: To tell you the truth, I think it's actually helped business. We've been the local curiosity for the last couple of days, and our sales have been pretty good. I've been watching carefully because I was going to let you know about it if my sales lagged. I really don't think it's a problem, especially now that one window will be fixed this afternoon.

CLARENCE: Have you had anybody look at the damage to the store?

STAN: Yes. Carl Topper, the contractor, built this store eight years ago, so I had him come over and look at it. Carl thinks he can begin repairs by the end of the week and can fix everything in one or two days at the most. Then I can have the glass put back on that side, have the lettering redone, and I'll be back in full swing.

As part of his investigation, Clarence Atwood, the claims adjuster, interviews Stan Schuman, the owner of Schuman Stationery Store.

CLARENCE: Have you contacted your own insurance company about the damage to the building?

STAN: Oh, sure. I'm covered by Crowley Fire and Casualty, and they said to go ahead and have the repairs done. They say I'm fully covered by my building policy, except for the deductible amount. Of course, after they pay for the damage, I'm sure they'll come to your insurance company expecting reimbursement.

CLARENCE: Well, there's no doubt about who ran into the store and did the damage, that's for sure. We think there might be faulty brakes involved, though, so Ruth might not be totally at fault—we'll just have to see. Would you mind telling me who else was working in the store at the time of the accident? I think I should talk to any witness.

STAN: The only employee who saw the accident happen was Millie Brown. You probably met her on the way in.

CLARENCE: Thanks. I'll go talk to her, take a few pictures of the damage, and then be on my way.

> **Food for Thought**
> Why do you think Clarence is concerned about Mr. Schuman's business activity since the accident? If the damage to the store was so extensive that the store had to be temporarily closed, or if the accident should cause a decrease in business volume, the owner would suffer a loss of income. Fortunately, it appears that there is no loss of income in this case. If there were, Ruth Manning could be responsible for it, and IIA Insurance Company might need to reimburse Mr. Schuman on her behalf.

Clarence obtains a statement from Millie Brown, but she does not add any new information. He examines the scene of the accident one more time, takes a few photographs, and gets back into his car.

How the accident occurred is fairly obvious at this point. The crucial question now is why. To get an answer, Clarence needs to talk to Ruth Manning and examine the Dodge at the body shop.

With Ruth's permission, Clarence tape records the interview. A claims clerk will place a copy of the tape in the claim file. (Clarence has also dictated some memos, recording his observations and conversations in the store. These, too, will become part of the growing claim file.)

Clarence receives some information from Ruth not already contained the accident report. He learns that Ruth had never needed to use the brakes until she reached the parking space in front of the store, so she could not say whether they had ever been working. She repeats her statement that the brake pedal went all the way to the floor when she tried to stop.

Clarence also learns that Ruth's doctor has told her that he expects her to have no further medical problems as a result of the accident. The car's airbag might have helped prevent a serious injury.

Clarence feels that he now has a clear mental picture of events from the time Ruth picked up the car until the time of the accident. There are three other items he wants to investigate before leaving:

1. He needs to look at the car to examine the brakes and see what damage has occurred to the car itself.

2. He wants to talk with the Anderson dealership about the faulty brakes.

3. He needs to find out the extent of Susan Cleamons' injuries.

He begins by talking with the manager of the body shop. The car looks about as Clarence had imagined. The body shop has already completed an estimate for Rick Manning. The manager expects the repairs to cost $4,000. Clarence asks the manager if he tested the brakes. The manager says that they look fine to him, but he did not check them thoroughly. Clarence opens the door and puts his foot on the brake pedal—the pedal goes down about two inches and feels normal, as far as Clarence can tell. He tells the body shop manager that he would prefer to have the car left exactly as it is because he might want an expert to examine the brakes and determine what might have gone wrong. The manager tells him that the car manufacturer's representative has already arranged to examine the car next Monday morning at nine o'clock.

Clarence then stops at the hospital to see if he can find out about Susan Cleamons' condition. Unfortunately, he learns that Susan's face is badly cut, that she has less severe cuts on other parts of her body, and that she might be permanently scarred.

Finally, Clarence visits Anderson Dodge. He is not greeted warmly. Everyone is obviously aware of the accident. Harry Anderson agrees to meet with Clarence but does not provide much information other than the name of his insurance company.

Clarence decides he has done just about all the investigating he can do for now. He tries to sort through everything he has learned to decide where he and IIA stand in this matter.

First, the car needs to be repaired. He is certain that Rick and Ruth Manning want the car fixed as soon as possible, but he would first like to have the auto examined by an independent expert to see if the brakes were faulty. Regardless of why the car was damaged, IIA Insurance Company has an obligation to pay for the repair of the car. But he realizes there will be a little delay before he is ready to authorize repairs. After making payment, it is possible that IIA would be able to recover its payment by **subrogation** either against the dealership or against the auto manufacturer itself if either of these parties proves to be responsible for the accident.

Second, Clarence expects a liability claim against Ruth Manning alleging that she is responsible for the property damage to the stationery store. Although Stan Schuman could file a claim directly against Ruth, Clarence expects that Stan will collect from his own insurance company, Crowley Fire and Casualty. Crowley will probably attempt to **subrogate** against Ruth Manning.

Third, and most important, is the potential liability for the bodily injury to Susan Cleamons, who might suffer permanent disfigurement if her facial cuts are serious.

Finally, Ruth Manning also has some medical bills that IIA will pay under the medical payments coverage of her insurance policy. Ruth's emergency room visit and two-day stay in the hospital have created a total bill of approximately $3,000. Since there appear to be no complications, however, the dollar amount of this claim is fixed.

As to who is responsible for the accident, Clarence knows that the answer lies in determining its actual cause. If Ruth Manning's driving ability (or inability) is found to be the cause of this accident, IIA Insurance Company is responsible for all damages and would have no rights to subrogate against the manufacturer or Anderson. If the Anderson dealership's faulty new car preparation is determined to be the cause, then Anderson (or Anderson's insurance company, assuming the business is properly insured) is responsible for paying all of the losses, and IIA can subrogate if it has already paid for repair of the Dodge. Finally, reason might be found to hold the auto manufacturer liable, if it can be proven that it manufactured a faulty brake system or improperly assembled the auto.

Subrogation, Subrogate

When the insurer pays the insured for a loss, the insurer takes over the insured's right to collect damages from any other person responsible for the loss. Otherwise, if an insured could collect from his or her own insurance company and also from the party responsible for the accident, the insured could end up better off after a loss than before. Insurance companies overcome this potential problem by stating that the insurance company takes over the right of recovery. The process of recovering these payments is called **subrogation**. In this case, IIA Insurance Company might **subrogate** against the car dealer or manufacturer because IIA is **subrogated** to the insured's right of recovery.

Clarence knows that several lawsuits might be involved to resolve all these issues.

THE LOSS RESERVE

One important step in the claims process is setting a **loss reserve**. A loss reserve must be established whenever the insurance company learns of an accident for which it might have to pay a claim. A loss reserve is the insurance company's best current estimate of the total dollar amount that will be paid in the future for an accident that has already occurred. In effect, the insurance company sets aside some money that will eventually be paid out to settle the claims arising from this accident.

A **loss reserve** is the insurance company's best current estimate of the total dollar amount that will be paid in the future for an accident that has already occurred.

Clarence Atwood meets with his supervisor, Craig Sartin, and they establish the loss reserves for the claims arising out of this accident. Although a reserve has been established, the reserve is only a best estimate of the amount IIA might eventually have to pay. This estimate is subject to change as the investigation continues and more information becomes available.

THE INVESTIGATION CONTINUES

To resolve the question of responsibility, the cause of the accident must be identified.

The manager at the body shop saw nothing obviously wrong with the brakes. Clarence also saw nothing wrong with the brakes when he examined the car. Clarence has ordered an examination by an expert auto mechanic to establish whether there was any flaw in the brakes. Once he gets this report, he hopes his questions will be answered.

Clarence works on adjusting other claims during the next few days while he is waiting for three separate reports—the expert's report on the faulty brakes, the physician's report on Susan Cleamons, and the report on the cost of glass and reconstruction work on the stationery store. The mechanic's report will help to establish the cause of the accident. The other reports will help to establish the dollar value of the loss. Once these reports are in, the loss reserve for the Manning case might be revised. Clarence also knows that he might need to investigate further before the claim is settled, depending on the brake expert's findings.

The report on the stationery store arrives first. The total cost of repairs is now estimated at $9,800. Stan Schuman's insurer is paying for the repairs (less Stan's deductible) and expects to recover its payment from Ruth or whoever is ultimately found responsible for the accident.

Because the report on the brakes is so important, Clarence decides to meet Andy Melcher, the expert auto mechanic, and watch while he performs his inspection. Clarence assumes he can obtain further information about Susan Cleamons' injuries on the same day, so he drives back to Plainfield and meets Andy Melcher and the car manufacturer's expert at the body shop.

The experts' inspection discloses that the brakes are not faulty. Andy agrees with the Dodge representative—the brakes are not faulty, and there is nothing to indicate that they were unable to operate properly at the time of the accident.

Clarence had hoped IIA would be able to defend Ruth by offering proof that she could not have stopped the Dodge and was therefore not responsible for the accident. Now, the only evidence that the accident was caused by defective brakes lies in a single bit of oral evidence—Ruth's description of the accident. Perhaps she could convince a judge or jury that her statement is accurate, but the chance of a successful defense seems weak. It de-

Clarence Atwood discusses the accident with Ruth Manning.

pends in part on whether or not Ruth is absolutely convinced that her recollections are accurate and how well she could stand up under questioning by attorneys for the manufacturer and the dealer.

What kinds of questions would Ruth have to answer on a witness stand? The car Ruth Manning usually drives is a late model full-sized Buick. Cars of this type have an automatic transmission and power brakes. It could be that Ruth Manning has become accustomed to braking with her left foot— a common practice. The Dodge five-speed, however, has a manual transmission. Forgetting about the stick shift, she could have pushed the clutch pedal "all the way to the floor," as she stated, and felt no braking action. Clarence decides to talk to Ruth again.

CLARENCE: I want to ask you something, Ruth. Did the stick shift on the Dodge cause you any problems that you can recall?

RUTH: Not really, Clarence. I grew up on a farm. I learned to drive an old pickup truck with a floor shift when I could barely reach the pedals. Rick and I owned manual transmission cars for quite a few years after we got married, but they don't put them in many big cars these days.

I was thinking so hard about the graduation party...I suppose I could have forgotten I was driving a car with a stick shift. I do tend to use my left foot to brake our Buick....

I don't really think the accident happened that way, but I guess it could have. To be honest, I guess it could have happened that way...maybe I did step on the clutch instead of the brake, but I don't really know....

Regardless of what really happened, it now seems very unlikely that IIA could provide a successful defense for Ruth. This case is like many that claims adjusters must handle—the facts are not clear-cut. In many instances, the true cause of an accident is never discovered with absolute certainty. Everyone involved must work with the facts in the best way he or she can, but opinions and perceptions can differ. If the facts do not clearly indicate *how* the accident occurred, lawsuits can result. **Litigation**, the process of carrying on a lawsuit, can become involved.

Under our legal system, when one person is injured or has property damage because of the acts of another, that person has the right to collect "damages" from the party at fault. In this case, Stan Schuman's store suffers

> **Litigation** is the process of carrying on a lawsuit.

property damage apparently caused by Ruth Manning. Stan wants to have his store repaired and has the right to sue to recover damages from the party that caused the property damage if the person at fault does not willingly pay for the repairs.

Under most circumstances, people prefer to settle a case among themselves rather than have a court handle it. When the parties involved can negotiate and reach agreement, it is called an **out-of-court settlement**. This saves everyone the time and costs that would be incurred in filing a suit and going through courtroom testimony and hearings.

An **out-of-court settlement** is often reached when people negotiate and reach agreement without having a court handle the case. Out-of-court settlements save everyone time and money.

Since Clarence now thinks it unlikely that IIA could successfully deny that Ruth Manning's driving was the cause of the accident, IIA Insurance Company should pay the resulting losses. There should be no problem in deciding the dollar amount of Ruth Manning's medical or auto repair bills or of Stan Schuman's repair bill. The amount payable to Susan Cleamons could be more difficult to determine and could lead to some disagreements.

Feeling that he has uncovered the cause of the auto accident, Clarence contacts Susan Cleamons' family to let them know he would like to speak with Susan about her claim when she is ready to meet with him. While talking with the family, Clarence hears the good news that even though her face was bleeding heavily when she was taken to the hospital, Susan's actual injuries were minor and she has already gone back to work. Clarence will contact Susan and arrange to pay her medical bills and replace her lost earnings, with, perhaps, an additional amount to compensate for her pain and suffering.

SUMMARY

In this chapter, we have examined the work of claims adjusters. Using an example, we have watched many of the things that adjusters do in order to make insurance work.

The claim adjusting process begins when an insurer or a producer is notified of a claim. Assuming the claim is or may be covered, it is reported to the insurance company claims department and is assigned to an adjuster. A claims adjuster must answer two key questions when handling a claim. First, coverage must be verified—is the loss covered by the insurance policy? Second, it is necessary to answer another question— what dollar amount should the insurance company pay? If the claims adjuster can answer these two questions and deal efficiently and fairly with everyone involved, the claims process runs smoothly.

An important part of the claim settling process is investigation—getting the facts. The adjuster seeks both physical and oral evidence to establish the facts. Once the claim is known, coverage is verified, and the preliminary facts are determined, it is necessary to set a loss reserve on the case. The loss reserve might be revised as the investigation progresses, until the claim is eventually closed.

Though a claims adjuster attempts to negotiate a fair settlement with all parties, negotiation is not always possible. Some liability claims are resolved only after litigation.

Many claims are not clear-cut. Despite extensive investigation, there might always be some uncertainty regarding the facts. In adjusting such claims, the adjuster must consider the probable outcome of a court trial before deciding whether to pay a claim or offer a defense.

Once it becomes clear that the insurance company is obligated to pay a claim, the payment should be made promptly in a fair and appropriate amount. The purpose of insurance is to protect. The claims adjuster is the person who delivers the protection that makes insurance work.

"They dropped the speeding charge but I've got to pay for the three storefronts and the railway station."

HERMAN copyright Jim Unger. Reprinted with permission of UNIVERSAL PRESS SYNDICATE. All rights reserved.

What Is Found in an Insurance Policy?

Touching the Adventures and Perils which the Underwriters are contented to bear and take upon themselves, they are of the Seas, Men-of-War, Fire, Lightning, Earthquake, Enemies, Pirates, Rovers, Assailing Thieves, Jettisons, Letters of Mart and Counter-Mart, Surprisals, Takings at Sea, Arrests, Restraints and Detainments of all Kings, Princes, and People, of what nation, condition or quality soever, Barratry of the Master and Mariners and of all other like Perils, Losses and Misfortunes that have or shall come to the Hurt, Detriment or Damage of the Vessel, or any part thereof, excepting, however, such of the foregoing perils as may be excluded by provisions elsewhere in the Policy or by endorsement hereon.

The above sentence might seem like the style of writing you would expect to find in a seventeenth-century legal brief. Is it surprising to learn that this is a one-sentence paragraph from the current edition (last revised in 1977) of an insurance policy covering an oceangoing ship? The wording looks as though it would be more familiar to Benjamin Franklin than to most people today.

This type of policy language was used in Great Britain during the late seventeenth century. The meaning of the words has been interpreted through many court decisions over the years. Even though the wording does not seem clear to a modern reader, insurers are reluctant to change a contract whose legal meaning has become so well established through centuries of use. As a result, much of the seventeenth-century wording is still being used in policies covering oceangoing ships.

You might be glad to learn that most other insurance policies are written in a more contemporary style. In fact, many insurance policies have been deliberately "simplified" in recent years. They use language that the typical policyholder should be able to understand. They are printed in large type with descriptive headings that identify the different sections of the policy.

Reprinted with special permission of King Features Syndicate.
Many modern insurance policies are printed in large type.

To illustrate what is found in an insurance policy, this chapter will look at one policy—the personal auto policy that IIA Insurance Company issued to Rick Manning. The personal auto policy (PAP) is a modern insurance contract that is widely used to provide car insurance coverage for individuals and families. You will see how the PAP addresses the claims described in the previous chapter.

> A **policy provision** is any statement in a policy.

TYPES OF INSURANCE POLICY PROVISIONS

Any statement in an insurance policy is referred to as a **policy provision**. Six types of policy provisions are found in property-liability insurance policies:

- Declarations
- Insuring agreement(s)
- Exclusions
- Conditions
- Definitions
- Miscellaneous provisions

Declarations

Declarations personalize a policy. They tailor it to fit the specific policyholder and his or her insurance needs.

The term "declarations" comes from the fact that the **declarations** contain some information that the policyholder declared (stated as facts) on the application for insurance, such as:

- The name and address of the policyholder,
- A description of the insured property or activity, and
- Other information from the application that was used in underwriting and rating the policy.

Declarations also contain information such as:

- The dates when coverage begins and ends,
- The policy limits and deductibles,
- The premium, and
- The names or numbers of all attached forms and endorsements.

Sometimes the applicant can choose optional coverages that are not purchased by everyone. In such cases, the declarations show which options apply.

Without the declarations, one person's insurance policy might be exactly like another person's. A unique set of declarations is provided for each policy.

> **Declarations** personalize a printed policy and tailor it to fit a particular policyholder and his or her insurance needs. The **declarations page** or pages of an insurance policy contain information that the policyholder declared (stated as facts) on the application for insurance. Examples are the policyholder's name and address.

Insuring Agreement

The **insuring agreement** states, *in broad terms*, the promises made by the insurance company. An insurance policy provides coverage only if the claim is within the scope of the promise expressed in an insurance agreement.

An insuring agreement is usually so broad that it includes coverage for some losses that the insurer does not intend to cover. For example, the liability insuring agreement of a PAP begins:

We will pay damages...because of an auto accident.

This insuring agreement is so broad that it would cover any auto accident. It would provide coverage for auto accidents happening while the family sedan is being used as a taxicab. It might even cover the damages that result when a driver intentionally smashes a car into another vehicle. Insurance companies do not intend to cover damages like these in a personal auto policy. A policy's "exclusions," described under the next heading, help clarify what losses the insurer does not cover.

A policy can contain more than one insuring agree-

> An **insuring agreement** is an insurance policy provision that states, in broad terms, the promises made by the insurance company. An insurance policy provides coverage only if the claim is within the scope of the promise expressed in an insuring agreement.

ment. The PAP contains four insuring agreements—one for each of four coverages:

Part A—Liability Coverage
Part B—Medical Payments Coverage
Part C—Uninsured Motorists Coverage
Part D—Coverage for Damage to Your Auto

These four insuring agreements are printed in every personal auto policy, but not everybody buys all four coverages. For example, people do not usually buy coverage for damage to their auto if the insurance premium for that coverage would exceed the value of the car. In a completed personal auto policy, the declarations show which coverages have been purchased for each listed auto.

Exclusions are policy provisions that restrict the broad terms of the insuring agreement by stating some exceptions to coverage—certain activities, loss causes, property, persons, and places for which the insurer does not provide coverage.

Exclusions

Exclusions restrict the broad terms of the insuring agreement by stating some exceptions to coverage—certain activities, loss causes, property, persons, and places for which the insurer does not provide coverage.

Why is it necessary for insurance policies to contain exclusions? One important reason is to *keep insurance premiums reasonable.* An insurance policy with no exclusions would cost more than most people would be willing to pay.

Some exclusions *eliminate coverage duplications.* For example, most on-the-job injuries are covered by workers compensation insurance, so other kinds of insurance exclude coverage for on-the-job injuries.

Exclusions are also used to *eliminate coverages that are not needed by the typical policyholder.* For example, a personal auto policy excludes coverage for theft of a television. Most policyholders would not be affected by this exclusion, and it is not the insurer's intention to provide coverage for televisions in this policy. (Special kinds of insurance are available for those whose insurance needs are not typical.)

In short, an insuring agreement describes a broad category of claims that *are* covered; exclusions describe some narrower situations within the general category that are *not* covered.

Conditions

Insurance policy **conditions** explain the duties, rights, and options of the insured and the insurance company. Conditions cover a broad range of topics, including

- The policyholder's duty to pay the premium,
- Steps the insured must take after an accident,
- The geographical area within which coverage applies,
- How disagreements between insurer and insured can be resolved, and
- The procedures to be used by the policyholder or the insurance company to cancel the policy.

Since many of these conditions are necessary with almost every type of property or liability insurance, the conditions in one policy are usually much like those in other kinds of policies. For example, though specific wording can vary from one type of policy to another, all policies state the insured's obligation to notify the insurance company promptly of any claim.

> The **conditions** in an insurance policy explain the duties, rights, and options of the insured and the insurance company.

Definitions

Most words in an insurance policy have the standard meaning that appears in a dictionary. The definitions in an insurance policy state the special meaning that applies to some words and expressions when used in that policy. In some policies, defined words are printed in **boldface type** or are placed in quotation marks ("") every time they are used with that special meaning. The definitions section of an insurance policy is like a built-in dictionary of special words and expressions.

> A **definition** is an insurance policy provision that explains the meaning of a word or term that is used elsewhere in the insurance policy. Words defined in some policies are printed in **boldface type** or in quotation marks (" ").

For example, the personal auto policy includes the following definition:

"Property damage" means physical injury to, destruction of or loss of use of tangible property.

This definition means that the term "property damage" includes not only damage or destruction of tangible property, but also the inability to use tangible property. In the claim described in Chapter 5, Stan Schuman might have been unable to use his store for a few days if the damage caused by Ruth Manning's accident had been worse. That loss of use, as well as the damage to the building itself, would be property damage.

Miscellaneous Provisions

Insurance policy provisions that are not really declarations, insuring agreements, exclusions, conditions, or definitions can be considered "miscellaneous provisions."

> **Miscellaneous provisions** are insurance policy provisions that do not fit into any of the other categories.

ARRANGEMENT OF POLICY PROVISIONS

Declarations are normally found at the beginning of a policy, but the other types of policy provisions can appear anywhere. Although some policies are arranged into easy-to-identify sections called "Insuring Agreement," "Exclusions," "Conditions," or "Definitions," each of these types of provisions can also appear in various places throughout the policy without any specific label.

Policy arrangement is illustrated in the Course Guide accompanying this book, which contains a copy of Rick Manning's personal auto policy (PAP).

Because the printed PAP covers a variety of people with many different types of autos who might be insured in many circumstances, it is a long policy containing four different insuring agreements and many exclusions, conditions, definitions, and miscellaneous provisions.

The rest of this chapter will require you to refer to that policy. When an item from the policy is mentioned in this book, it will refer to a bracketed number—for example, <1>. This bracketed number also appears somewhere in the policy in your Course Guide. Look for that number to find the section that is being explained.

Rick Manning's auto policy contains:

- A "Declarations" page <1>;
- One "Definitions" heading <8>;
- Four "Insuring Agreements" <12>, <18>, <20>, and <22>; and
- Four sets of "Exclusions" <14>, <19>, <21>, and <23>; but
- No "Conditions" heading.

Sections that fit the description of conditions are called "Duties After an Accident or Loss" <27> and "General Provisions" <29>.

©1981 Universal Press Syndicate   7-18

"I dreamt I was driving down a mountain road and the brakes failed."

USING AN INSURANCE POLICY

When an accident happens, both the insured and the claims adjuster are interested in determining the answer to the question:

- **Is the claim covered by the insurance policy?**

If it is covered, it becomes necessary to ask another question:

- **What dollar amount will be paid?**

It makes no sense to ask this second question until it is determined whether coverage exists.

In the accident described in the last chapter, Ruth Manning was the driver of a Dodge that crashed through a store window. Several claims resulted from this accident:

- A claim by the store owner, Stan Schuman, for property damage to the store,
- A claim by Rick Manning, the owner of the car, for the costs of repairing the collision damage to the car,
- A claim by the injured customer, Susan Cleamons, for her injuries, and
- A claim by Ruth Manning, the driver of the car, for her medical expenses.

This chapter will examine two of these claims—the first two in the list above—to show you how the language of an insurance policy can be examined to answer the questions about coverage and dollar amount. As described here, the process might appear tedious. In practice, experienced claims adjusters can answer most coverage questions without going through such a painstaking step-by-step analysis.

THE CLAIM FOR PROPERTY DAMAGE TO THE STORE

When the Dodge driven by Ruth Manning crashed through the window of Schuman's Stationery Store, it broke the store windows and damaged the brickwork surrounding the windows. This section will show how Rick Manning's PAP is used to determine the answers to the coverage questions posed by Rick Manning and by Clarence Atwood, the claims adjuster.

Is the Claim Covered by the Insurance Policy?

Whether a claim is covered can be determined by using the insurance policy to answer three questions:

1. Is this claim within the scope of an insuring agreement?

If not, the claim is not covered by the policy and there is no point in analysis. If the claim is within the broad scope of an insuring agreement, the next question is:

2. Does any exclusion eliminate or restrict coverage for this claim?

If a claim is within the scope of an insuring agreement and is not otherwise excluded, it is probably covered, but, to make sure, a third question must be asked:

3. Do any policy conditions affect the coverage for this claim?

The following sections explain these questions more fully and show how they can be answered.

Is This Claim Within the Scope of an Insuring Agreement? It appears that Ruth is legally responsible for the accident and will be called upon to pay for the damage to the store property. Is this claim for property damage within the broad scope of any insuring agreement in the policy?

The first sentence of the Part A—Liability Coverage insuring agreement <12> provides the answer to this question:

> We will pay damages for "bodily injury" or "property damage" for which any "insured" becomes legally responsible because of an auto accident.

The incident clearly concerns **damages** for property **damage** because of an auto accident.

Damage and Damages

These two words are similar, but they have different meanings.

Damage is loss or harm resulting from injury to a person, to property, or to someone's reputation. In insurance terminology the term is usually used in connection with injury to property. This is the meaning in phrases like "property damage" and "auto physical damage."

Damages is a legal term meaning money that the law requires one party to pay to another because of loss or injury suffered by the other party.

The phrase "We will pay **damages** for **property damage**…" can be loosely paraphrased as "We will pay money for injury to property…."

Ruth Manning, it seems, is legally responsible for these damages. If Ruth Manning is an "insured," this claim is clearly within the scope of the Part A—Liability Coverage insuring agreement.

Is Ruth an "insured"? Since "insured" is in quotation marks in the PAP, the term is defined in the policy. This particular definition does not appear in the Definitions section of the policy, but it is included within the first Insuring Agreement section <13>.

> "Insured" as used in this Part means:
>
> 1. You or any "family member" for the ownership, maintenance or use of any auto or "trailer."

What does the policy mean when it says "you"? Does this include Ruth? The first definition in the policy <9> says:

> Throughout this policy, "you" and "your" refer to:
>
> 1. The "named insured" shown in the Declarations; and
>
> 2. The spouse if a resident of the same household.

The declarations <2> name Rick Manning as "named insured." Ruth Manning is his spouse and resides in the same household. Ruth was using the auto at the time of the accident. And since "insured" means "You...," Ruth is an insured. Therefore, the insuring agreement could be translated this way:

> We [the insurance company] will pay damages [money] for..."property damage" [destruction or loss of use of tangible property] for which any "insured" [Ruth] becomes legally responsible because of an auto accident.

Based on this analysis, the claim for damages for property damage to the store building is within the broad scope of the Part A—Liability Coverage insuring agreement.

Does Any Exclusion Eliminate or Restrict Coverage for This Claim?

This question can best be answered by examining each separate exclusion that applies to the insuring agreement and asking whether the exclusion relates to the claim at hand. It often works best to read the insuring agreement together with each exclusion as a complete sentence or paragraph, skipping any portions that clearly have nothing to do with the particular claim. This process is illustrated by examining only the first two exclusions.

The first exclusion under the Part A—Liability Coverage insuring agreement <15> reads as follows:

> A. We do not provide Liability Coverage for any "insured":
>
> 1. Who intentionally causes "bodily injury" or "property damage."

The complete statement of coverage and exclusion, skipping the unrelated pieces, is obtained by reading the insuring agreement together with the exclusion:

> We will pay damages for..."property damage" for which any "insured" becomes legally responsible because of an auto accident.... We do not provide Liability Coverage for any "insured"...who intentionally causes..."property damage."

Ruth Manning did not intentionally drive the Dodge through the store window. The claim is within the scope of the insuring agreement and is not excluded by the first exclusion.

Using the same approach, the next exclusion can also be combined with the insuring agreement and read as follows:

> We will pay damages for..."property damage" for which any "insured" becomes legally responsible because of an auto accident.... We do not provide Liability Coverage for any "insured"...for "prop-

erty damage" to property owned or being transported by that "insured."

Ruth Manning did not own the stationery store. She was certainly not transporting it—the store was stationary. (Sometimes we just can't resist a pun.) Therefore, this second exclusion has no bearing on the claim.

The other exclusions can also be analyzed using the same approach. It is fairly obvious that most of the exclusions do not apply. However, the effect of exclusion B.2 <16> is not entirely clear unless other policy provisions are also considered. The exclusion says:

> We do not provide Liability Coverage for the …use of…any vehicle, other than "your covered auto," which is…owned by you….

The Dodge is owned by "you" (Rick Manning), but is it considered "your covered auto"? The Dodge is not listed in the policy declarations. Does "your covered auto" include the Dodge anyway? Unless it does, this policy provides no coverage. Since "your covered auto" is in quotation marks, the answer to this question is found in the definitions <11>:

> "Your covered auto" means… Any of the following types of vehicles on the date you become the owner:…a private passenger auto….

Recall that Rick Manning specifically called Connie Sue Rapp to add coverage for the Dodge to the policy even before he owned the car. Even if he had not called, the Dodge would have been automatically covered.

A few details were not explained completely in Chapter 4. When Rick called Connie Sue about the Dodge, she quoted a premium and assured Rick that the Dodge was covered. She also verified that the car would be titled in the name of Rick Manning, who would be the legal owner, rather than being titled in the name of his daughter Jill. Connie Sue also asked Rick to call after the car had been picked up and give her the **vehicle identification number** (**VIN**), or serial number, of the Dodge. Connie Sue also wrote a note for the Manning file and set up a ten-day diary to remind her to call Rick if he forgot to provide the Dodge's VIN. She would not submit a policy change form to IIA Insurance Company until she had all the information. She knew it would not be necessary because of the automatic coverage.

Vehicle Identification Number (VIN)

The **VIN** is the serial number of a car. Insurance applications request the VIN, and the number is then printed in the policy declarations <3>. This helps clarify precisely which car is the subject of coverage.

Various codes in the VIN also reveal how the car is equipped. This sometimes has a bearing on the insurance premium.

In modern cars, the VIN is located on top of the dashboard, where it can be read by a law enforcement officer looking through the windshield. This helps identify stolen cars, even when they are locked.

A new declarations page is usually sent to the policyholder whenever a policy change takes place. As this case shows, however, the Dodge is covered even though the declarations listing the Dodge have not been received—or even issued or requested by Connie Sue. The Dodge has the same coverage as the Buick that is described in the declarations.

Although it may seem surprising, automatic coverage on new exposures is provided by many insurance policies. Insurance works this way to meet changing insurance needs.

Even though her name does not appear in the policy, Ruth is an "insured." Even though it is not described in the declarations, the Dodge qualifies as "your covered auto." The property damage liability claim is within the scope of the Part A—Liability Coverage insuring agreement. Since none of the other exclusions eliminates or restricts coverage for this particular claim, it is covered—unless something further along in our analysis changes the picture.

Do Any Policy Conditions Affect the Coverage for This Claim? Whether any policy conditions affect the coverage for a particular claim is a question best answered by reading each condition. For experienced insurance people, this takes little more than a quick scan of the conditions because the same types of conditions are found in most insurance policies.

In the PAP, some conditions can be found within Parts A, B, C, and D of the policy; those conditions affect coverage only under the part where they are found. For example, Part A of the personal auto policy contains an "Out of State Coverage" condition <17>. This condition would affect only claims under the Part A insuring agreement; it does not have a bearing on the coverage under other parts of the policy. Like many insurance policy conditions, this one starts with an "if" statement that shows at a glance when it might affect coverage:

> If an auto accident to which this policy applies occurs in any state or province other than the one in which "your covered auto" is principally garaged,....

The entire condition relates to accidents away from the state where the car is kept. Since Ruth Manning's accident occurred in her hometown, this condition has no effect.

Most policy conditions are found in:

> Part E—Duties After an Accident or Loss <27>, and
>
> Part F—General Provisions <29>.

Neither of these sections is labeled "conditions." The conditions in Parts E and F apply to claims under Part A, as well as to the other policy sections.

The conditions in Part E—Duties After an Accident or Loss <27> describe the steps an insured should take following an accident. If the Mannings had not fulfilled these duties, IIA Insurance Company might have a right to deny coverage.

The conditions in Part F—General Provisions <29> also apply to claims covered by Part A. Some of them do have a bearing on the handling of the Manning claim, but none of them reveals that the claim for property damage to the store is not covered.

One important condition is titled "Our Right to Recover Payment" <30>. Although it does not use the word "subrogation," that is the concept it describes. As an example of subrogation, suppose that IIA Insurance Company had paid for the damage to the store but had evidence that the accident was actually caused by defective brakes. IIA would then have a right to try to recover its payment from whoever was responsible for the bad brakes.

Also important is the "Policy Period and Territory" condition <31>. A similar condition is found in most insurance policies. Ruth's accident did occur during the policy period, and it happened in the United States, so this condition does not affect coverage. If Ruth had driven the car into Mexico and the same accident had happened there—even though every other statement in the policy would seem to indicate that Ruth was covered—the policy would not apply because of this particular condition. This illustrates the importance of examining the conditions when using an insurance policy to determine coverage for a claim.

Questions To Ask When Analyzing an Insurance Policy After an Accident
1. Is the claim covered by the insurance policy?
To answer this question, ask the following:
    a. Is this claim within the scope of an insuring agreement?
    b. Does any exclusion eliminate or restrict coverage for this claim?
    c. Do any policy conditions affect the coverage for this claim?
If the answer to Question 1 is "Yes," then ask Question 2.
2. What dollar amount will be paid?

What Dollar Amount Will Be Paid?

We have not looked closely at the second, third, and fourth sentences of the Part A—Liability Coverage insuring agreement <12>. The paragraph reads:

> We will pay damages for "bodily injury" or "property damage" for which any "insured" becomes legally responsible because of an auto accident. Damages include prejudgment interest awarded against the "insured." We will settle or defend, as we consider appropriate, any claim or suit asking for these damages. In addition to our limit of liability, we will pay all defense costs we incur. Our duty to settle or defend ends when our limit of liability for this coverage has been exhausted.

Does IIA Insurance Company have a right to arrive at an out-of-court settlement with Stan Schuman, the store owner? Ruth might feel that IIA should defend the claim because she does not think the accident was her fault. Does she have a right to insist that the case go to court? Or if IIA's claims adjuster and Stan Schuman can agree on a dollar amount, does IIA have the right to pay Schuman and close the claim? This question is answered here <12>:

> We will settle or defend, as we consider appropriate....

Since "we" means the insurance company ("we" is defined after "you" in the Definitions section of the policy <10>), this clearly means that IIA has the right to decide.

If the claim involves costly litigation, will legal expenses reduce the amount of policy coverage that could go toward paying the claimants? The policy says <12>:

> In addition to our limit of liability, we will pay all defense costs we incur.

The limit of liability limits only the amount that will be paid as damages. "Defense costs" (such as attorney fees) are over and above ("in addition to") this limit.

What limit of liability is shown in the Declarations for this coverage? The Limit of Liability <5> for Coverage A is $300,000. Since the $300,000 limit applies to bodily injury and property damage together, it is necessary to consider Susan's bodily injury claim, as well as Stan's property damage claim, in answering the question "How much will be paid?" At first, it appeared that Susan Cleamons, the store customer, was seriously injured by flying glass. It seemed possible that Susan could collect hundreds of thousands of dollars in damages to indemnify her for her medical bills and to compensate for her disfigurement (the facial scars).

What if the damages for property damage to the store and the damages for bodily injury to Susan were greater than the $300,000 liability limit? Once $300,000 in damages have been paid, IIA Insurance Company will have exhausted its obligations to the Mannings. As the insuring agreement explains <12>:

> Our duty to settle or defend ends when our limit of liability for this coverage has been exhausted.

In summary, Stan Schuman's claim for property damage to his store is covered. The amount IIA would pay as damages would be determined by a court award or an out-of-court settlement. The maximum amount IIA would pay as damages for the property damage end the bodily injury combined would be the $300,000 policy limit. Any costs of defending the claim would be paid by IIA in addition to the amounts paid as damages. IIA has the right to decide whether it wishes to defend Ruth Manning in this claim, attempting to prove she was not responsible for the accident, or whether to arrive at a settlement and close the claim.

Most likely, settling Stan Schuman's claim for damages to the stationery store will be simple. Stan's own property insurance company will pay the repair costs charged by a local contractor. Stan's insurance company, in turn, will subrogate against Ruth Manning. Since there is little hope of successfully defending this claim, IIA Insurance Company will, on Ruth's behalf, reimburse Stan's insurer for the amount it spent in repairing the property. If the other insurer did not cover any of Stan's damages—perhaps because of a deductible in the property insurance policy—IIA would also reimburse Stan for those costs.

Alternatively, IIA Insurance Company might pay damages directly to Stan without involving Stan's insurance company. Either way, IIA ultimately pays for the loss and Stan is indemnified.

THE PHYSICAL DAMAGE CLAIM

When Ruth Manning and the Dodge crashed through the window of the Schuman Stationery Store, the Dodge was seriously damaged. A reliable repair shop has estimated the cost of repairs at $4,000. The car was brand new—it had been purchased only minutes before the accident. Would the Mannings' insurance policy reimburse Rick and Ruth Manning for the $4,000 they would pay to have the car fixed?

Is the Claim Covered by the Insurance Policy?

Before thinking about the dollar value of damage to the car, it is necessary to find out whether the claim is even covered. How? By checking the policy's declarations, insuring agreement, exclusions, conditions, and definitions.

Is This Claim Within the Scope of an Insuring Agreement?   This claim concerns damage to Ruth's auto. Therefore, one would look in Part D—Coverage for Damage to Your Auto.

The Part D insuring agreement <22> states:

> We will pay for direct and accidental loss to your "covered auto."

The damage was direct and accidental, and we have already seen that the Dodge qualifies as "your covered auto." Further analysis of the "your covered auto" definition would reveal that the Dodge automatically has the same coverages as the Buick that is described in the declarations.

The second sentence of the insuring agreement <22> reads:

> We will pay for...loss to "your covered auto" caused by..."Collision" only if the Declarations indicate that Collision Coverage is provided for that auto.

Does the Mannings' policy indicate that collision coverage is provided? If so, how is it indicated?

The Declarations page contains a statement that reads <4>:

> Coverage is provided where a premium and a limit of liability are shown for the coverage.

The Manning policy shows a premium of $200 <7> and a limit of liability for "Collision Loss," under the "Coverages" section, of "Actual Cash Value minus $500 deductible" <6>. Although this is the coverage shown for the Buick, we have seen that this coverage also applies to the Dodge.

Does Any Exclusion Eliminate or Restrict Coverage for This Claim? To answer this question, it is necessary to examine each of the exclusions in Part D—coverage for Damage to Your Auto <23>. If this is done, it will be seen that they clearly relate to situations that were not involved in Ruth Manning's accident. In short, none of the exclusions eliminates or restricts coverage for the damage to the Dodge.

"The good news is, I've saved you five bucks at the carwash tomorrow."

Do Any Policy Conditions Affect the Coverage for This Claim? Part D—Coverage for Damage to Your Auto contains four conditions in addition to a limit of liability provision. The Payment of Loss provision <26> begins:

> We may pay for loss in money or repair or replace the damaged or stolen property.

If the car is not so badly damaged that it is beyond repair, an insurance company will usually pay money that the insured can use to get the car fixed. If repairs would cost more than what the car is worth, an insurance company will usually pay the owner based on what the car was worth immediately before the accident. However, as this condition shows, IIA Insurance Company does not have to pay money to the Mannings to settle their claim. The insurance company has the right to repair the Dodge and return it to the Mannings. Or the insurance company has the right to replace the car. In this case, since the Dodge was brand new, replacement would mean providing another new Dodge with the same equipment.

Some conditions in Part E—Duties After an Accident or Loss apply specifically to this claim. Paragraph D <28> states, among other things, that:

> A person seeking Coverage for Damage to Your Auto must...take reasonable steps after loss to protect "your covered auto"...from further loss...[and] permit us to inspect and appraise the damaged property before its repair or disposal.

The Mannings complied with this condition. The car was towed to a repair shop after the accident. And IIA Insurance Company's adjuster and two brake experts were permitted to inspect it before any repairs began. Further examination would also show that none of the other conditions affects coverage for this claim.

What Dollar Amount Will Be Paid?

The Part D—Coverage for Damage to Your Auto "Limit of Liability" provision <24> reads as follows:

> Our limit of liability for loss will be the lesser of the:
> 1. Actual cash value of the stolen or damaged property; or
> 2. Amount necessary to repair or replace the property with other property of like kind and quality.

The term "actual cash value" is not defined. However, the policy does state <25> that an adjustment for depreciation and physical condition will be made in determining the actual cash value. The actual cash value of a car is generally considered to be the price for which it could be sold. Since there is an active market for used cars, it is easy to find out what any car is worth if one knows the year and model, what equipment it has, and the car's condition. A so-called "Blue Book" is published periodically that lists the average prices at which used cars of all kinds have recently sold.

Auto insurance companies evaluate auto physical damage losses by determining the value of the car before the accident. If the car can be repaired for less than that figure, the insurance company pays the cost of repair. If repairs would cost more than the car was worth, the insurance company will pay the car owner what the car was worth. The car owner could pocket the money and not buy another car, but most insureds usually decide either to buy a used car with the insurance proceeds or to use the money to help pay for a new car.

The Ruth Manning accident presents an unusual situation because the Dodge was so new. Since this car had had only about five minutes to depreciate, any insurance adjustment in this case would be based on the value of a new Dodge.

"When it was brand-new it cost $750. That's what I'm selling it for."

IIA Insurance Company has the choice of paying repair costs to the Mannings or buying them another new Dodge. Since new Dodges cost much more than $4,000 (the estimated repair cost), IIA Insurance Company will pay the cost of repairs.

Will IIA Insurance Company pay $4,000 to the Mannings so that the Dodge can be repaired? Not exactly. The Part D insuring agreement says <22>:

> We will pay for direct and accidental loss to "your covered auto"...minus any applicable deductible shown in the Declarations.

The declarations for Rick Manning's policy show that the "limit of liability" <6> for collision loss is "Actual Cash Value minus $500 deductible." The total damage equals $4,000, but IIA Insurance Company will pay $4,000 – $500, or $3,500—because of the $500 deductible.

SUMMARY

This chapter has explained what is found in an insurance policy. The personal auto policy (PAP) has been used as an illustration.

Insurance policies contain declarations, one or more insuring agreements, conditions, exclusions, definitions, and miscellaneous provisions.

Following an accident, an insurance policy can be analyzed to determine the answer to two questions:

- Is the claim covered by the insurance policy?
- What dollar amount will be paid?

A claim is covered by an insurance policy if:

- The claim is within the broad scope of an insuring agreement,
- No exclusions eliminate or restrict coverage for the claim, and
- No policy conditions adversely affect coverage for the claim.

This approach was then used in analyzing two of the claims that developed when Ruth Manning drove a new Dodge through a store window.

This chapter did not show how the PAP is used to determine whether Rick Manning's other claims are covered. Further analysis of the policy would reveal that Ruth's liability for damages resulting from the bodily injury to Susan Cleamons is covered by Part A—Liability Coverage. Likewise, Ruth's medical expenses are covered by Part B—Medical Payments Coverage. Chapter 7 will explain why these and other coverages are important in making insurance work to meet personal insurance needs.

What Is Personal Insurance? **7**

Insurance works to meet the insurance needs of individuals and families. Insurance purchased by individuals and families for nonbusiness loss exposures is referred to as *personal insurance*. The policies examined in this chapter provide personal insurance coverage.

The chapter begins by introducing the Hillmans—a family like many other American families. The Hillman family serves as a model for illustrating the personal insurance needs of the typical family. The family has many items of property that can be covered with *property insurance*. Also, any member of the family could become liable for bodily injury to somebody else or for damage to somebody else's property. These possibilities create a need for *liability insurance*.

After examining the Hillmans' personal insurance needs, the chapter will show how personal insurance works to meet those needs. The policies described here can be used to meet the property-liability insurance needs of most individuals and families.

THE HILLMAN FAMILY: A PROFILE

Leonard and Debbie Hillman live in Plainfield. Leonard owns and operates All-Sports, a large local retail sporting goods store. Debbie is the personnel manager of Allied Manufacturing Company, also in Plainfield. The Hillmans have two children—Patti, age fifteen, and Todd, age twelve. Napoleon, the family pet, acts as a watchdog when family members are at work and school.

The Hillmans' five-year-old house is on a large lot. It is a typical one-story ranch-style home with three bedrooms, a large recreation room, an attached carport, and a swimming pool in the back yard. The back yard is completely surrounded by a fence high enough to keep Napoleon on the premises.

The house and yard contain many kinds of sports equipment. A basketball net is located on a pole next to the driveway, and a bathhouse filled with scuba-diving equipment is next to the swimming pool. The recreation room contains a pool table and a ping-pong table, as well as exercise equipment. Some hunting rifles are securely locked in a closet. Leonard has the only key.

Other than the athletic and sports gear, a normal assortment of furniture, appliances, clothing, and other items is found in the Hillman home. The only items of special value are Debbie's diamond ring, currently worth $3,500, and a sterling silver tea service inherited from Debbie's grandmother.

The Hillmans have two cars. Leonard drives a late-model Ford minivan, which he also uses in the business. The minivan is also used on family camping vacations and trips to football games, where the family enjoys tailgate parties. Debbie uses a Toyota for driving to work and running errands.

PROPERTY INSURANCE NEEDS

Property insurance covers accidental losses to property of insureds. Property can be destroyed, damaged, or stolen—in which case the property owner suffers a financial loss related to the value of the lost property. Often, damaged or destroyed property cannot be used until it is replaced or repaired.

Perils are causes of property losses. Fire is one example of a peril.

Many things can cause a property loss. These various causes of loss are called **perils**. Fire is one example of a peril, but fire is certainly not the only peril that could cause a loss to property. A few other perils are hurricanes and other windstorms, explosions, and aircraft damage (as when an airplane crashes into a house).

What types of property do the Hillmans have that could be damaged by these or other perils?

The House

Like many other families, the Hillmans' most valuable possession is their house. Many perils might damage or destroy the house—fire, tornado, and earthquake are a few. Also, the house could be struck by an out-of-control car or truck or "decorated" with graffiti by vandals.

Are there any other perils that could damage the house? Think about this for a few minutes. You will probably find that the longer you think, the longer your list becomes. Even after a few minutes, you would not think of every possible peril. For example, did you consider the possibility of a flood? How about frozen water pipes bursting and causing damage to wall and floors? What about the possibility that a sinkhole would open up and the house would simply drop into the ground? All these perils have damaged or destroyed houses.

If the Hillman house were damaged or destroyed, it would be necessary to pay for repairs or reconstruction. While the house was being repaired or rebuilt, the Hillmans might have to stay in a hotel or rent temporary living quarters. This additional living expense could be costly.

Contents of the House

When a house is damaged, there is a good chance that the clothing, furniture, appliances, athletic equipment, and other items in the house will also be damaged or destroyed. Loss to the contents can also occur when the house itself suffers no damage. A **theft** could occur. For example, **burglary** could occur while the Hillmans are away, assuming Napoleon would not scare away the burglars. Or robbers might enter the house while the Hillmans are there and commit a **robbery** by threatening the family with guns.

> **Theft, Burglary, Robbery**
>
> **Theft** is any act of stealing.
>
> **Burglary** is a type of theft committed by someone who breaks into something (a building, for example) and illegally removes money or other property.
>
> **Robbery** is a type of theft committed by someone who threatens a person and forces him or her to give money or other property to the thief.
>
> These terms are often misused. Often, television and cartoon characters (see below) arrive home, see that somebody has broken into their house, and exclaim, "Our house was robbed!" They should more accurately say, "Our house was burglarized!"
>
> **Theft**, **burglary**, and **robbery** are all perils. Since burglary and robbery are kinds of theft, you can see that the labels for various perils sometimes overlap.

Hi and Lois

Reprinted with special permission of King Features Syndicate.
The terms "rob," "robbed," and "robbery" are often misused.

Some kinds of property are especially attractive to thieves. The Hillmans would probably be particularly concerned about Debbie's diamond ring and the silver tea set since these are both high-value items that are easy for a thief to sell. Some of the Hillmans' sports equipment would also be easy for a thief to sell. Guns, too, are often stolen. This is one reason Leonard keeps them securely locked in the closet.

Other Property

In addition to the house, the Hillmans have other structures. For example, we mentioned their swimming pool, bathhouse, basketball pole, and fence. Some of the perils that could damage the house could also damage these structures. However, there are differences. For example, it is unlikely that the swimming pool would be seriously damaged by a fire. On the other hand, the fence might be blown down by windstorm, struck by vehicles (if it is near a highway or a neighbor's driveway), or damaged by vandalism. And the basketball pole, located next to the driveway, might be damaged if somebody backs a car into it.

The Hillmans would also suffer a property loss if somebody should steal the scuba equipment from the bathhouse or if the equipment should somehow be damaged or destroyed. They also own patio furniture and other items that are usually kept outdoors where they are exposed to damage by windstorm, hail, and vandalism.

Autos

A **collision** is one vehicle running into or being struck by another vehicle or object.

The Hillmans' cars could also be damaged or destroyed by fire, windstorm, or flood, among other perils. A car could be stolen. Even more likely is the possibility that the car could be damaged in a collision. A **collision** is one vehicle running into another vehicle or object. One of the Hillmans' cars could sustain collision damage if, for example, (1) it runs into another car, (2) it runs into another object—such as a wall or tree, or (3) another car runs into it.

LIABILITY INSURANCE NEEDS

Liability means that a person, organization, or group of people is legally responsible, or **liable**, for the injury or damage suffered by another person, organization, or group of people.

Liability means that a person (or group of people) is legally responsible, or **liable**, for the injury or damage suffered by another person (or group of people).

Liability insurance covers the insured if the insured is legally responsible, or liable, for bodily injury or damage to the property of someone else. When the insured is accused of being liable for bodily injury or property damage, liability insurance will also pay the expense of trying to prove the insured's innocence.

Do the Hillmans need liability insurance? This question is best answered by considering the possible ways in which a member of the Hillman family could become legally responsible for bodily injury or damage to the property of someone else.

Auto Liability

Every driver has a duty to drive safely, but nobody's driving is perfect. Even though some drivers make more mistakes than others, it is obvious to everyone who has driven a car that accidents can happen. The chance of an accident is increased by **hazards** such as icy roads or fog.

Hazard

A **hazard** is anything that increases the chance of an accident. A hazard such as icy road or fog increases the chance of an auto accident. Likewise, a faulty kerosene heater is a hazard that increases the chance of a house fire.

A hazard might also increase the chance that any accident that happens will be a bad one. Refusal to wear seat belts creates a hazard of this type. Driving without seat belts does not cause auto accidents, but it does increase the chance of serious injury if an accident occurs.

Serious injuries, as well as serious property damage, can result from auto accidents that, in turn, are caused by unsafe driving. It is obvious that the Hillmans, like others who own or operate a car, need auto liability insurance.

Personal Liability

Technically, "personal liability" includes auto liability; drivers are personally liable for accidents they cause. In insurance jargon, however, the term **personal liability** refers to other, non-auto-related, general liability exposures that accompany a person's nonbusiness activities. Some examples follow.

There are many possible ways of becoming liable. The swimming pool presents an obvious hazard. Any guest of the Hillmans could be injured in a diving accident, could drown in the pool, or could be hurt by slipping on the deck around the pool. If the Hillmans invite a friend to use their scuba gear in the pool, a problem with the equipment or its use could cause injury or death.

Napoleon, the dog, might scare away burglars. Yet as far as liability is concerned, Napoleon presents a hazard. Many personal liability losses are caused when a previously friendly dog bites an unsuspecting friend, neighbor, postal service employee, or meter reader. When it comes to a question of who should carry the newspaper to the house, the newspaper carrier sometimes loses the argument with the family dog.

> The term **personal liability** refers to the general liability (non-auto-related) exposures that accompany a person's nonbusiness activities.

"Don't start looking for your glasses at 80 mph."

HERMAN copyright Jim Unger. Reprinted with permission of UNIVERSAL PRESS SYNDICATE. All rights reserved.

The Hillmans' many sporting activities also present the possibility of a liability claim. Perhaps their most dangerous sporting activity is hunting. Other sports also involve physical activities that could lead to injuries to others. Even ping-pong playing can injure a guest whose forehead might be gashed on a sharp corner of the ping-pong table. A guest's eye could be injured through the careless use of a pool cue.

The Hillmans could also become liable if they give or sell anything to somebody else that causes injury. For example, suppose they are having a tailgate party in the parking lot before a football game. Debbie sees they have more food than they need, so she offers some to a family in the next parking space. Although Debbie does not realize it, some of the food she gives away is spoiled and causes members of the family to require hospital treatment. Could this family sue Debbie? Not only could they sue—they could probably recover damages!

The possibilities for personal liability losses are endless. Embers from a trash fire could ignite a neighbor's roof. A neighbor might trip on a crack in the sidewalk. Todd or Patti might hit a baseball through somebody else's window.

These examples are enough to illustrate that every individual and family can cause injury to somebody else or damage to their property. When the injury or property damage is serious, large claims can result. Liability insurance is needed to protect the Hillmans against such claims.

PERSONAL INSURANCE POLICIES

Two insurance policies meet most personal insurance needs. These two are:

- The personal auto policy (PAP), and
- The homeowners policy.

The Personal Auto Policy (PAP)

The PAP is intended to meet the auto insurance needs of a typical family like the Hillmans. We examined the PAP in Chapter 6, where it was used to show how an insurance policy can answer questions about a specific claim. In this chapter, we will focus on the coverages of the PAP and how they meet a family's insurance needs.

The Parts and Coverages of the Personal Auto Policy (PAP)

Part A—Liability Coverage
Part B—Medical Payments Coverage
Part C—Uninsured Motorists Coverage
Part D—Coverage for Damage to Your Auto

Auto Liability Coverage.   The liability section of the PAP covers losses due to the insured's liability for bodily injury to others or damage to the property of others caused by an auto accident. Coverage applies to the "named insured," who is the person named in the declarations, and also to the spouse of the named insured and, in most circumstances, to other members of the household. Leonard and Debbie Hillman would be covered, as well as Todd and Patti (although the children would probably not be driving).

Insureds are covered while using the cars listed in the declarations. They are also covered while driving newly acquired cars (as we saw with Ruth Manning). Further, the Hillmans would usually be covered:

- If they borrow a neighbor's car or
- If they rent a car while on vacation.

(The PAP is intended to cover only occasional use of a nonowned car. It does not cover the Hillmans while they are driving another car that is regularly furnished to them or available for their use. For example, the PAP would not cover Leonard if he is driving the truck owned by his business, All-Sports, since that truck is regularly available to him. If it did, Leonard could, in effect, have free insurance on the truck.)

The PAP also protects other people who are driving one of the insured's cars that is listed in the policy declarations. If the Hillmans let somebody borrow one of their cars, the borrower is also covered by Hillmans' policy.

Of course, the PAP contains some exclusions. Suppose Leonard is using his Ford minivan to deliver some sporting equipment from his store and one of his employees is riding along. If the employee is injured in an accident, an exclusion would apply. The PAP would not cover the employee's claim to recover medical expenses because this claim would be paid by All-Sports' workers compensation insurance policy. Remember, one of the reasons for exclusions is to eliminate duplicate coverage.

Other exclusions would eliminate coverage if the Hillmans are using one of the cars as a taxicab or if, for example, Leonard regularly charges his neighbors a fee to haul their newspapers in his minivan to the recycling station. Those would be commercial uses. The car should then be insured under a business auto policy rather than a personal auto policy.

Auto Physical Damage Coverage. Property insurance—covering disappearance of, damage to, or destruction of the auto itself—can be purchased under the "Coverage for Damage to Your Auto" section of the PAP.

Like other auto policies, the PAP includes two sets of physical damage coverage—"collision" and "other than collision."

- **"Collision"** coverage applies to losses involving a collision (when a car strikes another vehicle or object). Collision coverage is available only when "other than collision" coverage is also purchased.

- **"Other than collision"** coverage applies to losses by perils other than collision. These other perils include theft, fire, windstorm, flood, falling objects, explosion, earthquake, contact with a bird or animal, hail, glass breakage, and any other peril that is not excluded. Insurance practitioners often use the term **"comprehensive"** to refer to the "other than collision" coverage, and policies other than the PAP might also use the label "comprehensive."

> **Other than collision** coverage, also called **comprehensive**, covers auto physical damage losses by nonexcluded perils other than collision.

Physical Damage Coverage Choices

Since collision coverage may not be purchased unless "other than collision" is also purchased, a personal auto insurance buyer actually has three options:

1. Coverage may be purchased for all perils that might cause damage to the car. The buyer purchases both "collision" and "other than collision" coverage. This combination, also known as "collision and comprehensive," involves the most protection and the highest premium.
2. "Other than collision" coverage ("comprehensive only") may be purchased for all perils except collision. Since collision causes the greatest amount of physical damage to autos, the premium is usually much lower without collision coverage, but the most important cause of loss is not covered.
3. Another choice requires no premium at all: Since the "damage to your auto" coverage of the PAP is optional, a person might choose to purchase no physical damage coverage. Although insurers will issue a PAP without the physical damage coverage, a person who has an auto loan might be required by the lender to have both comprehensive and collision coverage.

Because the Hillmans' cars are both fairly new, serious damage to either could cost several thousand dollars. The Hillmans would probably purchase coverage for collision loss ("collision") and coverage for other than collision loss ("comprehensive") on both cars. If the cars were older, they might consider purchasing only "comprehensive" to reduce their insurance premium costs. "Comprehensive" costs much less than "collision." For a very old car with little remaining value, they might decide to buy no physical damage insurance. Even a total loss of a car valued at $1,000 would cost the Hillmans only $1,000. They would probably think they could afford to take a chance on losing an uninsured car worth $1,000, but they would probably not want to lose a car worth $25,000.

CATHY copyright Cathy Guisewite. Reprinted with permission of UNIVERSAL PRESS SYNDICATE. All rights reserved.
The value of the car and the insurance requirements of a lender should be considered when buying auto physical damage coverage.

Auto Medical Payments Coverage.   "Medical payments," as the coverage is sometimes called, covers the medical expenses of the insured, as well as of anybody else riding in the Hillmans' car, if the expenses are the result of an auto accident. The expenses are covered even if the Hillmans are *not legally responsible* for the accident.

Auto medical payments coverage is usually available with a limit of $500 to $5,000 per person, with the amount of coverage selected by the applicant when insurance is bought. Of course, higher limits increase the premium.

Assuming the Hillmans have this coverage on their auto insurance policy, their own medical bills will be paid if they are injured in an auto accident. If any friends or guests are riding in the car when it is in an accident, their medical bills will also be covered. A borrower of the Hillmans' car would be covered while using the car, even if no member of the Hillman family is in the car at the time of the accident.

Since auto medical payments coverage applies even when the driver is not "at fault" (negligent or legally responsible) in an accident, the coverage is similar to the "no-fault" auto insurance coverages available in some states.

No-Fault Auto Insurance

"No-fault" auto insurance is sometimes considered as a way to reduce overall insurance costs by reducing the number of lawsuits while assuring that auto accident victims have a source of financial recovery. "No-fault" auto insurance means different things in different states, and the "no-fault" label is sometimes loosely applied to situations that do not strictly qualify as "no-fault."

Loosely, "no-fault" means that each policyholder has a right to recover financial losses from his or her own insurance company regardless of whose fault caused the accident. This so-called "no-fault" does not necessarily reduce lawsuits if insurance companies can subrogate or if injured accident victims still have the legal right to sue at-fault motorists to recover damages.

Strictly, "no-fault" auto insurance applies only to accidents under a state "no-fault" law that does two things: (1) It requires insurance companies to pay policyholders regardless of fault, *and* (2) it restricts the ability of accident victims to sue others for their injuries. Even when the so-called "right to sue" is restricted, a motorist may generally sue if the injury "crosses a threshold" (meets certain conditions) described in the law. The threshold might be "verbal" (described in words; for example, injury that is "permanent," "severe," or "disfiguring") or "monetary" (a specified dollar amount of medical bills). A "no-fault" law of this type can reduce legal expenses, provided it is not too easy to cross the threshold.

Critics of "no-fault" insurance hold that people should not be forced to give up their right to sue. Some states now provide a choice between lower-cost no-fault insurance and higher-cost insurance that preserves the "right to sue."

Uninsured Motorists Coverage.   Suppose the Hillman family is on vacation, riding in the Ford minivan, when the car is suddenly broadsided by another car, which has run a red light. All members of the family are injured and rushed to a hospital, where large medical bills—$20,000 or more for some family members—are incurred. The medical payments coverage would not pay for all their expenses, and it certainly would not reimburse the Hillmans for their pain and suffering or for the wages Leonard and Debbie lose while they are in the hospital. The Hillmans would attempt to recover damages from the other driver.

Suppose the other driver had never purchased liability insurance. The Hillmans would still have a legal right to recover damages from the driver (unless a no-fault law applied in that state). The Hillmans will be covered by the uninsured motorists coverage of their own PAP.

Uninsured motorists coverage also applies to accidents caused by a hit-and-run driver. As a practical matter, a known driver who is uninsured is almost as difficult to collect from as an unknown driver.

Uninsured motorists coverage can become important under certain circumstances.

The Homeowners Policy

The homeowners policy meets most of a typical family's property and liability insurance needs that are not covered by auto insurance. The homeowners policy that the Hillmans would purchase provides four *property* insurance coverages:

A. Coverage on the house itself—the dwelling building

B. Coverage on other buildings or structures on the premises

C. Coverage on household personal property

D. Coverage on loss of use of the dwelling building

The homeowners policy also provides two *liability* coverages:

E. Personal liability coverage

F. Coverage for medical payments to others

Coverage on the Dwelling Building.   This part of the policy covers the house itself. Structures attached to the house, such as an attached garage, are also covered. This is the part of the policy that would cover the Hillmans' house and the attached carport.

Coverage on Other Buildings or Structures.   Structures that are not attached to the house are also covered by a homeowners policy. Since the policy states a different limit for the dwelling building and for other buildings or structures, it is important to know what property is included under each coverage. In the case of the Hillmans, "other structures" would include the swimming pool, the bathhouse, the fence, and the basketball pole and net.

Coverage on Personal Property.   Personal property would include all of a homeowner's other property, such as the contents of the house (clothing, furniture, appliances, and other items), as well as any other items around the yard, such as a lawnmower, gardening equipment, and patio furniture. Autos are personal property, but they are excluded from the personal property coverage of a homeowners policy. Insureds are expected to buy auto insurance to cover their cars.

The Hillmans' scuba gear and sports equipment would be included as personal property, as well as Debbie's diamond ring and sterling tea service and Leonard's rifles.

Some items are more likely to be stolen than others. Homeowners policies provide only limited coverage on certain target items. Homeowners policies limit the dollar amount they promise to pay for theft of jewelry, furs, silver, guns, and some other items. For example, if the guns are stolen, the policy might limit coverage to $2,000.

Many households do not have valuable jewelry, furs, silver, or guns; they would not want to pay for coverage they do not need. The standard homeowners policy includes enough coverage on these target items to suit most families' needs. Households with valuable items can buy additional coverage on these items if they want it. Since the Hillmans do have the exposures, they might want to consider some specific insurance on their jewelry, silverware, and guns.

Coverage on Loss of Use.   Sometimes, it is impossible to live in a house following an insured loss. For example, it is usually impossible to live in a house while major fire damage is being repaired. The purpose of insurance is to indemnify insureds. This purpose is best served when insureds can survive a loss with as little interruption of their lifestyle as possible. The homeowners policy indemnifies insureds for the "additional living expenses" they incur in order to preserve their lifestyle.

Suppose a fire breaks out in the Hillmans' kitchen causing $10,000 damage to the building and damage to the contents. The damage is so severe that the building cannot be lived in until repairs are completed—a four-week period. During this time, the Hillmans rent rooms in a nearby hotel, eat in restaurants, and do their laundry at a laundromat. Homeowners insurance covers them for the *additional* expenses—expenses over and above their normal living expenses.

Personal Liability Coverage.   A homeowners policy covers claims for bodily injury or property damage for which the insured is legally responsible. Some exclusions eliminate coverage for auto liability and for business pursuits. Leonard should have commercial insurance to protect his business; this is not the purpose of homeowners insurance.

The personal liability section of the homeowners policy will cover the Hillmans if they are legally liable if, for example,

* A guest drowns in their pool;
* Napoleon, the dog, bites somebody;
* Leonard injures a stranger in a hunting accident;
* They give away food that happens to hurt someone;
* Embers from a trash fire ignite a neighbor's roof;
* A neighbor trips on a crack in the Hillmans' sidewalk; or
* Todd or Patti hits a baseball through a neighbor's window.

Personal liability coverage is usually purchased with a limit of liability of $100,000 or more—often as high as $500,000. The limit applies to each accident.

Coverage for Medical Payments to Others.   Actually, medical payments coverage should not be classified as liability insurance. Unlike personal liability coverage, the medical payments to others coverage does not require that the insured be legally liable for somebody else's bodily injury. In a loose sense, medical payments is "no-fault" coverage.

This coverage is sometimes characterized as "goodwill" coverage because it helps to avoid legal action between the insured and the injured person. For example, suppose Napoleon bites Leonard's nephew, who is visiting the Hillmans. A trip to the hospital emergency room for stitches costs $500. It is not necessary to determine whether the Hillmans, the insureds, as Napoleon's owners, are legally responsible for the injury or whether the nephew provoked the attack. It is not necessary for the nephew or his parents to get into a legal battle with the Hillmans. Regardless of liability, the Hillmans' homeowners policy will cover the bills under "medical payments."

Homeowners medical payments coverage is usually provided with a relatively low limit, such as $1,000 per person.

The policies designed for tenants and condominium unit owners are also called "homeowners policies." Tenants and condominium unit owners do not usually need insurance on the building or other structures. Therefore, the homeowners policies for tenants and condominium unit owners do not cover buildings or structures. Otherwise, they provide the same coverages as those found in other homeowners policies. Similar policies cover mobilehome owners and farm owners.

"Be careful how you sit in the chair. It's broken."

Other Personal Insurance Policies

Many families are adequately protected by a personal auto policy and a homeowners policy. Others need other types of insurance coverage. Some other coverages are briefly described here.

Personal Articles Floater Policies. As mentioned, the homeowners policy includes limited coverage on certain types of property such as jewelry, furs, silverware, and guns. People who own valuable items can purchase a "personal articles floater" to insure against loss of specified items. A personal articles floater can often be purchased as an endorsement to the homeowners policy. The endorsement is called a *scheduled personal property endorsement.*

The Hillmans should consider purchasing a personal articles floater to cover Debbie's diamond ring, the sterling silver tea set, and the guns. A personal articles floater would cover more perils than their homeowners policy and could have a dollar limit high enough to cover the value of these items.

Homeowners Medical Payments to Others Coverage Compared with Auto Medical Payments Coverage

Both the homeowners policy and the auto policy cover reasonable medical payments for injured guests without regard to fault. Both coverages are usually written with relatively small limits of liability. However, there is one important difference:

- The auto policy covers injuries to an insured, as well as to others occupying the insured's auto.
- The homeowners policy does not cover the medical expenses of an insured, but only those of other people who are injured because of the insured's premises, activities, or pets.

Umbrella Policy. An umbrella policy is a liability insurance policy that takes over where basic liability insurance policies leave off. Umbrella policies usually have a liability limit of $1 million or more, which is added on top of the limits for any other policies—such as a PAP and a homeowners—that cover liability.

The insured's auto or homeowners policy would provide basic "underlying" liability coverage. If the accident is so serious that damages exceed the limit of liability of one of those policies, the umbrella policy would pay this "excess" loss up to its limit of liability.

Umbrella policies have broad insuring agreements and relatively few exclusions. As a result, they cover some types of claims that are excluded by a typical basic insurance program. In such cases, a relatively small ($250 or so) deductible—known as a **self-insured retention**, or **SIR**—applies.

A **self-insured retention**, or **SIR,** is, in effect, a deductible in an umbrella policy. When a liability claim is covered by an umbrella, but not by another policy that covers liability, the insurer with the umbrella subtracts the SIR before paying the claim.

Exhibit 7-1 shows how the umbrella adds $1 million of liability insurance coverage on top of the underlying personal liability coverage of a homeowners, auto liability coverage of a PAP, and watercraft liability of a boat insurance policy. It also illustrates how the SIR acts as a deductible for losses covered by the umbrella but not by other policies.

National Flood Insurance Policy. Some floods cause widespread catastrophes that would create unmanageably large losses for a private insurance

Umbrella Loss—An Example

Leonard Hillman borrows a tractor from a farmer to do some landscaping work around his swimming pool. Leonard accidentally drives the tractor into the pool, and the resulting water damage requires expensive repairs to the tractor. The farmer expects payment from Leonard, but Leonard's homeowners, auto, and watercraft policies do not provide liability coverage for this unusual loss. However, Leonard's umbrella policy will cover all but $250 (the SIR) of this loss.

Umbrella losses usually involve large losses or unusual situations that are inadequately covered by a personal auto policy or homeowners policy.

Exhibit 7-1   Personal Umbrella Policy

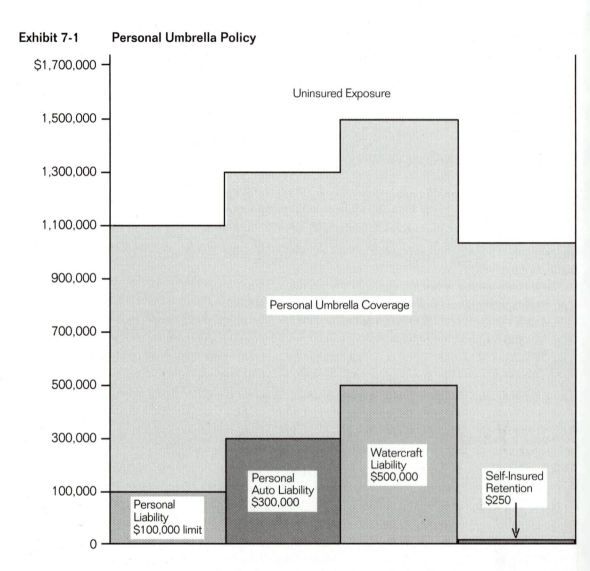

company that had issued many policies in the flood area. Most insurance
companies have been reluctant to offer flood insurance to homeowners under the theory that people in areas where floods occur every few years
would buy the coverage to a much greater degree than those in areas that
are not expected to have floods. (This is an example of "adverse selection,"
an underwriting problem mentioned in Chapter 3.)

The federal government has developed a program to make flood insurance available to homeowners through any licensed insurance producer.
Most flood insurance is now sold by private insurers, but excess losses are
subsidized by the federal government.

Other Personal Insurance.   Many other kinds of personal insurance are
available to meet special needs. For example, a family with a boat, an airplane, a motorcycle, or a camper might need another kind of policy. Whatever the insurance need, some type of coverage is usually available.

PERSONAL INSURANCE CHOICES

People who buy personal insurance need to make a number of choices, such as:

- What coverages to buy,
- What limits to select, and
- What deductibles to select.

Like other families, the Hillmans face such choices.

What Coverages To Buy

The Hillmans face choices related to auto insurance, homeowners insurance, and other coverages.

Auto. Along with the auto insurance coverages already described, the Hillmans might choose to buy such coverages as:

- **Rental reimbursement coverage**—which would pay the cost of renting a substitute car if their car is disabled in an accident,
- **Towing and labor coverage**—which would pay for road service and towing, and
- **Tape or CD coverage**—which would cover stereo tapes or compact discs in the car.

Rental reimbursement coverage is a PAP option.

Homeowners. The homeowners insurance choices are more difficult. The Hillmans need to choose between two or more homeowners forms available for people who own and occupy a home. The differences lie in which perils are covered in the various forms.

For example, a broad form homeowners policy covers a number of perils. A "special" homeowners policy covers household contents and other personal property for the same perils as the broad form homeowners policy.

However, it uses a different approach in covering the dwelling building and other structures. Instead of covering the **specified perils**, the policy covers all perils except for some that are excluded. This approach of covering all perils is sometimes referred to as "**all-risks**" coverage, even though many current policies do not use the word "all."

It is sometimes difficult to prove which peril caused a loss. With "all-risks" coverage, the **burden of proof** is shifted to the insurance company. The "all-risks" approach eliminates the need for the insured to have coverage to prove that the loss was caused by a specified peril. The effect is to provide fuller coverage—coverage for any peril that is not excluded. "All-risks" property insurance covers even perils that are not specified—as long as they are not excluded.

"All-Risks," Specified Perils, Burden of Proof

Specified perils property policies cover any loss that is caused by one or more of the covered perils that is named (specified) in the policy. The **burden of proof** in a specified perils policy is on the *insured*. To prove that a loss is covered, the *insured* must prove that it was caused by one of the perils described (specified).

"**All-risks**" property policies, also called "special" or "open-perils" policies, cover any loss unless it is caused by an excluded peril described in the policy. In an "all-risks" policy, the **burden of proof** is on the *insurer*. All losses are covered unless *the insurance company* can prove that the loss was caused by one of the excluded perils.

The burden of proof can be important in cases where a loss is obvious but its cause is not obvious.

When speaking with clients, insurance people avoid the term "all-risks." Instead, they might refer to "special" coverage or "open-perils" coverage, or they might simply refer to "the broadest coverage." Careless use of terms like "all-risks," "comprehensive," "blanket," or "full coverage" can leave the incorrect impression that the policy contains no exclusions. After learning that a loss is not covered, people sometimes sue the person who supposedly led them to believe it would be covered.

The **broad form homeowners policy** covers losses resulting from the following **specified perils**:

1. Fire or lightning
2. Windstorm or hail
3. Explosion
4. Riot or civil commotion
5. Aircraft
6. Vehicles
7. Smoke
8. Vandalism or malicious mischief
9. Theft
10. Falling objects
11. Weight of ice, snow, or sleet

12. Volcanic eruption
13. Accidental discharge or overflow of water or steam
14. Sudden and accidental tearing apart, cracking, burning, or bulging of steam or water heating systems
15. Freezing
16. Short circuits and brownouts

The **special homeowners policy** covers losses to the building from all perils *except* for such perils as:

- flood,
- earthquake,
- war,
- nuclear reaction or contamination,
- pipes freezing in a vacant or unoccupied house (unless reasonable care had been taken to prevent freezing),
- water freezing in a swimming pool,
- theft of building materials,
- vandalism to a house that has been vacant for more than thirty consecutive days, and
- wear and tear.

(The actual list of excluded perils is longer and contains considerably more detail.) The effect of this "all-risks" approach is to cover the building for all perils of the broad form homeowners policy plus some perils that are not named—except for those that are specifically excluded. Personal property coverage is the same as in the broad form homeowners policy.

An optional homeowners policy endorsement adds "all-risks" coverage on personal property. This endorsed homeowners policy would (subject to a deductible) cover even such things as fingernail polish spilled onto a table or bedspread or a television set knocked over by an unruly child. As might be expected, coverage this complete costs considerably more than the specified perils coverage. Since personal property losses are not usually as costly as losses to the building itself, most people decide that "all-risks" insurance on their household contents would cost too much in relation to the likelihood of losses that would be covered and the size of a possible loss. Not many people buy the homeowners policy that covers household contents on an "all-risks" basis.

Food for Thought

Did you realize that some homeowners policies and auto insurance policies cover more than others?

Both auto and homeowners insurance can cover just the basics, or they can cover other things as well. The basic policies have the lowest premiums, but they do not cover as many losses as policies that are more expensive. Insurance buyers need to decide whether they want just the basics—at the lowest cost— or whether they want the broader protection that comes with more expensive coverage.

Buying insurance involves more than simply finding a policy. Knowledgeable producers can help insurance buyers make the right choices.

Knowledgeable underwriters, claims adjusters, and others must recognize the differences among policies providing varying degrees of coverage.

Other Coverages.   Personal insurance buyers need to recognize that the personal auto policy (PAP) and homeowners policy are designed for the insurance needs of the typical family. Particular families have unusual needs that are not completely met by the "one size fits all" type of insurance policy.

The Hillman family, for example, has more sports equipment than the typical family. Except for the guns, this presents no property insurance problem because the homeowners policy covers sports equipment. It might cause extra liability concerns because many sports activities are hazardous and increase the chance that the Hillmans could become liable for injuries to a friend, guest, or stranger. An umbrella policy is a wise choice for any personal insurance buyer who wants to be sure that liability insurance limits are adequate.

The guns, as well as Debbie's ring and the sterling silver tea service, can be insured on a personal articles floater. The Hillmans, like other families, need to recognize that these items are not covered in full by a homeowners policy unless an endorsement is added. After finding out what it would cost to have these items covered on a personal articles floater or scheduled personal property endorsement, the Hillmans can decide whether or not to buy insurance on these specific items.

What Limits To Select

As a general rule, *property* insurance limits can be set at a dollar amount that equals the largest amount that could be lost if the property is destroyed. Because liability losses can become very large, selecting *liability* insurance limits is more difficult.

Property.   It is not necessary to select a dollar limit of coverage on the autos since they are covered for their value at the time of the loss. This value can readily be established by determining the price at which similar cars have recently sold.

It is necessary, however, to determine the value of the home. The homeowners policy presumes that most people will buy coverage for at least 80 percent of the home's replacement cost. Coverage to 100 percent of value is obviously more complete, but some people are reluctant to buy that much insurance since they think it unlikely that their house would ever suffer a total loss.

In homeowners policies, the limits for other coverages are automatically set at an amount equal to a certain percentage of the coverage on the dwelling building. These are usually as follows:

Coverages on Other Buildings or Structures	10%
Coverage on Personal Property	50%
Coverage on Loss of Use	20%

It is possible to raise or lower some of the amounts when circumstances make it necessary.

For example, assume the Hillman home has a **replacement cost** of $100,000. Also assume that Leonard decides to insure the home to 100 percent of its replacement cost value. His special homeowners policy would have the following coverage limits:

Dwelling Building	$100,000
Coverage on Other Buildings or Structures	10,000
Coverage on Personal Property	50,000
Coverage on Loss of Use	20,000

In the case of the Hillmans, it might be desirable to increase the "other structures" limit if the combined value of the swimming pool, bathhouse, and fence is more than $10,000.

> The current **replacement cost** of a building is the amount it would cost to construct the building today using materials of the same kind and quality. The replacement cost of a house does not include the value of the land because the land itself will not be damaged by most perils.

Liability.   Ideally, the insured would have liability insurance limits high enough to handle any foreseeable losses. Usually, the best way to accomplish this is to purchase an umbrella policy, which provides $1 million or more of liability insurance in addition to the coverage provided by auto and homeowners policies (as well as boat policies, if the insured has a boat).

Underwriters of umbrella policies require applicants to have at least a certain amount of underlying liability insurance—such as $100,000 of personal liability coverage on a homeowners policy and $300,000 of auto liability coverage. When an umbrella policy is combined with a PAP and a homeowners policy that meet these minimum requirements, the combined limits —exceeding $1 million—are high enough to protect against any but the most unusual liability claim.

Deductibles

A deductible is found in most property insurance coverages. However, except for umbrella policies, deductibles are less common with liability insurance.

A deductible is a portion of an insured loss that is not paid by insurance. For example, if there is a $500 deductible on the collision coverage of an auto insurance policy and an accident causes $4,000 of covered collision damage to the auto, the insurance company would pay $3,500.

From this description, it would seem that most people would want a low deductible. However, this overlooks the fact that deductibles reduce insurance premiums. As deductibles get higher, premiums get lower. With higher deductibles, fewer claims are paid (because more small claims are within the deductible amount), and fewer dollars are paid on large claims. That explains why insurers charge lower premiums on policies with higher deductibles.

Deductibles are desirable for insurance buyers because they help to reduce insurance premiums. Deductibles are also desirable for insurance

Food for Thought

Did you know that a building can have many different costs or "values"? People buying insurance need to know which "value" figure to use when deciding how much insurance to buy. For example, since the usual homeowners policy insures houses on the basis of replacement cost, a homeowners insurance buyer should consider the **replacement cost** when choosing insurance limits.

The **market value** of any property is the price at which it could be sold. You can easily see that this is different from the replacement cost value of a building. The market value includes the value of the land and can be higher or lower than replacement cost depending on the desirability of the location. Value of land and desirability of location do not change replacement cost value.

Except for a brand new building, the replacement cost is usually different from the **acquisition cost**—the price for which the building was originally built or purchased. The replacement cost depends on today's construction costs and the current cost of materials

The replacement cost of a building is almost always different from the **tax appraisal value** that tax appraisers establish as a basis for determining property taxes.

companies because it is costly for them to adjust many property claims for small amounts. Often, an adjuster's time and expenses would become as large as the amount of property damage itself. It simply does not pay to spend $50 in expenses to adjust a $50 claim.

Insurers usually recommend a deductible of *at least* $100 on auto physical damage insurance "other than collision" (comprehensive) and *at least* $250 on "collision." Higher deductibles are almost always available at a reduced premium. Homeowners policies usually have a deductible of at least $250 or $500, with higher deductibles available.

SUMMARY

This chapter has answered the question "what is personal insurance?" by describing the most common kinds of personal insurance. The personal auto policy (PAP) and the homeowners policy cover most needs of the typical individual or family. You saw some examples of how these policies would cover the needs of the Hillman family.

Other personal insurance policies can be used to cover additional needs. The umbrella policy covers liability over and above the liability coverage provided by the PAP and homeowners policies. The PAP and the homeowners policy can both be modified with some additional coverages. People

Reprinted with special permission of King Features Syndicate.

Personal insurance works best for those who make the right choices.

who do not drive a typical car or live in a typical one-family house can purchase other policies similar to the homeowners.

Whatever their needs, personal insurance buyers face a number of choices. They must decide whether to buy the basic, most inexpensive coverage or whether to purchase broader coverage. Individuals and families must decide what insurance limits to select, what deductibles to choose, and what optional coverages to buy. Personal insurance works best for those who make the right choices.

What Is Commercial Insurance? (Part 1)

8

Commercial insurance resembles personal insurance in many ways. However, the loss exposures faced by businesses can be much more varied than the exposures faced by families, so many more insurance choices might have to be made.

This chapter and the next show what commercial insurance is by examining the insurance needs of one particular business—All-Sports, a retail sporting goods store. After reading a profile of All-Sports, you will see that Paul Proctor is the producer who handles All-Sports' insurance review.

ALL-SPORTS: A PROFILE

All-Sports is a large retail sporting goods store operated by Leonard Hillman. (We reviewed the Hillman family's personal insurance in Chapter 7.) With twenty-two years in business, All-Sports is the only sporting goods store in Plainfield. All-Sports is located in a "strip" shopping center along a main highway. The other major store is Balboa's, a variety store.

All-Sports sells many kinds of sports equipment, including equipment and clothing for archery, baseball, billiards, bowling, boxing, camping, fishing, football, golf, hiking, hunting, ice skating, mountaineering and backpacking, roller blading, scuba diving, skateboarding, skiing, tennis, water-skiing, and weight lifting. Its customer service includes repair of tennis rackets, guns, rods, and reels, as well as fitting and drilling of bowling balls. Scuba-diving tanks are filled for customers, many of whom are members of a local diving club.

Besides making retail sales to the public, All-Sports provides a volume discount on sales to schools, clubs, and community sports organizations. A delivery van, boldly painted with the All-Sports logo, is often seen making deliveries.

An active advertising program and a pleasant store environment have contributed to All-Sports' popularity. All-Sports rearranges its displays to accommodate the various types of goods in high demand at any particular time. During the summer, items such as baseball, golf, swimming, boating, and fishing equipment are featured. Outdoor merchandise is often displayed in a corner of the parking lot. During the fall, fewer kinds of seasonal merchandise are highlighted, but the number of special displays increases in November and December because of holiday gift-giving and winter sports.

The store itself has roughly 5,000 square feet of sales and display space. The back room is used for storage of inventory and displays and also contains a loading dock and an office, where the computer is housed. Although Leonard Hillman makes most major business decisions, a store manager and bookkeeper are responsible for inventory control, billing, payments, and general accounting. The manager and bookkeeper also help out on the sales floor during busy periods.

PAUL PROCTOR APPROACHES ALL-SPORTS

For the past several years, Leonard Hillman of All-Sports has purchased personal insurance through Paul Proctor. Leonard has been impressed with the consistently thorough treatment he has received from Paul. Over the years, Leonard has learned that Paul Proctor is technically competent and that Paul's office provides friendly, efficient service. Several of Leonard's friends speak highly of Paul, who has a good reputation in Plainfield.

Paul Proctor has told Leonard several times that he would like to handle Leonard's business insurance. Last time, Paul asked what date All-Sports' business insurance expired. Three months before the "x-date," Leonard received a letter describing Proctor's commercial insurance facilities and asking for the opportunity to examine All-Sports' insurance needs.

Leonard is not very knowledgeable about insurance matters, and he is not sure whether All-Sports' coverage is up-to-date. For the past few years, the coverage has not been changed, and the current producer has suggested no changes. Leonard has been thinking it is about time for a review.

When Paul follows his letter with a telephone call, Leonard invites Paul to review All-Sports' insurance program. A date is set for a meeting at the store.

PAUL PROCTOR PREPARES FOR THE MEETING

Paul plans to use a survey questionnaire as a tool to help him check All-Sports' current insurance needs. The survey lists a large number of loss exposures often found in businesses. By using the survey as a reminder of possibilities and determining which of those possibilities exist at All-Sports, Paul reduces the chances that he will overlook an important insurance need.

Paul already knows what insurance coverages are generally needed by a typical retail store. These needs are obvious and do not usually require much specific attention. Paul will concentrate on discovering any unusual insurance needs so that he can recommend a complete set of coverages precisely matched to All-Sports' circumstances.

Paul will also pay close attention to the limits that should be carried on All-Sports' policies. In particular, he will pay attention to the value of property in various categories to provide property insurance with adequate limits. He will also be sure to recommend a high limit of liability insurance, probably by combining an umbrella policy with a sound program of underlying liability insurance.

The service that accompanies insurance coverage is also important. Paul will look for ways that IIA Insurance Company might be able to provide better service than All-Sports is receiving from its present insurer. For example, there might be ways in which All-Sports could benefit from IIA Insurance Company's excellent loss control services.

When he meets with Leonard, Paul also wants to "get a feel for" Leonard's attitude toward insurance. Is he the type of cautious business-owner who likes to buy every type of insurance he possibly can because it makes him feel secure? Is he the type of person who does not understand insurance, does not like insurance, and does not really want to buy any of it? Or is Leonard an analytical person who recognizes the role of insurance in covering large loss exposures but is willing to use deductibles or to omit insurance on exposures that would only lead to smaller losses? The insurance program that Paul designs should reflect Leonard's attitudes.

When Paul sets the appointment to review All-Sports' insurance needs, he asks Leonard Hillman to choose a time when they can meet for about an hour-and-a-half. Paul explains that he will first sit down with Leonard and get some basic information about the business. Then he would like a tour so that he can get a good mental picture of the store and the behind-the-scenes operation. After the tour, Paul will sit down again and get some of the more detailed information necessary to complete his analysis. Finally, Paul would like to get copies of All-Sports' present insurance policies.

After getting the basic information regarding All-Sports' insurance needs and taking down the information required to complete the necessary applications, Paul will return to his office and spend considerable time determining the best combination of coverages to recommend. He will then prepare a submission for IIA Insurance Company's underwriters to use in developing a quote. The quote might contain one or more options, if necessary. When he receives the quote, Paul will prepare a written proposal and will meet again with Leonard Hillman at All-Sports. This meeting will take place shortly before the expiration date of All-Sports' present insurance policies. If all goes well, Leonard will ask Paul to have IIA issue new policies as of the date when the old policies expire.

PAUL AND LEONARD MEET AT ALL-SPORTS

When Paul arrives at the store, Leonard invites him to the office and offers him a cup of coffee. Paul asks his first question:

PAUL: When I was getting ready for this call, it dawned on me that I had no idea whether All-Sports is a corporation and whether you own the building as well as the inventory.

LEONARD: All-Sports is a **corporation**, All-Sports, Incorporated, set up by my father when he founded the business. But I guess you could say I own the business, since my mother and my wife and I are the only stockholders. My accountant and lawyer say this is the best way to handle things.

The building is owned by a **partnership** that Ricky Balboa and I formed when we built this shopping center. The partnership is known as H & B Realty. H & B Realty owns all the buildings in this shopping center, as well as the land and the parking lot. I'm not worried about H & B Realty's insurance right now. That doesn't come up until June 1 of next year.

Paul makes the following note:

Shopping center buildings and land owned by H & B Realty
partners Hillman and Balboa
H & B x-date June 1!!!!

Food for Thought

Why do you think Paul made a note of H & B Realty's expiration date and added exclamation points? Paul will make an entry in his diary reminding him to contact Leonard again in March. At that time, Paul will see whether he can offer a quote to H & B Realty. An x-date is valuable information to an insurance producer.

Corporations and Other Forms of Business Ownership

A **corporation** is technically an artificial person. It can sue and be sued in its own name. Legally, it is a distinct "being" that is owned by stockholders.

A **partnership** is an association of two or more persons joined to carry on a business. Partnerships often use a business name, that is, the partners are "doing business as" (**dba**) some business name. Insurance policy declarations, for example, might list as the named insured "Leonard Hillman and Ricky Balboa dba H&B Realty."

A person might also own a business as an individual, in which case the business is known as a **sole proprietorship**. A sole proprietor might also use a "dba," such as "Alice's Diner," as a business name.

Each way of setting up a business has advantages and disadvantages. One risk-related advantage of a corporation is that the owner or owners of a corporation are not required to pay, out of their personal funds, any damages in a liability action that has drained all the corporation's assets. A large uninsured or underinsured liability claim against the corporation could drive All-Sports, Inc., into bankruptcy, but it would not cause Leonard Hillman to sell his home and other assets to pay a judgment. The buck generally stops, so to speak, with the corporation.

A similar judgment against H & B Realty could cause a personal loss to Leonard Hillman since the buck does not stop with the partnership. A partnership is not a separate legal being that shields its members from judgments. Each partner can be personally liable for the debts of the partnership.

A sole proprietor has unlimited liability for all claims against the business.

Paul now has some important information. He does not need to be concerned, at the moment, with insurance on the building. Any policies covering All-Sports' loss exposures should be issued in the name of "All-Sports, Inc.," since All-Sports is a corporation. If he eventually handles insurance on the buildings, the policy should be issued to "Leonard Hillman and Ricky Balboa dba H & B Realty."

Next, Paul asks some general questions about All-Sports to get a better feel for the business and its operations. Among other things, he asks

- How long All-Sports has been in business (twenty-two years),
- Whether there are any operations at other locations (except for deliveries and installations, there are not),
- Whether the business is growing, stable, or declining (it is showing steady growth), and
- What insured and uninsured losses the business has had.

Paul Proctor meets with Leonard Hillman in the All-Sports office.

Leonard summarizes the business operations and losses, which leads Paul to another question:

PAUL: Are your sales fairly even from month to month and from year to year, or is there a lot of variation?

Leonard reminds Paul that many sports are seasonal. Although All-Sports sells both winter and summer sports equipment, the biggest volume of sales is during the summer months from June through August, with another busy period during the December holiday sales season. All-Sports builds up its inventory of summer items during April and May and stocks up during October and November for the holiday sales season. Paul jots a note:

> **Peak seasons: June-August and December**
> **inventory levels seasonal**

Food for Thought

Do you think it makes any difference, for insurance purposes, if sales and inventory levels are seasonal?

Later, when Paul considers All-Sports' need for business income insurance, you will see that he is concerned that the coverage be adequate to handle an interruption during the busiest part of the year, when a loss would be most serious.

Paul also knows that property insurance covering the store's inventory has to have a limit high enough to be adequate for the times when inventories are at their peak. Yet carrying property insurance limits that exceed the maximum possible loss during "off" months simply wastes some premium dollars. Values in most businesses fluctuate, but this business might need much higher limits at peak times than at others. Paul might suggest **peak season** contents insurance, which provides different limits during different months of the year.

He might instead decide to suggest **reporting coverage**, which would require All-Sports to make a monthly report to IIA Insurance Company stating the current dollar values on all contents. If he uses the reporting approach, he will have to be sure All-Sports has accurate, up-to-date inventory records so that it is capable of producing accurate monthly reports.

PAUL: Have you had any burglaries during the past few years?

Paul knows a business like All-Sports can be a target for burglars. He listens carefully as Leonard responds. Leonard's answer might reveal something about his attitude toward insurance. Does Leonard believe All-Sports can afford to treat any burglary or robbery as a normal business expense, or does he prefer to insure the exposure? Has he taken any steps to control losses, such as installing a burglar alarm?

Leonard says there were two occasions during the last three years when somebody broke in and stole a few items, but he does not provide much detail.

LEONARD: Thank goodness we haven't had any serious problems. I worry about that—especially with the guns we sell in the store. Anybody who managed to steal the guns could really cause problems!

Paul jots another note:

> *Consider "all-risks" on contents—crime exposure*
> *Theft of guns a concern*
> *Check security of guns*

Before agreeing to cover the theft peril on a sporting goods store—especially one with firearms—Paul knows an underwriter will want information on locks, burglar alarms, and security measures at the store. He has decided to examine the store's security measures when he tours the premises so he can give the underwriter a preliminary description with his submission. If security is lax, IIA's loss control representative will probably make some strong recommendations.

In further conversation, Paul also learns that All-Sports owns only one truck, but that Leonard Hillman's minivan is also used for business purposes. Although Leonard has not mentioned the computer, Paul notices it in the office and decides to find out more about the system after taking a tour.

TOURING THE STORE PREMISES

Over his years in the insurance business, Paul has learned that he cannot find out everything about an account by sitting in an office. He needs to take a look at things.

As they leave the office, Leonard points out the bowling ball drilling machine and the repair equipment in the back room. Paul notices many shelves holding tagged items and asks,

PAUL: Those items on the shelves with tags…are they all here for repair?

LEONARD: Yes, they are. We do quite a volume of repair business. Nobody else in this county can handle some of the repairs we do. In fact, we do all the warranty service in the state on Fisch-Storey rods and reels.

PAUL: I had no idea your service department was so large. What do you think is the maximum dollar value of customers' property in your service department at any one time?

LEONARD: If you include the scuba tanks we refill and the tennis rackets we restring, I guess the values could get as high as $10,000. Is that something that needs special insurance?

Paul explains that customers' property should be separately listed to be fully covered and makes a note:

> *Bailee Exposure—equipment being repaired*
> *Max value $10,000*

Paul asks whether it is difficult to refill scuba tanks. Putting air into tanks seems easy enough, but Leonard explains that a mistake could cost the life of a diver.

LEONARD: Only one person in this store is authorized to refill tanks. He's a diver himself—used to be a frogman in the Navy. I know he's careful because he got into trouble once when somebody gave him a bad tankful of air. He knows the importance of his job, all right!

Paul makes another note:

> *Completed Operation hazard: refilling scuba tanks*
>
> *Ex-frogman does all refills*
>
> *Boiler and Machinery? Check coverage on pressure tanks*

Bailee

A **bailee** is a person or business that has in its care, custody, or control property that belongs to someone else. The value of bailed property should be separately considered if the property is to be properly covered. Paul now has the information he needs to be sure customer property is covered in the policies he will recommend.

Paul is now ready to move on to the selling area of the store, but Leonard pauses to raise another question.

LEONARD: Sometimes we let customers come back here when we're filling their tanks or working on their equipment, so we can show them exactly what we're doing. Do you think that's a good idea? I see some shops with signs that say something about an "insurance company requirement" that customers must stay out of the shop area, and I sometimes worry that we wouldn't be covered if one of my customers gets hurt back here.

Boiler and Machinery Insurance

Why did Paul make a note about boiler and machinery insurance even though he saw no boilers and little machinery?

Paul saw that the scuba tank refilling operation involved the use of an air compressor with a large pressurized air tank. Tanks containing pressurized air or gas are "unfired pressure vessels." They are "unfired" because they have no burner and therefore no flame. However, they contain pressure like a boiler or other fired pressure vessel, and they can explode if something goes wrong.

Boiler and machinery insurance covers explosions of boilers and other pressure vessels, as well as breakdown of various types of machinery. **Boiler and machinery inspectors** are specialists who periodically inspect insured objects to detect problems that could lead to an explosion or breakdown. Because their inspections are thorough, many losses are prevented.

When Paul analyzes the information he has developed about All-Sports, he will consider whether boiler and machinery insurance is an appropriate way to handle All-Sports' air compressor and tank.

Many insurance companies do not write boiler and machinery insurance but refer the boiler and machinery coverages to a specialty insurance company. The largest boiler and machinery insurer is Hartford Steam Boiler Inspection and Insurance Company.

PAUL: Before quoting on your insurance, IIA will probably want to have one of their loss control representatives take a look at your store. They may have some recommendations that address that question.

Paul goes on to describe the services provided by IIA's loss control representatives and gives some examples of ways the loss control representatives have helped several of Paul's customers. He explains that IIA might recommend that All-Sports put up a sign to discourage customers from entering the shop area, but he assures Leonard that this type of "insurance company requirement" does not mean All-Sports will not be covered if a customer is injured in the shop area despite the sign. However, Paul explains, an insurance company might decide not to renew a policy if it learns that its loss control recommendations are being ignored, so All-Sports will find it best to comply with any recommendations.

Leonard takes Paul through the store, pointing with pride to the attractive displays and the variety of merchandise. When they get to the gun display case, Paul pauses to study its security. Leonard explains that guns are kept in a locked showcase during the day, except when they are being shown to a customer. When the store is closed, a heavy padlocked chain is run through the trigger housing of all rifles and shotguns. Handguns are moved to the office safe.

LEONARD: It would still be too easy for somebody to make off with one or more of these guns when they're on display, but if we kept them all chained or locked in the safe we'd never sell any. If the insurance company has any better ideas on how I should handle the guns, I'd be glad to hear them.

Paul promises to look into this problem and makes another note:

Gun security adequate? Need display to sell guns!

Before returning to the office, Leonard leaves the selling area to show Paul the rest of the back room. As they approach the loading platform at the back of the building, Paul again thinks about crime exposures. How easy would it be for someone to break in through the loading platform area? Is the area well-lighted at night? Is the back of the store patrolled by police? Is any type of alarm system in place? Paul considers these questions as Leonard describes how shipments are delivered. When Leonard pauses, Paul mentions his concerns:

PAUL: I see that the large loading-dock door is open even though you're not making any shipments or deliveries. Don't you think this could invite some thefts?

LEONARD: We leave the door open for ventilation. It can get pretty warm back here at times. I've never had any thefts here...at least, not to my knowledge.

PAUL: How about after working hours? Have you had any break-ins? Is this door area well-lighted?

LEONARD: About four years ago we had a break-in through the back door over there beside the loading platform. They didn't take much, though. Anyway, after that I had an alarm system installed on all the doors. We turn it on whenever the store closes. We had one attempted break-in since it was put in, and the system obviously worked. It seems the burglar left empty-handed when the alarm went off.

While they are discussing theft, Paul raises a more delicate issue:

PAUL: Have any of your employees ever tried to steal from you?

Leonard describes a few incidents involving part-time clerks who were caught with merchandise and were promptly fired. He explains that he checks the inventory record himself from time to time and feels he has control over things. He checks bank deposit and withdrawal slips and makes most of the deposits himself. When Leonard is busy, the bookkeeper or office manager might drive a personal car to the bank with the deposit. The only people he thinks would have a chance to steal much are his bookkeeper and store manager, and he trusts both of them.

Paul points out that stock clerks, checkout clerks, and all the others who work at All-Sports have a chance to steal and that small items like sports watches can easily be slipped into a clerk's pocket. Paul also explains that most serious employee thefts are committed by trusted employees because those who are not trusted get less of a chance. He jots a note:

> *Recommend employee dishonesty coverage*
> *Emphasize office staff*
> *but note need for all employees*

While they are at the dock, Paul asks about property in transit:

PAUL: What do you carry in that truck of yours, Leonard? I see it all over the county. I'm wondering how much insurance you should have on the contents of your truck.

LEONARD: I guess we could have as much as $30,000 worth in there at times when we're delivering to one of our volume customers. Isn't that covered by our truck insurance?

Paul explains that neither a business auto policy nor insurance on the store

"That's the last time I go on vacation."

contents would adequately cover that much property away from the store while it is in transit. Paul jots another note:

> *Property in transit: $30,000*

PAUL: By the way, who drives the truck most of the time?

Leonard explains that nobody in particular is a regular driver. Sometimes it is one of the high school students working part-time, sometimes the ex-frogman, sometimes the office manager.

THEY RETURN TO THE OFFICE

As they walk back to the office, Paul asks a few more questions about All-Sports' full-time and part-time employees. As they sit down he asks a pointed question:

PAUL: What's your total annual payroll?

Leonard gives Paul last year's payroll figure and explains that next year's payroll will probably be about 5 to 10 percent higher. Paul makes a note:

> *add 5 to 10% to last year's payroll*

He also jots down the payroll amount.

Paul follows with a few more "money" questions. He asks for a dollar value on the store's inventory and also for the dollar value of all furniture, fixtures, office supplies and equipment, and miscellaneous store contents. He asks what the highest total dollar value of all personal property would be at any one time during the busy season and what the lowest value would be during the off-season. He asks how much cash the store might collect in any single day, how often the money is taken to the bank, and how much money might be in the moneybag when the deposit is made. He makes notes of Leonard's answers to all these questions.

Paul also asks about projected sales during the coming year. Leonard has been able to answer the other questions by referring to accounting records or thumbing through bank deposit slips or computer printouts. To answer this question, he uses the store intercom to talk to the office manager.

Food for Thought

Why do you think Paul is asking all these questions about All-Sports' money? Is he being nosy? Is he trying to figure out how much premium All-Sports could afford? Is he merely trying to get a better idea just how big the business is?

The answers to these questions do indicate how big the business is. But Paul is not asking for these dollar figures as a matter of curiosity. He wants to be sure the amounts of insurance requested in his submission correspond to what All-Sports could lose. And to determine the premium, IIA's underwriter and rater need to know how big a risk is involved. The size of the risk is related to "how big" the business is.

For example, the size of the risk from damage to the store's contents is related to the dollar value of those contents. Paul will complete an application requesting property insurance limits that are appropriate in light of the dollar value of the contents. The quoted fire insurance premium, which is based on the policy limits, will then be proportional to the value that could be lost in a fire.

Likewise, the size of the payroll is proportional to the chance of employee injuries that would be covered by workers compensation insurance. The more employees the business has and the more hours they work, the higher the year's payroll will be. For businesses as a whole, as the number of employee-hours during the year increases, the number of employee injuries during the year increases.

Similarly, sales figures relate to the chances of a liability claim from a defective product sold by the store and injuring a customer. And the amount of cash in the store or in the moneybag helps indicate the potential size of a robbery loss.

Some of the figures Paul gets, such as the payroll and sales, are estimates. The exact dollar amount of next year's payroll cannot be known now. It depends, among other things, on how much part-time help is needed, how much overtime pay is involved for full-time employees, and whether any employees are hired or fired, or resign. Premium auditors (remember Perry Andrews in Chapter 4?) will determine the exact figures after the year is over, at which time the premium will be adjusted for the difference between the estimated and the actual figures.

Paul tries to use sound estimates now to avoid problems later. A low payroll estimate now would reduce the workers compensation premium that will be quoted, but it would lead to a substantial deficit when the final premium is determined by the premium auditor later. Paul hopes to keep All-Sports as a customer, and he realizes that few things "turn off" a customer so rapidly as an unexpectedly large audit premium. Of course, it does not make sense to estimate on the high side, because this raises the initial premium. Although the insured gets back any extra premiums after the audit, the money has been tied up and unavailable to the insured.

LEONARD: Vic, will you check that budget projection for next year that we ran on the computer and see what figure we came up with for total sales?

After jotting down the answer, Paul asks a few questions about the computer. He learns that a "perpetual inventory" tied to the cash registers and scanners enables All-Sports to know, at the end of each week, the amount and cost of all items in inventory. He also learns that the computer is used to process the payroll and to handle accounts payable and accounts receivable.

Accounts receivable insurance pays for the cost of reconstructing accounts receivable records that have been damaged or destroyed by a covered peril. Even more important, it covers any payments that cannot be collected because records cannot be reconstructed.

PAUL: Did you ever stop to think what would happen if your accounts receivable records were destroyed? Your customers owe you thousands of dollars, but without records you wouldn't be able to collect from any of them. Would you be interested in insurance to cover the cost of reconstructing the accounts receivable records? **Accounts receivable insurance** would even cover the payments you can't collect because the records cannot be reconstructed. If you like, I can include that coverage in the quote.

Food for Thought

Do you think insurance would be the best way to handle All-Sports' accounts receivable exposure? Or do you think Leonard might be right in saying All-Sports does not need accounts receivable insurance because duplicate records are kept at a separate location?

Without knowing how many dollars could be involved in an accounts receivable loss, and without knowing how much—or how little—accounts receivable insurance would cost, this question cannot be satisfactorily answered.

However, it does illustrate the point that insurance is not the only way to handle exposures to loss. All-Sports has almost eliminated the chance of having a serious accounts receivable loss. All-Sports is probably better off spending a little time and money to keep duplicate records than it would be by buying insurance and doing nothing to prevent losses.

Of course, prevention and insurance can be used at the same time. With accounts receivable insurance, premiums are substantially lower when duplicate records are kept. Many other kinds of insurance also have reduced premiums when the insured has or adopts loss control measures that tend to reduce insured losses.

LEONARD: I don't think we need that coverage. At the end of every week we have the computer print out a current listing of accounts receivable for me to take home. I figure if the store burns down I'll still have the records at home. We could lose a few days' records but should even be able to reconstruct many of them. Most of our big-ticket sales to charge account customers would not be forgotten that quickly.

Paul asks for dollar values on the computer hardware and software. The computer is the nerve center of All-Sports' business. Leonard might be interested in a special policy that will cover computer-related losses.

After getting this information, Paul explores another important topic:

PAUL: How much money would you lose if the business had to be shut down for a while?

LEONARD: What are you getting at? And what does that have to do with my property and liability insurance?

PAUL: Well, suppose you had a fire that started in one of the light fixtures in the showroom and burned through the roof before it was extinguished. Chances are you would have to shut down while the place was being repaired. The store wouldn't have many paying customers while the doors were locked!

Worse yet, what if the building were to burn to the ground? You could be out of business for months! Say it took six months to rebuild your store—that would mean six months with no sales. You would have no income and certainly no profits. But a lot of your expenses would continue, and you might even have to set up a temporary office in a trailer in the parking lot, or something, that would create some extra expenses.

Business income insurance would cover your lost profits and meet those kinds of expenses. You don't have to suffer a financial loss if your business is closed, if you have the right business income coverage.

Do you think six months is a reasonable time to use in estimating the worst possible interruption? Could you be back in business within six months if this building had to be rebuilt and restocked?

LEONARD: Six months sounds about right.

PAUL: Let's go over your sales and expense figures and see how much business income insurance you should have. Since your business is so seasonal, we'll take into account the possibility of an interruption during the summer season when your income is the highest.

Using a business income insurance worksheet form, Paul and Leonard calculate how much business income insurance is needed to cover the loss that would result from a six-month shutdown.

Paul asks a few more questions from his questionnaire and eventually begins to discuss the delivery truck. He asks for a list of drivers and their ages. Leonard promises to have the office manager go through the personnel files and send Paul this list. Paul jots a note:

> *Drivers' names and ages*
> *Vic (office manager) will send*

Business income insurance is designed to help a business survive an interruption in its earnings after fire or some other covered peril damages business property. Business income insurance indemnifies a business for its loss in profits caused by the interruption and also pays the business expenses that continue during the interruption.

Normally, profits and the money to pay expenses are earned with the income of an active business. Business income insurance, in effect, makes up for what would have been earned during the period when a business is temporarily inactive because business property has been damaged by a covered peril.

Food for Thought

Why does Paul ask for losses during the previous three years? He knows IIA will need that information because three years is the time period usually considered for insurance underwriting and rating purposes.

Paul also asks what insured losses All-Sports has had during the previous three years and makes notes of Leonard's answers.

The last thing Paul asks for is a specific description of the truck—year, model, and VIN (vehicle identification number). Leonard picks up a file from his desk.

LEONARD: Here's my insurance file. The answer is probably in there somewhere. When you made this appointment you said you'd like to borrow copies of my current policies, so I had my bookkeeper pull this file. How long will you need to keep it?

Paul should only need a few days to review the file and make copies of any important forms. He explains this to Leonard, thanks him for the file, and takes a quick look through it.

PAUL: I see you're carrying a $250 deductible on personal property in the store and that your deductibles on the truck are also pretty low. Did you ever think about raising those deductibles to reduce your premiums?

LEONARD: I asked about that last time I reviewed our insurance with my agent. If I remember right, he said the discounts for the higher deductibles probably wouldn't be enough to make them worthwhile. But I'll tell you what: If you can show me a reasonable discount, I'd be glad to consider a $500 or even a $1,000 deductible.

I can afford to handle a $1,000 loss if I need to. Just last month I took a $900 loss when we ordered a bunch of imprinted uniforms for the local high school team—the Eagles—and they came through with sparrows because we put the wrong code on the order form. It's too late now to get replacements for this season. If only I'd double-checked the order…say, you can't sell me any "stupidity insurance," can you?

Paul has learned what he needs to know about Leonard's attitude toward deductibles. Both men laugh about Leonard's "stupidity insurance" joke and end the meeting.

SUMMARY

In this chapter we have seen how a producer and a businessowner can go about discovering insurance needs. We have seen that there are different ways of organizing businesses and that a corporation is different from a partnership or a sole proprietorship.

We have also had a chance to observe some of the circumstances that can affect a given business's insurance needs. For example, seasonally fluctuating inventory patterns need to be considered when setting limits for direct property insurance coverages. And fluctuating sales patterns need to be considered for business income insurance.

Some relationships between loss control and insurance needs have also become apparent. You have seen that crime prevention is important for a business like All-Sports, which has a number of items attractive to thieves. The safety of the shop area and the customer injury hazard also need to be considered. An insurer's loss control expertise can be valuable to an insurance buyer concerned about safety.

Commercial insurance needs are often different from personal insurance needs. We have seen that Paul is concerned about workers compensation, employee dishonesty, large values of property in transit, accounts receivable, sizable computer operations, and customers' property, among other things. Paul has also needed to obtain considerably more information to determine "how big" the business is so that he can recommend appropriate amounts of insurance. Paul's information on values, payrolls, and sales figures will also enable the underwriter to determine an appropriate premium to quote.

In Chapter 9, we will see how Paul uses this information to develop an insurance program that works to meet All-Sports' needs.

What Is Commercial Insurance? (Part 2)

9

P aul Proctor has set aside a day to work on the All-Sports submission. He begins his analysis by examining the All-Sports insurance file, along with the other information he accumulated during his visit to All-Sports, as described in Chapter 8. Paul had a hunch that there would be much room for improvement. His hunch was on target.

Paul gathers the IIA Insurance Company applications he will need and begins to prepare his submission. As he begins to work on each application, he reviews his notes regarding coverages and dollar values, and he decides what coverages to recommend. At the same time, he makes another set of notes summarizing the differences between his recommendations and All-Sports' present insurance program.

MEETING ALL-SPORTS' BUILDING AND CONTENTS INSURANCE NEEDS

Like families, businessowners are concerned about insurance on buildings and their contents. Some kinds of business property require special insurance coverages, and some perils are more important to businesses than to families. Also, just as a family needs to be concerned with additional living expenses if they cannot live in their house for a while after it is damaged, a business might be unable to operate because of damage to business property. A business interruption might be accompanied by a loss of business income.

Paul Proctor works on the All-Sports submission.

Building

Many business owners occupy a building they own. However, this is not always the case. Some business owners are tenants. They rent the building, or a portion of the building, where their business is run—just as some people rent houses or apartment units.

Paul has learned that All-Sports is a tenant. Therefore, All-Sports does not need to insure the store building.

Contents

Virtually every business owns some **personal property**. For a retail store like All-Sports, the largest amount of personal property is usually its merchandise for sale, known as **stock** or **inventory**. A store would also have furniture and fixtures in the office, sales area, and storeroom. Equipment owned by All-Sports is used for drilling bowling balls, filling scuba tanks, and making repairs. Miscellaneous equipment and supplies such as cash registers, office supplies and equipment, and display materials are also found in the store.

Contents (personal property) might be damaged if the building is damaged by some peril. Contents might also be damaged by some peril that does not affect the building. For example, much of All-Sports merchandise can easily be shoplifted. Also, it is more likely that burglars would be attracted to a sporting goods store than, say, a furniture store.

Personal Property and Real Property

Personal property includes everything except land, and buildings and other structures attached to the land. Land, buildings, and other structures are r**eal property**.

Merchandise, furniture, and supplies are examples of personal property. For convenience, insurance people sometimes use the word "contents" to refer to personal property in or near buildings.

(The "personal" in "personal property" is used in a different way than from the "personal" in "personal insurance." The "personal" in "personal insurance" refers to individuals and families as a class of insurance buyers.)

Stock and **inventory** are other terms for the merchandise a store intends to sell. Other types of business also use these terms to refer to their materials or products on hand.

Building and Contents Insurance

Building and contents policies cover property at the location or locations described in the policy. They can provide coverage for buildings or for personal property,

> **Building and contents insurance policies** cover property at the location or locations described in the policy. A building and contents policy can provide coverage for buildings or for personal property, such as contents inside the buildings. Many policies cover both buildings and personal property.

such as contents inside the buildings. All-Sports has no need for building insurance but certainly needs insurance on the store contents. Building and contents insurance always covers some perils besides fire. Paul examines the policy to see whether All-Sports' insurance covers a list of specified perils, or whether it has "special" (sometimes called "all-risks") coverage including all causes of loss except for excluded perils.

As part of his analysis, Paul also checks whether the amount of insurance on All-Sports' contents is up-to-date. All-Sports could be underinsured since retail prices have been increasing, but the store's insurable values have apparently not been reviewed for several years.

Present Coverage.   All-Sports, Paul sees, has a building and contents policy covering its contents on premises for the specified perils of fire, lightning, windstorm, hail, aircraft damage, riot and civil commotion, vehicle damage, explosion, smoke, vandalism, sprinkler leakage, and sinkhole collapse.

All-Sports' present insurance policy will cover the **actual cash value** if any covered property is damaged or destroyed by a covered peril. Subject to any deductible, the loss will be paid in full if policy limits are adequate and if the requirements of a **coinsurance clause** are met. The policy limit is the maximum amount that will be paid for businesses that are underinsured.

Paul sees that All-Sports' present policy contains an 80 percent coinsurance clause. Analyzing the value figures provided by Leonard Hillman, Paul discovers that the present policy limit is insufficient most of the year. When he adds up the value of furniture, office equipment, and other insured property, it appears that the business barely meets the requirements of the 80 percent coinsurance clause at the time of year when inventories are at their lowest level. All-Sports will suffer a penalty for underinsurance if it has a loss at any other time.

> **Actual Cash Value, Depreciation, and Replacement Cost**
>
> A building and contents insurance policy like All-Sports' covers the actual cash value of all covered property in All-Sports' store. This means that the property's actual cash value is the most the insurance company will pay if the property is destroyed.
>
> The **actual cash value** of property is figured by determining what it would cost to replace the property and then adjusting this replacement cost by subtracting an amount that reflects depreciation.
>
> **Depreciation** is loss in value that develops as items age, wear out, or become obsolete. In a sense, depreciation represents value that has already been used up before the loss occurred.
>
> Often, buildings, contents, or both are insured for their replacement cost. When insurance covers the **replacement cost** of the building, the insurance will pay the cost to restore the building, without any deduction for depreciation, assuming the policy limit is adequate.

Coinsurance Clause

A **coinsurance clause** in a property insurance policy reduces the amount that will be paid for a loss occurring when property is underinsured. The value of the property, as reflected in the policy limit, is supposed to reflect "how big" the risk is. If by choosing too low a policy limit the policyholder has indicated that the risk is smaller than it really is, then the premium will be too low. A coinsurance clause sets a "penalty" for underinsurance (reduced payment of any claim) when the policy limit is substantially lower than the value of the covered property.

All-Sports' present policy contains an 80 percent coinsurance clause. This means that All-Sports is supposed to have a policy limit that is equal to at least 80 percent of the actual cash value of the insured property. If All-Sports carries enough insurance to meet this requirement, all losses are covered in full, after subtracting the deductible. (For losses that exceed the policy limit, the policy limit is the maximum dollar amount that will be paid.)

Some property insurance policies do not contain coinsurance clauses.

Recommendations. First, Paul recommends a "special" (or "all-risks") type of insurance policy that will cover fire and all other perils except for some—such as flood, earthquake, and wear-and-tear—that are specifically excluded in the policy. This will provide important protection against burglary losses, as well as coverage for damage by sudden accidental water leakage and other perils. Paul will get quotes with $250, $500, and $1,000 deductibles.

Second, Paul recommends an increase in policy limits. He could suggest continuing the 80 percent coinsurance clause, with a new dollar limit that would equal 80 percent or more of the highest dollar values expected during the coming year, but Paul has an even better idea. He recommends a **reporting policy**. An estimated premium will be charged at the beginning of the year. All-Sports will have to send in a **report** every month that states its actual values. The final premium will be computed based on the average values on hand throughout the year.

The effect of a "reporting" policy is that All-Sports will pay only for the amount of insurance it actually needs. A reporting policy can be ideal for a business with values that fluctuate.

It is very important that a business with a reporting policy be able to submit accurate reports on time every month. If this has not been done, a penalty might be deducted from any claim payment. Paul would not recommend a reporting policy if he had not learned that All-Sports keeps accu-

Reporting Policy

A **reporting policy** can be ideal for a business with property values that fluctuate a lot during the year because a business with a reporting policy pays for only the amount of insurance it actually needs.

An estimated premium, called a **provisional premium**, is paid at the beginning of the year. Each month, the insured submits a report on its current property values. At the end of the year, the premium is recomputed based on the average of the monthly values.

The policy limit on a reporting policy is set higher than the maximum expected exposure. A business that purchases a reporting policy must submit its reports accurately and on time. As long as values remain within the policy limit and reports are accurate and timely, covered losses will be paid in full (after subtracting any applicable deductible).

rate, up-to-date inventory records with its computer. If All-Sports becomes his client, he will have his customer service representative, Connie Sue Rapp, set up a diary system to make sure the reports come in on time every month. Connie Sue will also check the reports to be sure they do not exceed the policy limit; if they do, she will take steps to have the limit raised.

Paul's third recommendation is for business income insurance, an important coverage that All-Sports has overlooked in the past. Based on the business interruption worksheet he and Leonard filled out, Paul recommends a type of business income insurance suitable for a store with seasonal sales fluctuations that would expect a maximum interruption of six months following a serious loss. Even though All-Sports does not own the building it occupies, damage to that building could cause an interruption in All-Sports' operations. So All-Sports' business income insurance will cover its loss of income if the loss results from damage to the building, to All-Sports' personal property, or to both.

Direct Versus Indirect Losses; Time Element Insurance

Building and contents insurance covers the **direct losses** resulting from damage to that property. Business income insurance covers indirect losses resulting from the same incident.

When property burns, the reduction in value of the property (a direct loss) is almost instantaneous. The **indirect loss** (the loss of earnings) takes place over a period of days, weeks, or months, depending on the severity of the fire. The longer it takes to restore the property, the bigger the business income loss; thus, the passage of time is an important element in these **indirect losses**. Because of this "time element," business income and other similar types of indirect loss insurance are sometimes called **time element insurance**.

MEETING ALL-SPORTS' GENERAL LIABILITY INSURANCE NEEDS

The possibility of being legally responsible for someone else's injury or for damage to someone else's property is as important to businesses as to individuals and families. A business can be held responsible for the acts committed by its employees and owners.

Premises and Operations Liability

A business might be responsible for bodily injury or property damage caused by conditions on its *premises*. The premises of a sporting goods store, though not unduly hazardous, do present some exposures. Customers can be injured while shopping. They can trip, slip, run into counters, knock over displays, and otherwise suffer injury whether they are in a grocery store or a sporting goods store. Perhaps the chance of injury is slightly greater if customers are tempted to lift weights, operate rowing machines, and check the sharpness of hunting knives. Paul has seen swing sets displayed in the parking lot in front of the store; they cannot possibly be disassembled or guarded at night. They might present a hazard leading to children's injuries for which All-Sports could be liable.

A business might also be responsible because of ongoing activities in its business *operations*. These activities might be considered *operations in progress*. Suppose All-Sports' employees are trying to install a basketball pole on a school playground and it topples and crashes onto a nearby car, breaking the car's windshield. All-Sports would probably be held liable for the property damage to the car.

Distinguishing between liability arising out of *premises* and liability arising out of *operations in progress* can be difficult. The distinction is not terribly important, however, since the two are insured by the same coverage.

Completed Operations Liability

Suppose All-Sports installs a basketball pole but does not properly anchor it. During a basketball game a week later, the pole suddenly falls and injures a player. This is an example of liability because of a *completed operation*. The injury is caused by some work that All-Sports has completed, rather than by an operation in progress.

Products Liability

Suppose All-Sports sells a toboggan that suddenly veers off-course and crashes into a tree the first time it is used. The customer breaks a few bones. She incurs some medical bills and loses two months' income because she cannot work. It would seem that the injury was the result of a product that was (1) defective when it left the factory, (2) damaged between the factory and the customer, or (3) damaged by the customer. The customer could sue both the store and the manufacturer. The store would need products liability coverage to provide defense and, if necessary, to pay any damages awarded by the court or agreed to in an out-of-court settlement. Many sports-related injuries are serious.

General Liability Insurance

Remember the "personal liability coverage" of a homeowners policy, which covers the liability arising out of the premises and activities of a

"Lily, give me a price on those bee-keeper hats."

family and its liability for products (such as food) sold or given to someone else? A similar type of coverage, known as **general liability insurance**, can be used to cover some of the major liability expo-

> **General liability insurance** covers some of the major liability exposures of a business, including liability related to the premises, operations in progress, products, and completed operations of a business.

sures of a business, including liability related to the premises, operations in progress, products, and completed operations of a business. This is the coverage that Paul examines next.

Present Coverage. All-Sports' has general liability insurance that provides coverage if All-Sports should become liable for others' bodily injury or damage to the property of others. The policy includes coverage of the major liability "hazards" mentioned above—premises, operations in progress, completed operations, and products. As expected, the policy excludes coverage for liability related to the operation of an auto because any business with auto operations is expected to have separate auto insurance.

Like all general liability policies, All-Sports excludes coverage for damage to property owned by others but in All-Sports' care, custody, or control. Another coverage, discussed later, is needed for the customers' property being repaired in All-Sports' back room.

Recommendations. Paul recommends that All-Sports continue to carry general liability insurance like its present coverage, with the same policy limits. He will also see if IIA's loss control representative can recommend some measures to reduce the chances that a customer could be injured in the back room, in an effort to prevent premises and operations liability claims.

Products liability coverage is especially important because it will pay for bodily injury or property damage that takes place away from the All-Sports store and is caused by a product sold by All-Sports. **Completed operations liability coverage** will pay for bodily injury or property damage caused by work that All-Sports has completed—such as repair work to customers' property. As with all liability insurance, the insured must be legally responsible for the injury or damage. The insurance company will handle the costs of defending the store if it chooses to try to prove that the injury or damage was not the responsibility of the insured.

> **Products and Completed Operations Liability Coverage**
>
> **Products liability coverage** pays for bodily injury or property damage that takes place away from the insured's premises and is caused by a product sold by the insured.
>
> **Completed operations liability coverage** pays for bodily injury or property damage caused by work that the insured has completed—such as repair work to customers' property.
>
> Some activities—such as installing an accessory in customer-owned equipment—involve both a product (the accessory) and an operation (the installation). It is usually unnecessary to decide whether a given claim relates to a product or to a completed operation. Products and completed operations coverages are written together, as parts of the same coverage.

> The **medical payments coverage** of a general liability policy will pay for injuries to customers and other members of the public who are injured on the store premises, regardless of whether the store is legally responsible for the injury.

The policy Paul recommends will include premises **medical payments coverage**. Like the medical payments coverage of the homeowners policy, the medical payments coverage of a general liability policy will pay for injuries to outsiders—customers and other members of the public who are injured on the store premises, regardless of whether the store is legally responsible for the injury. A customer who gets "carried away" trying an exercise machine might have to be carried away on a stretcher. If the customer's medical expenses can be paid without any argument about liability, All-Sports will preserve its goodwill. In Paul's opinion, this element of goodwill is important for retail stores. In his sales talks, he sometimes refers to medical payments coverage as "goodwill insurance."

MEETING ALL-SPORTS' AUTO INSURANCE NEEDS

Auto Liability

Businesses, like individuals and families, can be held responsible for bodily injury and property damage resulting from the ownership, operation, or use of a car or truck. All-Sports needs auto liability insurance because of its delivery truck.

Even if it did not own a car or truck, All-Sports would still need auto liability insurance. Leonard or an employee might use a vehicle rented or borrowed by All-Sports, or they might use their own cars to run business errands. All-Sports could be liable as a result. Since auto accidents can be serious, All-Sports has an exposure to loss in almost any situation involving the business use of a car or truck.

Auto Physical Damage

All-Sports' truck could be damaged in a collision, and it might also be damaged by other perils—such as vandalism, fire, glass breakage, and flood.

Business Auto Insurance

Although All-Sports' present insurance program does cover the delivery truck, Paul once again sees room for improvement.

Present Coverage.   All-Sports' business auto policy declarations, which are in the file Leonard provided, contain the year, model, VIN, and purchase price of the store's truck. Paul copies this information onto an IIA Insurance Company business auto application form and reads on.

Paul's state requires that persons or firms registering cars and trucks carry a certain minimum amount of auto liability insurance. All-Sports is carrying more than the minimum limits of coverage, but Paul thinks All-Sports' limits should be higher.

The policy covers All-Sports liability for bodily injury or property damage caused by an auto accident involving All-Sports' truck. If a claim or suit is brought against All-Sports as a result of such an accident, the insurance company promises to defend All-Sports, to arrive at a settlement if it chooses, and to pay any settlement or judgement up to policy limits.

The policy covers liability from accidents involving All-Sports' truck only. It provides no coverage for accidents involving employees who might use their cars to go to the bank or to run another business errand. It provides no coverage for liability arising out of rented cars, yet Paul has learned that All-Sports occasionally rents a larger truck to deliver assembled gymnastic equipment. The policy also provides no coverage if All-Sports should borrow a car or truck for any reason.

All-Sports has comprehensive and collision coverage on the truck. Even though the truck does not travel long distances, any bulky vehicle that backs up to loading docks, maneuvers through city traffic, and so forth has a higher than average possibility of collision loss. A commercial vehicle parked behind the store at night certainly faces the chance of a vandalism loss.

All-Sports has uninsured motorists coverage but no medical payments coverage on the truck. This is not unusual for a business vehicle since the occupants are usually employees who are entitled to workers compensation benefits if they are injured.

Recommendations. Paul recommends higher liability limits and will also recommend an umbrella policy to provide an additional layer of coverage. Paul recommends continuing to carry comprehensive and collision coverage because of the value of the truck. However, the $100 comprehensive deductible and the $250 collision deductible seem low—especially since All-Sports is willing to carry higher deductibles on its other property insurance coverages. Here Paul sees an opportunity to improve the insurance program by providing less coverage—by raising these deductibles he will reduce the premium for auto physical damage insurance.

He enters his recommended liability coverage limits and physical damage deductibles on the IIA Insurance Company business auto policy application. The combined effect of these two changes will probably lower the premium slightly, Paul estimates. The higher physical damage deductible could cost All-Sports a few hundred dollars if the truck is damaged in an accident. However, the higher liability limits could provide hundreds of thousands of dollars of additional protection if a person is seriously injured in an accident. It seems like a reasonable trade-off to Paul.

Paul recommends expanding the liability insurance coverage to apply to "any auto," rather than covering only liability resulting from All-Sports' truck. This expansion of coverage is not expensive, but it will protect All-Sports on those occasions when the store manager or bookkeeper goes to the bank using a personal car, as well as other instances when All-Sports could become liable for an auto accident. Although such an accident is much less likely than an accident with the truck, auto liability losses can be large. This is simply not something to take a chance on, in Paul's judgment.

Paul considers the advantages and disadvantages of adding auto medical payments coverage to the policy. Even though the truck is normally driven and occupied by on-the-job employees, whose medical expenses would be paid by All-Sports' workers compensation insurer, there is always the chance that the Hillman family, an employee, or a friend would use the truck after business hours to move a large personal item or to move to another apartment.

Paul decides to get a quote for $5,000 of auto medical payments coverage. Although All-Sports could probably handle a $5,000 loss—or even a $10,000 loss if two people were injured—without insurance, the coverage is relatively inexpensive. Paul will let Leonard decide whether to buy this coverage. In his proposal, he will list it as an option.

MEETING ALL-SPORTS' WORKERS COMPENSATION INSURANCE NEEDS

All-Sports needs workers compensation insurance because it has employees.

Workers Compensation Insurance

Workers compensation insurance pays certain benefits required by law to employees who are injured in the course of their employment.

When an employee is injured or contracts a disease that is job-related, the employer is required to pay for the cost of medical care, a portion of lost wages, and possibly certain other benefits (such as benefits to the survivors of an employee killed on the job). This is true regardless of who caused the injury or sickness. With a few exceptions, such as intentionally self-inflicted injury, a job-related accident or a job-caused disease is the employer's responsibility.

The amount that must be paid by the employer is specified by law in each state. The workers compensation policy contains no policy limit because it pays whatever dollar amount the law requires of the employer. In effect, the limits are in the law rather than in the policy.

To make sure that employers can meet their obligation to pay what the law requires to injured employees, most employers are required to purchase workers compensation insurance.

> **Workers compensation insurance** pays certain benefits required by law to employees who are injured in the course of their employment.

In some states, a large portion of workers compensation insurance is written through a workers compensation insurance pool or a residual market program. In Paul Proctor's state, workers compensation insurance is sold by private insurance companies. In some states it is sold by the state, in competition with private insurers. In several so-called "monopolistic" states, the state has a complete monopoly on workers compensation insurance; in these states, a state fund provides the required workers compensation coverage.

Present Coverage.   All-Sports has the workers compensation coverage required by state law.

"They've decided it *was* a job-related accident."

Workers compensation insurance pays benefits to employees injured in job-related accidents.

Recommendations.   There is little if any variation in coverage among the workers compensation policies offered by different insurance companies. All policies, in effect, say, "the insurance company promises to pay whatever the law requires the employer to pay under the workers compensation statute of the state."

Paul will recommend that workers compensation coverage be shifted to IIA Insurance Company along with the other coverages. An IIA Insurance Company policy will provide no improvement in coverage and no significant change in premiums. However, IIA's loss control services could help All-Sports reduce its future workers compensation losses.

OTHER COVERAGES

Paul Proctor has already found several ways to improve the coverage of the four policies in All-Sports' insurance file. He has also identified a number of additional policies that should be considered.

Umbrella Liability

Paul will recommend a **commercial umbrella policy** with at least a $1 million limit of liability. Similar to a personal umbrella policy, a commer-

A **commercial umbrella policy** will provide "excess" coverage in the event of a liability claim that is big enough to exhaust the limits of All-Sports' general liability or auto liability policy.

cial umbrella policy will provide "excess" coverage in the event of a liability claim that is big enough to exhaust the limits of All-Sports' general liability or auto liability policy. The umbrella policy will also cover some major liability losses that "slip between the cracks" of the general liability or auto liability policy; these are subject to a $10,000 **self-insured retention** (SIR), which operates like a deductible.

Underwriting guides generally require that an applicant for commercial umbrella coverage have a sound basic liability insurance program with adequate limits (the exact requirements are made known to producers) so that very few things will "slip between the cracks." Appropriate general liability coverage is required, as well as auto liability coverage that includes nonowned and hired cars. If the business has more than a modest amount of property of others in its care, custody, or control, this bailee exposure must also be covered by an appropriate type of insurance. Although not mentioned earlier, qualifying for umbrella coverage is another reason Paul will recommend increasing the auto liability insurance limits. It also explains why Paul recommends bailee coverage, discussed next.

Food for Thought

Many businesses do not buy umbrella policies. Is umbrella liability coverage really necessary?

An umbrella policy has been characterized as "coverage for the kinds of things that usually do not happen, just in case they do." Liability claims too big to be covered by basic policies with reasonable limits do not happen very often. Bodily injury or property damage liability claims over $10,000 that are not covered by general liability and auto liability insurance are rare. This means that umbrella liability claims are rare. So why do many businesses buy commercial umbrella policies?

First, any of the rare claims that occur are big ones, involving thousands, if not millions, of dollars in damages. One of the most important reasons for buying insurance is to cover exposures that could possibly lead to huge losses.

Second, umbrella liability coverage is relatively inexpensive. These insurance policies cost surprisingly little when you consider that they can obligate an insurance company to pay $1 million—or more—if an insured loss happens.

Umbrella liability policies are an excellent illustration of the way insurance operates as a system to help businesses share their risks. Many businesses pay a relatively small premium to buy an umbrella policy. A few businesses have large losses that are covered by umbrella liability insurance.

Because of the large potential claims involved, most insurers reinsure a portion of their umbrella policies. Umbrella insurance losses are not only shared by policyholders, but are also shared by insurance companies as well.

Bailee Coverage on Customers' Property

A **bailee** is a person or business that has in its care, custody, or control personal property that belongs to someone else. All-Sports is a bailee because it has customers' property in the store awaiting repair, being repaired, and awaiting customer pickup after repair. This property could be damaged through All-Sports' negligence, in which case All-Sports would be legally responsible for the damage. The property could also be damaged simply because it is on All-Sports' premises when a fire or some other peril occurs for reasons beyond All-Sports' control.

If lightning would strike the store, causing it to burn to the ground, All-Sports could refuse to reimburse customers whose property was destroyed on the basis that the lightning bolt was not caused by All-Sports' negligence.

Generally, the courts would support All-Sports in this position. As a "bailee for hire" (customers hire All-Sports to fix their sports equipment), All-Sports is responsible to use a high degree of care, but it does not have a duty to guarantee the safe return of the property regardless of circumstances.

Needless to say, many of All-Sports' customers would not be entirely pleased with such a position. Either All-Sports would end up with many unhappy customers, or else—and more likely—Leonard Hillman would make a management decision to replace all the damaged customer property at considerable expense.

All-Sports has $10,000 worth of customers' property on its premises. Such a large amount of customers' property is not automatically covered as "contents" on All-Sports' building and contents policy, but it could be added as a separate item. Another type of policy—**bailees customers coverage**—could also be used in this situation. Either policy will pay for losses to customers' property even if All-Sports is not legally responsible for the losses. Bailees customer insurance is a type of **inland marine** insurance.

> **Bailees customers insurance** covers losses to customers' property in the custody of a bailee. Most policies provide coverage regardless of whether the insured is liable for the loss. This helps the insured bailee to maintain customer goodwill.
>
> Laundries and dry cleaners, who have a great deal of customer property in their custody, are among the types of business that usually buy bailees customers insurance, a type of inland marine insurance.

Inland Marine and Ocean Marine Insurance

Isn't "inland marine" a strange term? "Marine" is from the Latin *marinus*, meaning pertaining to the sea. How can anything "marine" be "inland"? And what do tennis rackets and other customers' sporting goods have to do with the sea? This is one of those situations in which insurance terminology makes no sense without a history lesson.

The oldest insurance policies dealt with transportation. That was long before the days of cars and trucks. The earliest marine insurance covered boats and their cargo. When an ancient sailing vessel ran into trouble, often the only evidence of the loss was the fact that the ship did not get where it was going. Insurers in those days were not particularly concerned with covering certain perils. They paid losses whenever any peril whatsoever caused a ship to disappear. These ancient marine underwriters used an approach similar to today's "all-risks" insurance.

As time went on, transportation activities spread beyond ports and docks. Insurance was needed to cover cargo in transit by train and by motor truck. Fire insurance underwriters were most accustomed to insuring property at a single, fixed location, against certain familiar perils. It seemed natural, at the time, for marine underwriters to expand their activities to cover cargo that was not transported over water but inland. The term **inland marine** was coined to distinguish marine insurance on inland exposures from the marine insurance on waterborne exposures, called **ocean marine**. There was a demand for inland marine insurance on many types of property that was subject to being moved.

For many years, inland marine insurance was kept separate from fire insurance. Gradually, fire insurance underwriters broadened the perils they covered, and rules changed so that insurance companies were permitted to deal with more than one "line" of coverage.

Today, inland marine insurance coverages are described in a long document known as the **Nation-Wide Marine Definition**. Most of the inland marine coverages have something to do with transportation or communication. But in some cases the relationship to transportation is remote; in these cases, the fact that a coverage is defined as "marine" is based more on history—the way insurance developed—than on logic.

All-Sports needs transportation insurance—another inland marine coverage—because it transports cargo on its truck. Of course, collision is not the only peril that could cause a loss. An entire truckload of merchandise could be stolen or damaged by a fire or explosion.

Based on the information he has received, Paul completes a section of the IIA Insurance Company inland marine application, requesting $30,000 coverage for "owners' goods on owners' trucks."

One of the options on the application form is for theft coverage. This would cover All-Sports if someone stole all or part of the contents of the truck. Paul knows that IIA's underwriters are not very eager to provide theft coverage on a truck full of sporting goods. Thefts of this type can generally be prevented by not leaving the truck unattended or unlocked while it holds merchandise. Paul does not request the theft coverage, but he jots a note to himself:

> *In proposal:*
> *Point out to Leonard*
> *no theft coverage on truck contents*
> *Leave room for him to initial and acknowledge*
> *Suggest instead keep eye on loaded trucks*

Food for Thought

Why do you suppose Paul will want Leonard to "initial and acknowledge" the fact the proposed coverage will not cover theft on truck contents?

In this situation, Paul is recommending coverage that falls a little short of the broadest possible coverage. Even though he carefully explains to Leonard the reasons for this recommendation, it is possible that Leonard could forget the discussion in a few months. If a theft of truck contents occurs, Leonard might insist that he understood that his insurance would cover theft. If Leonard could convince a judge that Paul had, indeed, misled Leonard, whether intentionally or through an error or omission, Paul might have to pay of the loss with his own funds. (Or he might have part for the loss paid by his own insurance agent's professional liability insurance, sometimes called "errors and omissions insurance.")

Having Leonard initial this part of the proposal will call his attention to it in a way that helps him remember this coverage gap. Should Leonard ever forget the discussion, Paul will have his initials as proof that this gap was not, in fact, an error or omission on Paul's part.

Electronic Data Processing (EDP) Coverage

Since the computer is personal property, All-Sports would have some coverage for its computer under the insurance on contents. The business income policy would also provide coverage if the business is interrupted because of damage to the computer by fire or some other insured peril. All-Sports' building insurance would also cover computer disks and tapes but would only pay to replace them with blank disks or tapes; it would not cover any loss of information or programs recorded on the destroyed "media" (a term for computer disks or tapes).

Paul considers whether to recommend an EDP policy, a type of inland marine policy specially tailored to the needs of a business with extensive computer equipment and media. The EDP policy would pick up coverage on the computer, so Paul could subtract the computer's value from the building and contents insurance policy. It would also cover the programs and information stored on the tapes and disks.

After evaluating his options, Paul decides not to recommend an EDP policy to All-Sports. The special personal property coverage he recommends will provide so-called "all-risks" coverage on the computer and media, but not on information or programs recorded on the media. Duplicate copies of important programs and records can be stored in Leonard Hillman's home, the same way the accounts receivable records are handled. Paul will recommend duplication as a loss control measure, but he does not see a pressing need for additional insurance. He makes a note to discuss these points with Leonard.

Boiler and Machinery Coverage

Paul has noticed that All-Sports uses unfired pressure vessels in the scuba tank-filling operation. An explosion could turn the air tank into an unguided missile that sails through All-Sports' roof or, worse, cuts a path right through the back room and store.

All-Sports' present contents insurance covers the peril of explosion and does not exclude explosion of an unfired pressure vessel. The special personal property policy Paul recommends will also cover such explosions, but neither policy would provide coverage for an explosion in the tank of a steam boiler. If All-Sports had a boiler, Paul would recommend boiler and machinery coverage. Since the heating and air conditioning systems are the responsibility of the building owner, H&B Realty, Paul decides that All-Sports needs no separate boiler and machinery coverage.

Crime Coverage

The coverages Paul has already selected will cover some crime losses. "Special" ("all-risks") coverage on All-Sports' store contents will include coverage for burglary of merchandise or other contents, but it will not cover money or securities.

A lot of money goes into All-Sports' cash registers every day—particularly during the busiest seasons. The money is put into a moneybag when bank runs are made. A person carrying a bank bag with a few thousand dollars in cash makes an easy target. The "all-risks" protection of "theft, disappearance, and destruction coverage" on money and securities would be costly. It would tend to provide more coverage than All-Sports seems to need under the circumstances. Yet Paul thinks All-Sports should at least have robbery coverage that would cover money and securities both on premises, while the store is open, and off premises, to cover Leonard or one of his employees on the way to the bank. Since daily bank deposits are made, All-Sports has little need to keep more than petty cash and money to make change in the office safe overnight. Paul completes the application for robbery coverage. Paul also jots a note:

> *Note in proposal:*
> *No coverage for burglary of money*
> *Recommend daily bank deposits, without exception*
> *Have Leonard initial and acknowledge*

Employee Dishonesty Coverage

The policies Paul has recommended so far do not deal with the possibility that one of All-Sports' employees might be dishonest. The office manager or bookkeeper could conceivably manipulate the records and embezzle a large amount of money before Leonard discovers it. One way of doing this would be by "forgetting" to record some of the cash before it is deposited in the bank and pocketing it instead. Without even handling cash, one of the office employees could arrange for checks or bank deposits to be credited to a dummy account. Likewise, an employee who "forgets" to run some large cash sales through the cash register could also pocket quite a bit of money without being discovered.

Employee dishonesty does not involve only the loss of money. Merchandise can be pocketed, carried home in the trunk of a car, or even hauled away in All-Sports' own delivery truck to an employee's garage. Although a business like All-Sports takes periodic physical inventories, the count never comes out exactly right on all items. Many shortages are the result of record-keeping or delivery errors, but some can be caused by employee dishonesty. If the shortages are mistaken for record-keeping errors, a dishonest employee could operate for a long time before being discovered.

Leonard seemed to realize this problem when Paul mentioned it during their meeting. Many business people fail to identify the dishonesty exposure until it is too late.

> **Employee dishonesty coverage** applies to theft of money or other property by an employee.

Paul will include **employee dishonesty coverage**, also known as **fidelity coverage**, in his proposal. Loss caused by the dishonest acts of any employee—either theft of money or theft of other property—will be covered up to the policy limits. The type of coverage Paul will recommend does not require that a specific employee be identified by name as the culprit, so long as it is clear that dishonesty by an employee or employees was the cause of All-Sports' loss. The policy, however, will exclude coverage for losses that cannot be conclusively shown to be the result of employee dishonesty. If a physical inventory discloses a shortage of, say, divers' watches, employee dishonesty coverage will not pay the "loss" unless there is reasonable evidence that the shortage was indeed due to employee dishonesty.

IIA Insurance Company might want to check All-Sports' hiring practices and bookkeeping procedures before agreeing to provide this coverage. Are employee references checked before an employee is hired? Do sound procedures require one employee to count bank deposits and another to match them with bank records? As a final step, Paul jots another note:

Regarding employee dishonesty:
Stress employee stability in cover letter to IIA
Remind Leonard about reporting any dishonesty at once

This last note relates to a condition in policies providing employee dishonesty coverage. The condition says, in effect, that as soon as All-Sports learns that any of its employees have been dishonest, the insurance company will not cover any loss resulting from future dishonest acts of that employee. In general, All-Sports should fire anybody who has been caught stealing. If, for any reason, Leonard Hillman would decide not to fire that employee, All-Sports itself now faces the risk of any future theft by that employee. (In extreme cases, the insurance company might agree to renew coverage for that employee if he or she is shown to be completely rehabilitated.)

Package Policy

Although Paul has been thinking in terms of a number of different coverages, this does not mean that he will be delivering to All-Sports a pile of different policies. Most property and liability insurance coverages will be combined by IIA Insurance Company into a single **package policy**.

> A **package policy** combines a number of property and liability insurance coverages into a single insurance policy.

A package policy offers convenience for the insured, the producer, and the insurance company because it reduces the number of policies that would otherwise have to be dealt with. Package policies also receive a package discount. Insurance companies are willing to reduce premium costs when they can sell a number of coverages as part of a package.

COMMERCIAL INSURANCE CHOICES

As Chapters 7 and 8 and this chapter have shown, setting up a personal or commercial insurance program that meets the insured's needs involves a number of choices. Many of the same types of choices apply to both families and businesses, although commercial insurance tends to be more complicated.

Choices are made by everybody involved with insurance, not just insurance buyers.

- Insurance companies must choose what coverages and services to offer.
- Underwriters must choose whether or not to offer certain coverages to applicants and what price to charge.
- Insurance producers must choose what coverages to recommend to their prospects or clients.
- And finally, insurance buyers must choose which coverages and services they need and determine from whom they will purchase those coverages and services.

This chapter has focused on the choices made by a producer. Paul Proctor's coverage and service recommendations were made based on his knowledge of All-Sports' needs and of IIA Insurance Company's policies, services, and underwriting attitudes. Paul's customer service representative, Connie Sue Rapp, will use Paul's notes to complete a submission to IIA Insurance Company's underwriting department and will later prepare a proposal for Paul to present to All-Sports.

The following section summarizes some of the choices with commercial insurance and illustrates them with examples from the All-Sports case.

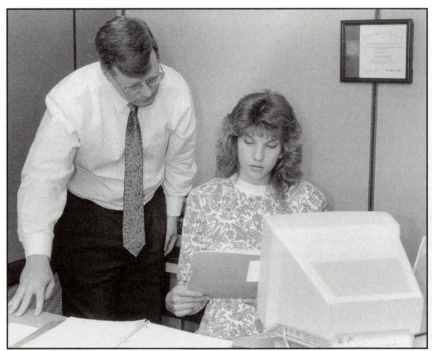

Connie Sue, Paul's customer service representative, will use Paul's notes to complete a submission to IIA Insurance Company's underwriting department and will later prepare a proposal for Paul to present to All-Sports.

Policy Limits

In general, policy limits should be related to the possible size of an insured loss. The specific ways in which this is handled vary between property insurance and liability insurance.

Property Insurance.   Property can be totally destroyed, but most property claims involve partial losses. If the limit of a property insurance policy is equal to or greater than the insurable value of the property, both partial and total losses will be covered in full (subject to any deductible).

If the policy limit is less than the total insurable value of the covered property, the property is underinsured. Total losses will not be paid in full because insurance policies never pay more than the policy limit.

Partial losses will be paid in full unless the insured has failed to comply with the requirements of any coinsurance clause in the policy. For example, if the policy has an 80 percent coinsurance clause and the policy limit is equal to 80 percent of the total insurable value of the property, the insured has enough insurance to pay for partial losses involving 80 percent or less of the total. Total losses or losses of more than 80 percent will not be covered in full. In short, a property insurance limit should normally be no less than the amount required by the coinsurance clause, and a higher limit is often advisable. For full coverage for a total loss, the limit should equal the full insurable value of the property.

The insurable value of any property depends on the valuation clause in the policy. The valuation clause describes the method that will be used to determine property values following a loss. As we have seen in this chapter, commercial property is usually valued on either an actual cash value or a replacement cost basis. When both options are offered, the choice between actual cash value and replacement cost coverage must also be made. When actual cash value coverage is purchased, the coinsurance requirements are based on the actual cash value of the property. That is, there is a penalty for underinsurance unless the policy limit equals at least the specified percentage of the actual cash value of the property. When replacement cost coverage is purchased, policy limits should be based on the replacement cost of the property.

All-Sports' expiring building and contents policy had policy limits that were barely adequate when the store's inventory was at its lowest point. All-Sports would have suffered a coinsurance penalty any other time of the year if it had continued to carry insurance on that basis. Paul Proctor could have recommended a policy with higher limits, but he instead selected a reporting policy that is even better at meeting the needs of a business with fluctuating values.

Paul also paid close attention to values in the coverage dealing with business income, property in transit, robbery, and employee dishonesty.

Liability Insurance. Although direct property losses are limited to the value of the property, and business income losses are limited by the firm's earnings, there is no ceiling on most liability insurance loss possibilities.

In fact, most liability insurance claims probably involve amounts well under $100,000. Though widely publicized when they occur, multimillion-dollar liability claims do not happen very often.

All-Sports' general liability insurance limits were adequate to cover almost any foreseeable claim, and Paul Proctor recommended no change. Paul was aware that auto liability claims often involve serious injuries and recommended higher limits of coverage than what had been carried.

Paul also recommended an umbrella policy with limits of at least $1 million to provide an extra margin of safety. Although the "underlying" general liability and auto liability insurance should take care of almost any foreseeable claim, a very large liability claim could have such a serious effect on All-Sports' ability to remain in business that Paul believes an umbrella policy is worth the premium.

This approach is a sound one for most businesses. It is like wearing a belt and also wearing suspenders. A basic liability insurance program is designed to cover most insurable exposures, with limits high enough to cover most claims. An umbrella policy adds protection for the very big claims "that usually don't happen, just in case they do." However, not all businesses choose such extensive coverage.

No choice of limits was involved with workers compensation coverage. Workers compensation insurance does not have a policy limit; instead, the policy agrees that the insurer will pay whatever amounts are specified by law for employee injuries.

Deductibles

Deductibles are found in most property insurance coverages. They are less common in liability insurance.

Property Insurance.   Higher deductibles mean lower premiums because the insurer must pay fewer losses. Choosing more coverage and lower premiums can be difficult. The decision, as we have seen, depends in part on how much of a loss the insured is willing to bear without any insurance reimbursement.

In the All-Sports case, as with many other businesses, the firm must occasionally take a business loss because of an uninsurable event, such as ordering the wrong type of athletic uniforms. Since All-Sports could take in stride a $900 loss from "stupidity" in ordering uniforms, chances are it could also afford to bear a $1,000 loss that could otherwise have been insured with a lower deductible. Whether All-Sports should take the chances associated with a higher deductible is a decision Leonard Hillman must make after finding out how much premiums will be reduced by the higher deductible. Tax considerations might enter into the decision, but a discussion of them is beyond the scope of this book.

Some kinds of property insurance usually do not have deductibles. Business income and employee dishonesty coverage are in this category.

Liability Insurance.   The umbrella policy recommended for All-Sports, like most umbrella liability policies, contains a large "self-insured retention," or SIR, for claims that are covered by the umbrella, but not by one of the "underlying" policies. The $10,000 SIR in All-Sports' policy is typical, but the amount varies from one insurance company to another.

Coverages

Although most businesses purchase the basic building and contents, liability, auto, and workers compensation insurance, many additional policies are available. Many endorsements can also be used to modify the basic coverages. The possibilities are almost endless.

In the All-Sports case, we have seen building and contents insurance coverage expanded with a "special," or "all-risks," type of form, which covers many more perils. Business income insurance covers time element losses that were not previously insured.

Inland marine policies provide bailee and transportation coverage. Crime insurance deals with robbery and employee dishonesty coverage.

Services

Service is important to all insurance buyers. The range of services is broadest with commercial insurance.

We saw an example of one important service in the insurance review provided by Paul Proctor, using a survey questionnaire as a tool. This service is needed by many businesses like All-Sports; Leonard Hillman, like many other businesspeople, has little expertise in insurance matters. The producer's services might be as important as IIA Insurance Company's coverages and services.

The insurance company's services include loss control service. As suggested in this chapter, loss control representatives do much more than serve as eyes and ears for underwriters. Their safety expertise is very important as well in helping policyholders to prevent and reduce their losses.

Price

Nearly all insurance buyers consider not only limits, deductibles, coverages, and services, but also price. It costs the insurance company more to provide more coverage and service. Buyers are not always willing to pay more, and they often choose to do without some coverages or services to reduce insurance premiums.

For many insurance buyers, price is the single most important factor in the buying decision. Price played a very important role in the Allied Manufacturing case, which you saw earlier in this book. Factors affecting insurance prices will be described in more detail in Chapter 10.

In short, insurers can compete on the basis of price, and they can also compete on the basis of the limits, coverages, and services they provide.

SUMMARY

Businesses have a wide variety of property and liability insurance needs. This chapter has not tried to describe all the commercial property and liability insurance coverages that are available. To do so would require a much longer book. Instead, this chapter has used All-Sports as an example to illustrate the kinds of insurance needed by one particular business. In the process, it has also explained factors that are considered in making commercial insurance buying choices. Although the specific needs of other business might vary substantially, the kinds of choices illustrated here apply in many situations.

What is commercial insurance? Commercial property and liability insurance is a widely varied set of coverages that work to meet the needs of businessowners.

How Are Premiums Determined?

How are insurance premiums determined? That question will be answered in this chapter. You will learn that premiums for many kinds of insurance are developed by applying "rates" to "exposure units." You will find out about the "rating systems" that are used to calculate insurance premiums. You will also come to understand some reasons behind the systems. In the final section of this chapter, you will see that many of the things you studied in earlier chapters also affect the cost of insurance.

An **insurance rating system** is an orderly method for arriving at an appropriate premium. Insurance rating systems can be divided into two broad categories:

- **Class rating** places similar insureds into categories, or "classes," and applies the same rate to all insureds in the same class.
- **Individual rating** is used when every insured is unique. Each insured is assigned an insurance rate that reflects its own unique characteristics.

Before explaining class rating and individual rating, it is necessary to explain how **rates** and **exposure units** are used to calculate **insurance premiums**. We will begin by briefly discussing insurance premiums.

INSURANCE PREMIUMS

An **insurance premium** is a periodic payment by the insured to the insurance company in exchange for insurance coverage. The word "periodic" means that the

> An **insurance rating system** is an orderly method for arriving at an appropriate premium.

> **Class rating** places similar insureds into categories, or "classes," and applies the same rate to all insureds in the same class.

> **Individual rating** is used when every insured is unique. Each insured is assigned an insurance rate that reflects its own unique characteristics.

An **insurance premium** is a periodic payment by the insured to the insurance company in exchange for insurance coverage.

payment must be made at certain time intervals. Each premium payment buys protection for a particular time period.

The premium charged for an insurance policy should be "commensurate" with the exposure. That is, there *should be* a close relationship between the premium charged and the risk—the possibility of financial loss—assumed by the insurance company. It is not easy for insurers to calculate a premium for each policy that accurately reflects the loss potential of the insured.

An ideal insurance pricing structure also encourages the insured to practice loss control. Basically, this means that an insured that exercises sound loss control should pay less for the insurance than one that does not.

The people who develop systems for calculating insurance premiums are called actuaries. The **actuary** uses complex mathematical methods to analyze past loss data and other statistics. This information is used for determining future premiums.

An **actuary** uses complex mathematical methods, usually with the aid of computers, to analyze loss data and other statistics and develop systems for determining future premiums.

In many cases, different insurance companies charge different premiums for the same coverages. Insurers want premiums to match losses that are expected to happen in the future, but losses do not always happen as they were predicted by actuaries, and actuaries for different insurers might differ in their predictions. (The weather forecasts on different radio stations do not always agree, either, because reasonable meteorologists can differ in their evaluations of available data. Any prediction of future events can be made with only limited accuracy.)

Insurers are not the only ones who care whether premiums properly reflect exposures. Insurance buyers also compare the cost of insurance with the potential losses the insurance would cover. They tend to stay away from insurance companies whose prices seem too high.

People tend to buy insurance from the insurer with the lowest prices. Thus, insurance companies will generally write more business if they offer lower prices. However, premium levels can be reduced only so far before underwriting losses result.

Insurance premiums provide the funds with which an insurance company pays claims. Insurance premiums also pay the insurance company's expenses and, the insurance companies hope, provide a margin for profits and contingencies. Earnings on investments

Two Desirable Features of Insurance Premiums

Insurance premiums (1) should be commensurate with the risk and (2) should encourage insureds to practice loss control.

Insurance premiums should be **commensurate with the risks** (should properly reflect the exposures) they cover. There should be a close relationship between the premium charged and the risk assumed by the insurer.

Insurance premiums should **encourage the insured to practice loss control**. This goal is addressed by insurance rating systems that lower the premium to reflect factors that reduce losses or raise the premium to reflect factors that tend to increase losses.

supplement the income from insurance premiums. To some extent, investment income can reduce the amount insurers would otherwise have to charge as premiums. If an insurance company is to succeed in the long run, its premium income and its investment income, together, must be at least adequate to pay claims and expenses—preferably, with some money left for profits and contingencies.

INSURANCE RATES

An **insurance rate** is the price of insurance for each unit of exposure. The rate is multiplied by the number of exposure units to arrive at a premium.

An **insurance rate** is the price of insurance for each unit of exposure. The rate is multiplied by the number of exposure units to arrive at a premium.

Using Rates To Calculate Prices and Premiums

Calculating an insurance premium is much like determining how much a purchase costs at the vegetable stand. Assume you are buying two peaches priced at $0.20 per peach. To determine your cost, you would multiply the rate per peach times the number of peaches.

Rate per Unit	Times	No. of Units	Equals Price
$0.20 per peach	X	2 peaches	= $0.40

The same formula is used if you buy five pounds of peaches at the vegetable stand at a price of $0.49 per pound:

Rate per Unit	Times	No. of Units	Equals Price
$0.49 per pound	X	5 pounds	= $2.45

In both examples, the total cost is composed of a rate ($0.20 or $0.49) for some standard unit of purchase (peach or pound) multiplied by the number of units (two peaches and five pounds, respectively). The choice of standard units is a matter of convenience. Peaches might be priced "per peach" or "by the pound"; gasoline in the United States is usually priced by the gallon, but in many other countries it is priced by the liter.

Sometimes rates are expressed as a rate per some quantity of a product. For example, although it would be possible to charge a certain amount for each egg, raw eggs are usually priced by the dozen. If you purchase sixty eggs to cook up a giant-sized omelet, and if eggs cost $1.00 per dozen, you have to divide the number of eggs by a dozen (12) to determine the number of units for which you will be charged:

Number of Items Divided by Unit Size=
Number of Units
60 eggs/12 = 5 dozen eggs

The price is then determined by applying the formula used before:

Rate per Unit	Times	No. of Units	Equals Price
$1.00 per dozen	X	5 dozen	= $5.00

People calculating insurance premiums follow essentially the same process. Based on rates provided by actuaries and published in rating manuals, the final price of insurance (the premium) is determined by multiplying the rate per unit times the number of units.

Rate per Unit   Times   No. of Units   Equals *Premium*

The formula is the same as before, except that the word "premium" is substituted for the word "price." For example, if the rating manual shows a rate of $475 per auto to provide collision coverage for one year, this rate is multiplied by the number of autos to arrive at the annual premium. For a firm like All-Sports, with one auto to insure, the computation would be simple:

Rate per Unit	Times	No. of Units	Equals Premium
$475 per auto	X	1 auto	= $475

For a business like Allied Manufacturing, with many different kinds of autos, there may be different rates for each of the various models. In such a case, the rating procedure is more complicated.

Many insurance rating units are expressed in dollar amounts, such as "$100 of insured value" or "$1,000 of payroll." This is not unlike eggs, which are priced in "dozen" units, and the calculation approach is the same. Suppose a building and contents policy has a rate of $0.70 per $100 of building insurance and a building is being insured for $200,000.

Number Of Items Divided By Unit Size = Number Of Units
$200,000/$100 = 2,000 units

Rate per Unit	Times	No. of Units	Equals Premium
$0.70	X	2,000	= $1,400

EXPOSURE UNITS

The units used in insurance rating are referred to as **exposure units**. Since the purpose of insurance rating is to develop premiums commensurate with exposures, **the exposure units selected for rating each insurance coverage should bear a relationship to the size of the exposures**. To be more specific, the number of exposure units should be a fair measure of expected loss frequency and severity. As the number of exposure units increases, the potential number of losses or the amount to be paid for each loss should increase.

> Exposure units are the standard units used in insurance rating.

What factors determine the selection of an appropriate rating base? Consider the following example. Suppose that you need to develop a system for determining general liability insurance premiums for movie theaters; the same system would be used in all theaters. General liability insurance covers bodily injury and property damage liability. There are some ways in which a theater could become liable for damage to the property of theatergoers. For example, grease in the mechanism of a theater seat might soil a customer's clothing. However, the most serious claims would probably involve bodily injury. People can be injured in a number of ways—for example, by tripping over an obstacle that cannot be seen in a darkened theater.

What would be an appropriate rating base for this exposure? Logic might tell you that liability losses would be related to the number of people who enter the theater, to the length of time they stay, and, perhaps, to the number of people in the theater at any one time (because it is more difficult to evacuate a large crowd swiftly when there is a problem). What exposure unit would you select as a rating basis to determine the premium for one year? Some possible rating bases might be the number of tickets sold each year, the total amount collected from ticket sales each year, the number of films shown each year and their length, the square foot area of the theater, or the number of seats.

Each of these possible rating bases might bear a relationship to the size of the exposure. In addition, each possesses some characteristics that are desirable in a sound rating base. Each is **readily measurable**. The square-foot area of the theater building can easily be determined and usually does not change during the year. The number of seats is easy to count and, again, does not usually change. Other suggested rating bases rely on figures that could be readily determined if the necessary records are kept.

It is also desirable that an exposure base be **"inflation sensitive"**—that is, insurance premiums should go up during periods of inflation if insurance premium dollars are to keep pace with claim and expense dollars. When insurance rates are not inflation sensitive, rates can gradually become inadequate, requiring rate revisions. The use of an inflation sensitive rating base tends to adjust automatically for the changing value of the dollar. (The use of an inflation sensitive rating base does not entirely eliminate the need for rate changes, which might still become necessary for other reasons.)

Size of building, number of seats, number and length of movies, and number of tickets are not inflation sensitive, but the dollar amount paid for tickets is. (The cost of theater tickets tends to rise during inflationary periods. Even if the **number** of tickets remains the same from year to year, the **dollars** received each year from ticket sales would increase if ticket prices are raised.) Inflation sensitivity might favor selecting "per $100 of ticket sales" as a rating base rather than selecting another measure. Rating based "per $100 of ticket sales" would be simple but might not relate as closely to the exposures as some other rating base. For example, "per $100 of ticket sales" would apply the same rate to first-run movie theaters—which charge higher prices—as to second-run movie theaters—which charge less per ticket. Other factors (such as location) also affect theater prices.

Another desirable feature of a rating system is **simplicity**. You could consider combining two factors. For example, you might use a rating base that considers both dollar ticket sales (which are inflation sensitive) and the number of tickets sold (which directly reflects the number of theatergoers), but this would make your rating system more complicated and you would lose the advantages of simplicity. To keep the system simple, it is desirable to use only one rating base.

"Admissions" is the exposure base that is currently used. It is simple and readily measurable. Each ticket sold is considered one admission. Since the number of admissions relates directly to the number of people visiting the

Four Desirable Features of Exposure Units
Ideally, a standard exposure unit should:
1. reflect the exposures,
2. be readily measurable,
3. be inflation sensitive, and
4. be reasonably simple.

theater during the policy term, it reflects the exposure. However, it lacks one desirable feature—inflation sensitivity. This is considered the best compromise, since other exposure bases would not be as desirable in other ways. It is not unusual for the selection of an exposure base to involve some compromises.

DEVELOPING AND USING INSURANCE RATING SYSTEMS

Insurance rating systems are developed by insurance companies and independent insurance service organizations. Insurance companies and insurance service organizations, as well as state insurance departments, employ actuaries who help develop and monitor insurance rating systems.

Insurance Service Organizations

Insurance service organizations set up classes, or categories, to use in collecting and analyzing reliable loss data that is used by insurers.

Insurance Services Office (ISO), the largest insurance service office in the country, performs a variety of services. Among other things, ISO develops statistical classification systems and collects statistical data on insured claims from a large number of insurance companies. It also analyzes this information and uses it to develop loss cost data. Insurance companies that subscribe to ISO's services may use this loss cost information in setting their own insurance rates.

Insurance service organizations continually collect loss information from many insurance companies. Loss data from many insurance companies for each of the different rating classes is combined. Combining this data makes the information more reliable because loss prediction is most accurate when it is based on the actual losses of a large number of exposure units.

Insurance service organizations then analyze the loss data to determine the average "loss costs" per exposure unit in each rating class. The largest insurance service organization is Insurance Services Office (ISO).

Loss Costs

Loss data reflects **historical loss costs**. This name is used because historical loss costs involve only past losses. Data on historical loss costs is often adjusted to anticipate losses that can be expected in the future. These expected future losses are called **prospective loss costs**.

Historical loss costs, which involve only past losses, indicate the dollar losses relating to each exposure unit in the past.

Prospective loss costs indicate the amount of money an insurance company can expect to need to pay claims for each exposure unit. Of course, it is not enough for insurance companies to collect just enough money to pay claims. An insurance company must also cover its expenses and allow for profits and contingencies.

Therefore, each insurance company determines how much to add to prospective loss costs to arrive at the rate it will charge to those in each rating class.

The result is that each insurance company uses loss cost information to develop its own set of rates per exposure unit. These rates reflect both prospective loss costs and the insurer's expenses and are published in the insurance company rating manual or stored in the insurance company computer. These rates are also "filed" with the state insurance department where required. In many cases, the state insurance department might also reject, modify, or approve the rates that will be used.

> **Prospective loss costs**, which are based on past losses plus some adjustments, indicate the dollar losses relating to each exposure unit that can be expected in the future.

CLASS RATING

Many kinds of insurance are **class rated**. That is, a **classification and rating system** groups together all insureds with similar characteristics into the same rating class. All members of the class are charged the same rate for insurance, although their premiums will be different if they have different numbers of exposure units. (For example, one theater might sell 50,000 tickets a year, and another might only sell 10,000.)

The basic idea of an insurance classification and rating system is that insureds with similar characteristics have similar potential loss frequency and severity. Even though there may be wide variation in actual losses from one insured to the next, aggregate losses among all members of the class should be predictably different from the losses of all members of another class who have different characteristics.

For example, suppose you are responsible for developing an appropriate classification plan for liability insurance on school buses. Should all school buses carry the same rate for insurance, or are there characteristics that would enable you to develop classes of school buses? (Although classes normally ride in school buses, school buses appear in insurance rating classes.)

It would be logical to classify buses according to where they are driven. Road, weather, and traffic conditions vary from state to state, county to county, and city to city. You would probably develop some kind of classification system that divides a large area into smaller territories. Each bus in the same territory would have some similar characteristics.

Another factor to consider would be bus size. Large buses can injure more people or cause more damage in an accident than smaller van-type buses. It would seem logical to use at least two size categories—and possibly more.

A number of other factors could also be built into your rating system, but you would want to keep the system as simple as possible. Also, if you increase the number of classifications too far, the number of the similar units in each classification would decrease to the point that the purpose of grouping was lost. A rating classification system that was so highly refined that it had only one bus in each class might be even less useful than a system that applied the same rate for every bus. (As a matter of fact, school buses are divided into four size categories based on "number of passengers." They are further classified according to geographical territory and "radius of operations.")

The term **homogeneity** is used to describe similarity among insureds in the same rating class. The term can be remembered by relating it to homogenized milk. Dairy farmers realize that nonhomogenized milk separates into two categories when allowed to stand—the cream rises to the top. Homogenized milk has **homogeneity**—the entire jug of milk has the same characteristics. The cream is dispersed and suspended evenly throughout, and it is not possible to identify different categories of milk within the jug.

> The term **homogeneity** is used to describe similarity among insureds in the same rating class. All insureds in the same class of a sound classification and rating system should be fairly homogeneous. **Perfect homogeneity** (completely identical loss characteristics) is impossible, but **workable homogeneity** is feasible for many types of insurance.

As suggested earlier, if it is impossible to find a perfect exposure base—one that is simple yet contains all the other desirable characteristics. **Perfect homogeneity** is also impossible in insurance classes. A good classification and rating system is based on **workable homogeneity**. That is, insureds are broken into enough classes, based on one or more characteristics, so that each class of similar insureds has loss potential that is different from the loss potential for other classes of insureds. For example, school buses are broken into only four groups based on passenger capacity, even though more capacity groupings would certainly be possible.

INDIVIDUAL RATING

Individual rating systems are used when every insured is unique. Insureds could not be placed into "workably homogeneous" classes under such circumstances. When large numbers of reasonably homogeneous loss exposures do not exist, the only alternative is to devise a rate for each insured reflecting the exposure characteristics of that particular insured.

This is the approach that would be taken in developing a fire insurance rate on a large, unique factory building. The specific building is inspected by a person using a point system that adds or subtracts points for such things as type of construction (masonry, wood, and so on), number and type of fire extinguishers, nature of the occupancy, capabilities of the local fire department, as well as the supply of water available at nearby hydrants. The number of points determines an insurance rate for that particular building. The rate is "published" so that producers, underwriters, raters, and other interested parties have access to it. The published rate is applied "per $100 of insurance" to determine the premium for fire insurance.

Sometimes it is necessary to insure an exposure for which there is no established premium-determining system. In such cases, the underwriter has to rely heavily on his or her judgment, a practice that is referred to as **judgment rating**. Judgment rating is a type of individual rating.

Judgment rating does not mean that an underwriter simply "pulls a rate out of the air." The underwriter usually has experience with insurance cov ering comparable exposures. This experience gives the underwriter a "gut" feeling as to what premium amount would be appropriate. For example, successful experience in insuring cross-country rail shipments of coal and iron ore might help an underwriter to decide what to charge for insuring the shipment of some other bulk cargo.

> **Judgment rating,** a type of individual rating, is used to develop a premium for exposures for which there is no established premium-determining system. With judgment rating, the underwriter relies heavily on his or her experience in setting the premium.

EXAMPLES OF INSURANCE RATING PLANS

In this section of the chapter you will examine the methods used to determine premiums for some particular kinds of insurance. In each case, you will see whether the coverage is class rated or individual rated. You will also be shown what exposure units are typically used as a rating base and the characteristics of the coverage that make this a workable approach. Where applicable, you will also observe some premium modification techniques that might apply.

Personal Auto Insurance

Personal auto insurance is class rated, using rating systems with a large number of rating classes. One rating plan has 262 different rating classes within each geographical rating territory. Since there are hundreds of territories across the country, actual rating classes number well into the thousands.

A system with so many different classes would not provide workable homogeneity for a type of insurance with relatively few insureds (because there would be so few insureds in each class). However, the 169 million licensed drivers in America provide enough exposure units to permit a highly refined classification system.

(The large number of auto insurance buyers makes auto insurance rates politically sensitive. No other category of insurance rates seems to be watched as closely by insurance regulators.)

"If you spend over $20, it includes free vehicle insurance against vandalism in our parking lot."

HERMAN copyright Jim Unger. Reprinted with permission of UNIVERSAL PRESS SYNDICATE. All rights reserved.

Traditional auto insurance classification and rating systems classify drivers and their autos according to the following factors:

- Territory where the car is "garaged"
- Age, sex, and marital status of drivers
- Whether youthful drivers have had driver training
- Whether youthful drivers are "good students"
- Whether the vehicle is used for pleasure, for commuting to work, in business, or on a farm
- Whether the car is standard, high performance, or a sports car
- Whether the policy covers a single car or more than one car (in which case there might be a discount)
- Whether any drivers have been licensed for fewer than three years
- Age of the car (for physical damage insurance)
- Cost of the car when new
- Tickets received during the past three years for traffic violations (five years for some serious violations)
- Accidents during the past three years

Food For Thought

Some states prohibit the use of sex and marital status as a basis for auto insurance classification and rating. What are the advantages and disadvantages of "unisex" rating?

Over the years, statistics show a distinct difference in the accident experience of males and females. That is why males and females have traditionally paid different auto insurance premiums.

Critics of these traditional systems do not deny the differences in accident experience. However, they question whether the differences are based solely on differences in sex and suggest that other rating factors should, perhaps, be used instead. In addition, they suggest that it is socially unacceptable to charge different premiums to people who are classified according to factors (such as sex) that are essentially beyond their control.

Insurance premiums have to be at a level that will pay for losses and expenses and provide a margin for profits and contingencies. Systems that ignore sex could meet this goal. However, many insurers are concerned that abolishing sex-based classification and rating systems would be the first step in abolishing all classification systems, which, they hold, provide a necessary basis for insurance premium determination.

Do you agree that it is necessary to classify insureds in order to charge each insured an appropriate insurance premium? Might rating factors other than sex and age—maybe "miles driven" and "years of driving experience"—provide equally valid results? Do you think that "unisex" auto insurance rating would inevitably lead to banning other classification and rating plans despite actuarial differences in the experience of the different classes? Would life insurance still be possible if "age discrimination" in life insurance rates were prohibited? Don't feel bad if you cannot answer these questions. People who have considered them at great length have not agreed and will probably continue to debate the issues.

The last two items (tickets and accidents) help to encourage loss control. Drivers who have had at-fault accidents or have been convicted of serious traffic violations will pay substantially more than those with a record of safe driving.

Studies have traced the accident experience of specific makes and models of cars. It is now possible to predict that certain types of cars are more likely to be stolen, more likely to sustain serious damage in an accident, or more likely to have injured occupants than are others. Some insurers' classification and rating plans reflect these damageability and susceptibility factors.

Sure your rates are high. You don't have an airbag.

Reprinted with permission of Insurance Information Institute.

Other insurers have classification and rating systems that do not use all of the factors listed here, but instead use factors that we have not discussed. In each case, the purpose is to place insureds into groups, with the members of each group having similar loss potentials.

Since most personal auto policies run for six months, the standard exposure unit for auto insurance rating is "one auto for six months." Of course, the premiums also reflect the coverages that are purchased since there is a premium charge for each coverage. The premium also depends on policy limits and/or deductibles for each coverage.

For example, the manual premium for six months' liability coverage for a standard auto, used for pleasure and operated by an adult, is as follows in the rating manual for one territory:

Limit	Premium
$ 35,000	$124
$ 50,000	$136
$ 75,000	$146
$100,000	$153
$200,000	$172
$300,000	$181

The premiums would be much higher for a young male, inexperienced behind the wheel, who had caused several accidents.

It is worthwhile to notice the difference in premiums for different amounts of liability coverage. Some people are surprised to see how little more it costs to buy liability insurance coverage with much higher limits. However, the pricing makes sense when you realize that the vast majority of liability claims involve less than $10,000. That is why insurers can offer so much more coverage for so little extra premium. But even though most liability claims are small, higher liability limits are still a good choice. To a person who happens to cause a serious accident, the additional coverage can be very important.

A similar pattern appears with other types of liability insurance. Compared to the premium for the lowest available limits, it costs relatively little to increase liability insurance limits.

Homeowners Insurance

Like auto insurance, homeowners policies are class rated. There are millions of homes in America, and a number of classifications have been developed, each including a large number of similar homes.

Most states are divided into rating territories, reflecting differences in crime and vandalism claims or exposures to windstorm, hail, or other climatic conditions. Within each territory, further classification is based on two factors:

- **Construction type**—generally frame or brick, since wood frame houses burn more readily and therefore have higher premiums than solid brick houses; and

- **Protection class**—a rating of the local fire department's capabilities and the availability of fire hydrants and other water supply sources.

Protection class is a rating of the local fire department's capabilities and the availability of fire hydrants and other water supply sources, usually on a scale from 1 to 10, with 1 being best and 10 having essentially no fire protection.

After an insured's classification category has been determined, tables in the rate manual are used to find an appropriate premium

The premium is based on:

1. The type of homeowners policy purchased (for example, broad or special), and
2. The policy limit (amount of insurance) purchased to cover the dwelling building.

This is all that is needed to determine the premium for one year of coverage on a standard homeowners policy with the lowest liability and medical payments coverage limits. Simplicity is possible because, as you might remember, the amounts of insurance for other structures, for household personal property, and for additional living expenses are set at a fixed percentage of the dollar limit on the dwelling building itself (unless specific steps are taken to use different limits).

Additional charges are added when higher liability coverage limits or other coverage options are purchased. Discounts are subtracted for such options as higher property coverage deductibles.

Many insurance companies base their rates on loss costs developed by ISO or another insurance information and service organization that draws from the experience of many insurers. Some insurance companies choose to modify those loss costs when setting rates. Loss costs based on a cross-section of homeowners business of many insurers might not adequately reflect the losses expected by one particular insurer. For example, IIA Insurance Company might have underwriting guidelines that accept only homes built within the last fifteen years. If experience shows that these newer homes will have fewer serious losses than the combination of new and old homes used in developing loss costs, IIA Insurance Company might use lower loss cost figures when developing its rates.

The typical home seldom has an insurable loss, and most homes therefore have no loss history. However, some insurers' discounts for alarm systems and other rating devices attempt to identify and reward homeowners with reduced loss potential by charging them a reduced premium.

Commercial Building and Contents Insurance

Commercial building and contents insurance can be class rated

"I get a real deal on fire insurance."

Insurance rates are lower for structures with sound protection and low loss potential.

or individual rated, depending on the building. Both class rates and individual rates are stated as rates "per $100 of fire insurance."

Some commercial buildings and their contents are of a type that have a large number of similar exposure units. Take, for example, the typical gasoline station and mini-market. A large number of these gas stations can be found in every state, all with essentially the same physical characteristics. For these and other buildings, the rating bureaus publish class rates.

Other commercial buildings are unique. One-of-a-kind buildings cannot be grouped with other buildings, so it is necessary to develop fire insurance rates on their own individual characteristics. Inspectors examine such buildings to establish a fire insurance rate for each particular building. Separate rates are published for each building and its contents. In a multiple-occupancy building, different contents rates might be published for each tenant.

Package discounts are often built into insurance company rating plans when building and contents insurance is part of a commercial package policy that also includes liability insurance and other coverages.

Individual rating encourages loss control since rates are lower for structures with low loss potential. Underwriters are sometimes permitted to "schedule" credits (discounts) or debits (surcharges) if they can identify some characteristics that are not considered in the rating system but that affect a property's loss potential. This practice is called **schedule rating**.

> **Schedule rating** can be used when underwriters are permitted to "schedule" credits (discounts) or debits (surcharges) if they can identify some characteristics that are not considered in the established rating system but that affect the loss potential of a particular insured.

Commercial General Liability

General liability insurance is class rated. Each classification describes a particular type of business operation. Insureds in the same line of business are grouped together because they have similar potentials for loss. For each classification, the manual indicates the applicable rates for various liability coverages.

The activities of many businesses fall into more than one category. Generally, the single category that best describes the business determines the rate for all liability coverage. Only when the insured conducts separate and distinct businesses would more than one classification apply. The major exception is the construction business, where the variation in hazards requires each construction operation to be separately classified.

Allied Manufacturing Company manufactures farm implements. According to the ISO classification scheme, it would fall into classification 56651, "Machinery or Machinery Parts Manufacturing—farm type." Premises and operations liability coverage rates would be found next to that code in the rating manual. Products and completed operations rates would be found in another area.

Wilkinson, Cartoonists & Writers Syndicate

Several different standard exposure units are used in rating commercial general liability insurance. Some of the most common are:

- Payroll—rates apply per $1,000 of payroll.
- Gross sales—rates apply per $1,000 of gross sales.
- Area—rates apply per 1,000 square feet.
- Admissions—rates apply per 1,000 admissions. (For a movie theater, each ticket sold would constitute one admission.)
- Total cost—rates apply per $1,000 of total cost as defined and are generally used as a basis for determining premiums on contracted work.
- Units—various exposures are rated on a "unit" basis. One example is the number of living units in an apartment.

The standard exposure unit selected for businesses in each classification is one that reflects the extent of exposures by businesses in those categories. Within workable limits the exposure unit also possesses the other desirable features described earlier. That is, it is readily measurable, inflation sensitive, and reasonably simple to work with.

What exposure unit(s) do you think would be most appropriate for Allied Manufacturing? In fact, gross sales is the standard exposure unit for coverage for businesses in code 56651, "Machinery or Machinery Parts Manufacturing—farm type." Generally speaking, for manufacturing firms in this class, those with higher gross sales are more active and therefore have a greater liability loss potential. Gross sales also reflect the volume of products sold. Gross sales figures can readily be verified by examining records kept by all manufacturers.

What exposure unit(s) do you think would be appropriate for a retail store, such as All-Sports? The standard exposure unit, again, is gross sales. If All-Sports' store had $2 million in gross sales, the manual rate for "Sporting Goods or Athletic Equipment—Stores," code 18206, would be multiplied by 2,000 to arrive at a premium for that coverage. Remember the formula explained earlier in this chapter:

Number of Items Divided by Unit Size = Number of Units
$2,000,000 gross sales/$1,000 = 2,000 units

Area (floor space) was used for years as the basis for rating most retail stores because the potential for customer injury is closely related to the size of the store. However, square-foot area is not inflation sensitive, so rates based on area needed to be revised more often than rates based on, say, gross sales if the rates were to be kept commensurate with the exposure. Whenever possible, insurers try to use inflation sensitive rating bases rather than bases like square-foot area or number of apartment living units.

The approach described so far makes no allowance for any type of rating adjustment that reflects the insured's loss control activities. Any business in a particular class might have a potential for more losses—or for fewer losses—than other members of its class because of characteristics that go beyond the mere type of business. Small businesses are generally charged a manual premium under the theory that any differences in their loss potential cannot readily be distinguished from the loss potential of other businesses in the same category. Larger businesses, with a much greater number of exposure units, can be evaluated to some degree based on their past loss records. The process of doing this is known as **experience rating**.

Experience rating is a process by which the insurance premiums of larger businesses can be modified to some degree based on their past loss records. Underwriters usually refer to the insured's loss history as **past experience**, even though the word "past" is technically unnecessary.

Experience rating compares a firm's actual losses during the three most recent years with the losses that were expected when manual premiums for those years were developed. If the firm had fewer dollar losses than expected, the experience rating formula provides a discount; if losses were greater than expected, the formula adds a surcharge.

Additionally, underwriters can *schedule* credits or debits based on judgments regarding certain characteristics of the insured. And when liability coverage is written as part of a package involving property coverage, a *package discount* can be applied.

Workers Compensation

Workers compensation insurance is class rated. The classification system resembles the one used to develop premises and operations premiums for general liability insurance rating on a payroll basis. There are approximately 600 classifications for workers compensation insurance. This classification system groups employers so that the rate for each classification reflects the exposures common to the business described by that classification.

ISO is not involved in workers compensation rating plans, but other service organizations are. The **National Council on Compensation Insurance (NCCI)** is the rating bureau responsible for developing workers compensation insurance loss cost data in most states. In some states, all insurers are required to use the same workers compensation insurance rates. However, other states permit insurance companies to develop their own workers compensation insurance rates.

Because workers compensation benefits prescribed by the laws of the states differ, loss potentials also differ by state. Therefore, each insurer's rates are different in each state. The standard exposure unit is $100 of payroll. Each $100 of payroll is multiplied by the manual rate to arrive at a manual premium.

A **premium discount** is applied to policies on larger businesses to reflect the fact that some of the expenses of selling and servicing workers compensation insurance do not vary in proportion to the premium.

Premiums may also be adjusted by the application of an **experience modification**. In the case of workers compensation insurance, the so-called "experience mod" is developed ("promulgated") by the service organization, which bases the "mod" on the loss experience of the insured business. When experience modifications are used, premiums move up and down from year to year in relation to an insured's **past** loss experience.

> The **National Council on Compensation Insurance (NCCI)** is responsible for developing workers compensation insurance loss cost data in most states.

> A **premium discount** is applied to workers compensation policies on larger businesses to reflect the fact that some of the expenses of selling and servicing workers compensation insurance do not vary in proportion to the premium.

> An **experience modification ("mod")** for workers compensation insurance is based on the loss experience of the insured employer.

Inland Marine Insurance

A variety of rating plans are used in inland marine insurance. Some coverages are class rated, using loss cost data developed ("promulgated") by service organizations. This approach is taken with very common types of insurance, such as a "jewelry floater" covering an engagement and wedding ring set.

Other inland marine policies cover unique, one-of-a-kind exposures that must be individually rated. For example, chances are there is no rating manual with a rate for a float in the Weevil Boll Parade, so an underwriter who is asked to insure such an item of mobile property would have to

OF COURSE i HAVE "PAST EXPERIENCE" ... WHAT OTHER KIND iS THERE?

3-1

ZIGGY copyright ZIGGY AND FRIENDS, INC. Dist. by UNIVERSAL PRESS SYNDICATE. Reprinted with permission. All rights reserved.

Experience modifications adjust the premium to reflect past loss experience.

charge a premium based on personal experience and judgment of the float's loss potential. The underwriter would not get the rate entirely "out of the air," but might examine rates for physical damage insurance on a semi-trailer and consider the rates typically used to insure a single one-day-long shipment of perishable cargo before arriving at a premium for this unusual exposure.

OTHER FACTORS IN PREMIUM DETERMINATION

This chapter has provided a simplified overview of the systems used to determine insurance premiums. Of course, individual insurance companies might vary in the premiums they charge even when they use the same system to make rates. Elsewhere in this book, we mention other things that affect premium levels. Some such items are briefly repeated here to reemphasize their relationship to insurance premiums.

Marketing System

In Chapter 2, you examined the various insurance marketing systems. Every marketing system has costs that are reflected in insurance premiums. However, some marketing systems involve a different mix of costs than others. For example, a direct response marketing system involves considerable mail and telephone expenses. On the other hand, a system with commissioned or salaried agents has agent expenses to consider.

Underwriting Standards

In Chapter 3, you examined the processes involved in underwriting insurance submissions, with the use of an underwriting guide that describes the insurance company's attitudes towards accepting various applicants. Some insurance companies are extremely selective in their underwriting standards, and they accept only applicants who have loss experience much more favorable than other insureds of the same type.

Insurance companies with strict underwriting standards can and often do charge lower premiums because they expect fewer losses. On the other hand, some insurance companies set relatively high rate levels. They might attract applicants willing to pay a higher premium because they have been rejected by companies with stricter standards.

"Which estimate do you want? How much it's gonna cost to repair it or how long it'll take you to get insured again?"

Reprinted by permission of NEA, Inc.

In short, underwriting standards affect premium levels that must be charged if premiums are to be commensurate with the exposures covered by a given insurer.

Insurance Company Ownership

In Chapter 3, you learned that stock insurance companies are owned by stockholders and that mutual insurance companies are owned by policyholders. Both stock and mutual insurance companies need to increase their assets to build an allowance for major losses and other contingencies.

Stock insurance companies also need to generate a profit for outside investors in the form of a dividend paid to stockholders. This is reflected in the premiums that must be charged.

A portion of a mutual insurance company's income is returned to policyholders in the form of a dividend. Dividends can never be guaranteed. Yet some insurance companies have been fairly consistent in paying dividends in the past. Since dividends are, in a sense, a return of premium dollars, they also affect insurance premiums.

Services

In Chapters 4 and 5, you had a brief look at many of the activities performed by insurance companies while insurance coverage is in force. There is some variation in the service provided by insurance companies, which is reflected in different expense ratios for different insurers. For example, some insurers provide more extensive loss control services than others. The insurer's services—and the efficiency with which it provides them—affect its expenses, which, in turn, affect the premiums that must be charged.

Coverage

In Chapters 7, 8, and 9, several personal and commercial insurance coverage options were presented. You had a chance to see, for example, that some property insurance policies cover a relatively limited number of perils while others cover losses by all perils that are not excluded. In short, some insurance policies provide broader coverage than others of the same type.

All else being equal, premiums are generally higher on insurance policies that provide more coverage. However, because so many variables are involved, it is not safe to assume that the insurance policy with the highest premium also provides the most coverage. On the other hand, the policy with the lowest premium is not always the best buy.

Investment Income

Insurance rating systems have been discussed in this chapter, but premiums are not the only source of income to insurers. To some extent, all insurance companies consider investment income when they decide what premiums they will charge their customers. Both investment profits and investment losses have an effect on the premium insurers charge, so investment results can raise premiums as well as lower them.

Cash Flow Considerations

During periods of high interest rates, everybody wants to hold onto money as long as possible. While you hold your money, you can use it or invest it. Once you turn it over to somebody else, you no longer have that advantage.

Insurers want to collect premiums as rapidly as possible. Of course, they want to cover the cost of providing insurance coverage and to avoid bad debts. Insurers also want premiums so that they can generate investment income. Policyholders—particularly large businesses with hundreds of thousands of dollars of premium—also want to hold the money as long as possible before paying premiums. That way, the policyholder can generate its own investment income or use the money to generate profits in its own business.

Because both insurers and insureds are concerned not only with "how much" but also with "how soon," premium amounts also depend in part on any payment plans. An insured that pays the annual premium in twelve monthly installments will pay more dollars for insurance than an insured who pays the entire premium "up front." However, the increased dollar cost might be more than offset by the longer time during which the insured gets to use the money.

SUMMARY

In this chapter, you have seen some things that insurers do to develop premiums that are commensurate with the exposures they cover and encourage loss control. Those who reduce their loss potentials are rewarded with lower premiums than those who do not. You have seen how insurance rates are multiplied by the number of exposure units to determine a premium. You have also seen why certain exposure units are selected as a rating basis. An ideal exposure unit should reflect the exposures, be readily measurable, be inflation sensitive, and be reasonably simple to use.

Two rating systems were analyzed—class rating and individual rating. After briefly examining the roles of various people who use insurance rates, you examined the rating plans used for various kinds of insurance.

The final section of the chapter serves as a reminder that insurance premiums are based on many things—including the marketing system, underwriting standards, and the type of insurance company ownership. The services provided by the insurer, the coverage purchased by the premium, and the extent of investment income is also considered when rates are developed. Cash flow considerations can also affect a premium since both insurers and insureds want to hold onto money as long as possible and are willing to pay for the privilege.

Premiums are determined different ways and for different reasons. The systems used are complicated, but they work—and they help make insurance work.

Insurance in a Changing World

H ave you ever looked at an album of wedding pictures? Just as a series of pictures helps you imagine (or remember) the entire sequence of events at a wedding—including those not captured by the photographer—so the series of scenes in this book has provided clues to help you visualize the entire insurance business. When you put down the book of wedding snapshots—and when you put down this book—you move from a world that is standing still on paper to the real, live motion-picture world of reality, the constantly-changing world that surrounds you.

Almost anyone with insurance experience will agree that insurance is always changing. The insurance business is dynamic, with new developments constantly taking place. The newspaper headlines shown on the following page remind us that changes in the insurance business often involve important issues that influence many people. Many changes in insurance will affect your personal life as well as your job.

This chapter will examine several areas of change. As you read this chapter, try to imagine how the dynamic nature of insurance could affect your insurance career. Looking to the future, you might want to think about preparing yourself for the many opportunities that lie ahead. The closing section of the chapter provides some ideas that might help you plan your career.

INSURANCE CYCLES

One reason insurance is always changing is that the insurance business tends to operate in cycles. Each cycle lasts several years. One phase of the

Education
Key to Future

A-rated insurer fails

Today's Emphasis
On Professional
Development

Restructuring Carves Out P-C, Life Units

New York Considers Another
Workers' Comp. Rate Increase

Winter Storm Insured Loss
May Top $1B

Record P-C Losses Won't Harden Entire Market

Staying Ahead
Of The Game

Insurers Are Major Users Of Electronic Printing

Future of cost containment

cycle is called a hard market, and another phase is referred to as a soft market. During a **hard market**, insurers become more selective, and it becomes more difficult to get insurance, even at higher prices. Eventually the market "turns" and gives way to a **soft market**. Prices begin to drop, and insurance coverage becomes more readily available until the market turns again. Cycles can be expected, but each cycle seems to be unique. Both hard markets and soft markets create change and uncertainty for insurers and insurance buyers.

It is always difficult to predict when the market will turn. It is also difficult to identify all of the forces that cause insurance cycles. One of the strongest forces is competition, which leads insurers to modify their pricing and underwriting standards as other conditions change. Other forces include changing interest rates, changes in insurance regulation, changes in the legal system, and changing medical costs.

> **The Insurance Cycle**
> Hard markets and soft markets are part of the **insurance cycle**.
> During a **hard market**, insurers become more selective, making it more difficult to get insurance, even at higher prices.
> During a **soft market**, insurance prices are lower, and insurance is readily available.

CHANGING CONSUMER NEEDS

No type of insurance would exist unless somebody wanted to buy it. Many forms of insurance were developed because of consumer demand.

Most consumers do not understand insurance very well. Yet it can be among the more expensive things they buy. Not surprisingly, consumers often feel stress when they make insurance decisions. For many people, the contact with insurance companies comes at a time when they have experienced an accident or some other stressful event. Consumers have become bolder in stating their needs and demands. In recent years, consumer advocates and the news media have often focused on insurance issues.

Basically, insurance consumers want to be treated fairly and to get their money's worth. Most

"I've always said we should look into birdbath insurance!"

Reprinted by Permission: Tribune Media Services

Most forms of insurance were developed because of consumer demand.

consumers want easy access to reliable, affordable insurance, and they want prompt, efficient, and courteous service from insurers and their representatives. Unfortunately, rising insurance costs have often made insurance seem unaffordable. It can be difficult for consumers to believe they are receiving their money's worth. Insurance service has not always been prompt, efficient, and courteous. Service problems, when they occur, are especially annoying for people who are already under stress.

Generally speaking, consumers want the same things that insurers want to provide. In exchange, insurers expect their customers to be fair and to act responsibly. Reflecting these ideas, insurers and consumers groups worked together and created the Insurance Consumer's Bill of Rights and Responsibilities, shown below.

Insurance Consumer's Bill of Rights and Responsibilities

The Insurance Consumer's Bill of Rights and Responsibilities is your guide to fair insurance practices, protection of your insurance dollars, and honest, reliable representation.

Preamble

We pledge to support these principles as a first step in creating greater understanding of what consumers should expect in buying and using insurance, and to define clearly the responsibilities expected of consumers in return. Using these goals as a yardstick, consumers, agents, and insurers will be able to measure progress as we work together to build the best possible insurance system for the American people.

Bill of Rights

The Right to Protection

The right to purchase insurance that meets your needs, regardless of where you live or work, priced fairly according to your specific risks, without regard to race, color, or creed.

The Right to Be Informed

The right to have your policy printed in clear, easily readable type and written in understandable language; the right to have policy provisions explained to you accurately before purchase; the right to be told in advance, if possible, when the price or terms of your policy are to change, and why.

The Right to Choose

The right to be offered available options for protection; the right to enough time to adequately consider your purchase; and the right to make an informed choice of the coverage that best meets your needs for quality protection, fair value, price, and personal service; the right to a competitive marketplace where several insurance companies compete for your business.

The Right to Be Heard

The right to have a voice in major decisions that affect you, whether made by insurance companies, insurance agents, or insurance regulators; the right to prompt and constructive replies to suggestions and inquiries; the right to be informed about and participate in consumer organizations that are involved in insurance issues.

The Right to Redress

The right to prompt settlement of just claims; the ability to have access to third parties for mediation and to have access to a responsive state insurance department for further redress.

The Right to Service

The right to be treated with dignity, honesty, and fairness; the right to receive prompt and fair attention to claims, policy changes, and inquiries; the right to be served by an insurance professional who strives to provide you with the best insurance value.

Bill of Responsibilities

The Responsibility to Be Informed

The responsibility to understand the concept of insurance, to read each insurance policy and attempt to understand its terms and, when lacking understanding, the responsibility to seek answers from an insurance professional.

The Responsibility to Help Control Losses

The responsibility to minimize risk through safe driving, loss prevention, vehicle and home maintenance, and caring for your health.

The Responsibility to Report Accurate Information

The responsibility to file insurance applications and report claims accurately and in a timely manner.

The Responsibility to Keep Updated and Accurate Records

The responsibility to maintain in writing the name, address, and telephone number of your insurance agent and your insurance company, and all policy numbers and vehicle make, model, and identification numbers; the responsibility to maintain an updated inventory of household possessions.

The Responsibility to Comply with Policy Provisions

The responsibility to comply with the specific conditions outlined in your policy, including paying premiums on time, cooperating with insurance companies when they defend your claims, and reporting changes that may affect your coverage.

The Responsibility to Report Fraudulent Practices

The responsibility to report to law enforcement and insurance authorities any questionable practices by insurers, agents, consumers, auto body shops, doctors, lawyers, or any other parties seeking to defraud or circumvent the insurance system or consumers.

Reprinted by permission of National Association of Professional Insurance Agents and Consumer Insurance Interest Group.

CHANGING INSURANCE REGULATION

All legal businesses are subject to government regulation. Insurers are primarily regulated by state governments. Each state and the District of Columbia has an **insurance department** headed by an **insurance commissioner** (their titles vary). Insurance regulators belong to the **National Association of Insurance Commissioners (NAIC)**, which coordinates insurance regulation among the states. Still, each insurance department acts in response to the unique laws and authority granted by that state's legislature. Therefore, insurance regulations vary from state to state. Some people believe it would be better for the federal government to regulate insurance nationally, but others see strong advantages in regulation by the states.

Insurance Regulation

Insurance is regulated by the states. Each state has an **insurance department** headed by an **insurance commissioner**. All insurance commissioners are members of the **National Association of Insurance Commissioners (NAIC)**, which coordinates insurance regulation among the states.

Rate regulation is the control by state insurance regulators over the rates and classification and rating systems used by insurers.

Insurance regulation affects many insurance activities, such as producer licensing, claims practices, and the wording of insurance policies. We will concentrate here on only two areas of insurance regulation—rate regulation and financial supervision.

Insurance Rate Regulation

Some state regulators supervise insurance rates very closely and require approval of all changes before new rates may be used. On the other hand, some states allow insurance companies to use whatever rates they choose, under the theory that competition will keep insurance rates from going too high and the costs of paying losses and of meeting expenses will keep rates from going too low.

Rate regulation can be different for different types of insurance within a given state. Property and liability insurance rate regulation can take one of the five approaches explained under the following headings.

With **mandatory rates**, the state insurance department or a state-approved service organization develops insurance rates that must be used by all insurers.

Mandatory Rates. In some states, for some types of insurance, the state insurance department or a state-approved rating bureau develops insurance rates that must be used by all insurers. **Mandatory rates** are not used in many states, and they are usually used for only one type of insurance—such as personal auto or workers compensation.

When mandatory rates are the only rates that may be used, there is a complete lack of price competition. However, insurers still compete in ways other than price—generally through the services they provide to customers.

Prior Approval. In states with a **prior approval** law, the state insurance department must approve rate changes before they can be put into effect. To obtain approval, the insurance company "files" its proposed rates with the insurance department. The insurance company might be required to defend or to modify its proposed rates before they are approved by the state insurance department.

A **prior approval law** requires that the state insurance department must approve rate changes before they can be put into effect.

The actual rate filing may be made by an individual insurer or by a service organization filing the rates on behalf of member insurance companies. Typically, a company can choose to "deviate" from its filed rates if it notifies the insurance department and can satisfy the department that the deviation is appropriate.

Rate filings often must contain not only the proposed rates, but also the statistics on which the rates are based. The insurance company must then wait until rates are approved before any changes can be made. Sometimes, if the state takes no action on filing within a specified time period, such as ninety days, the request is deemed to have been automatically approved. If the request rate change is disapproved, another change might need to be filed and an additional time period might pass.

> **Rate filings** are documents submitted to ("filed" with) a state insurance department that contain the proposed rates and also, when necessary, the statistics on which the rates are based.

Under a prior approval system, there is some tendency for rates to be a step behind the times. Past losses are used by actuaries working in the present to develop current insurance rates that are matched to losses that will happen in the future. The systems described under the following headings provide a faster response to rate changes.

File and Use. In many states with a file and use law, insurance companies are permitted to use new rates *as soon as* they have been filed with the state insurance department. The state insurance department reserves the right to disapprove rates if it can show that they violate statutory requirements.

> With a **file and use law**, insurance companies are permitted to use new rates as soon as they have been filed with the state insurance department.

A variation of this approach, sometimes called "use and file," permits insurers to use new rates *before* making a formal filing with the state. However, a filing must be made within some specified time period—often fifteen days—after the new rates become effective.

No-Filing ("Open Competition"). With a **no-filing law**, rate filing is not required. Insurance regulators do not approve or disapprove insurance rates. Each insurer is free to develop its own rates and rating systems that— at least in theory—reflect the insurer's costs as well as competitive pressures. Changes may be made at any time. Generally speaking, rates cannot fall too low, or else insurance premiums would not be enough to pay losses and expenses and to provide for profits and contingencies. On the other hand, rates that are higher than competitors' rates tend to drive customers away.

> With a **no-filing law**, also called **open competition**, no rate filing is required because insurance regulators neither approve nor disapprove insurance rates.

Setting rates in a competitive environment is a delicate balancing act, with cost pressures on the one hand and the pressure of competition on the other. It is particularly difficult since insurance costs, which are largely related to *future* losses, cannot be accurately predicted.

Flex Rating. One of the newer approaches to rate regulation, flex rating, combines some features of open competition and prior approval. Under a flex-rating law, insurers can modify their rates without prior approval as long as the rate change is within a certain percentage range, known as a "band." The size of these bands varies depending on the state and the type of insurance, but most are between 10 and 25 percent.

> With a **flex-rating law**, insurers may raise and lower rates within a certain range ("band") without specific approval from state regulators.

Effects of Changing Rates and Rate Regulation

All the preceding types of rate regulation exist today. Yet there is more competition than in the past. Independent rating systems are on the increase, and underwriters are able to exercise much flexibility within some commercial rating plans.

What is the effect of price competition on the insurance business? Some people argue that competition is beneficial in any business because it encourages efficiency. Insurance companies facing heavy price competition have an incentive to keep their expenses as low as possible, thus providing service at lower cost to customers. Others warn, however, that open rating could allow insurers to get carried away with self-defeating "cutthroat" price competition, and a number of insurance companies could go bankrupt. If that happens, policyholders might not have their claims paid and the public could suffer, rather than receiving benefits. Needless to say, insurance company failure to pay claims would not increase public confidence in insurance companies.

> **Rate suppression** occurs if government regulators hold insurance rates at a level below their true economic cost.

In some cases, insurance rates are held down because insurance regulators limit insurance rate increases for political reasons. **Rate suppression** occurs if government regulators hold insurance rates at a level below their true economic cost. It is difficult to determine the true economic cost of insurance because it covers future events. Although insurers might honestly believe certain rates are suppressed, regulators who study the same data might feel the rates are adequate.

The people who make insurance rates have a difficult challenge. First, they must develop systems for collecting data. Using the data, they try to develop rates that will lead to premiums that are commensurate with the insurance companies' predicted losses and expenses, with an allowance for profits and contingencies. Then, they must prepare a filing and actually file the rates in many states. If necessary, they must be prepared to defend the proposed rates and work with the people in the state insurance department to modify them.

Underwriters, producers, and other people who use the rates must exercise judgment in applying any classification and rating system in a way that corresponds with the filing given to the state regulators.

Insurance regulators have a responsibility to the public to ensure that insurance rates are adequate but not excessive. But regulators also face political pressure to hold rates down.

If you are involved with insurance rates you can count on changes. Insurance rates and classification and rating systems change for many reasons—including the effects of past loss experience, inflation, and competition. You will have to adjust for the changes as they occur, perhaps learning new procedures in the process. You might also be required to explain some of these changes to others. Insurance rating systems have become quite complicated in some situations.

Financial Regulation

An insurance company that runs out of money cannot fulfill its promises. Insurance regulators want insurance companies to remain financially sound. They approach this goal in many ways.

First, insurance regulators set standards for how much money is required to form an insurance company. Before an insurance company can be licensed, it must demonstrate that it has met these financial standards.

Second, insurance regulators require insurance companies to submit detailed "Annual Statements" of their financial condition. Through each insurance company's complex accounting system, every premium, loss, expense, and investment dollar eventually affects the Annual Statement.

Regulators study Annual Statements carefully to be sure each company has enough assets to meet its financial obligations, or liabilities. Assets and liabilities are not easy to measure precisely. Regulators require insurers to use a conservative approach to measuring their assets and liabilities. It is better for an insurer to understate its financial strength than to overstate it.

> **Assets and Liabilities**
> **Assets** and **liabilities** are shown in financial records.
> **Assets** are items of value. Cash, stocks, bonds, and buildings are assets.
> **Liabilities** are financial obligations. These include debts that have not been paid as well as bills that can be expected to come due in the future. In its financial records, an insurer's liabilities include **loss reserves** and **unearned premium reserves**.
> Since you have studied **liability insurance**, does it confuse you now to find **liability** used in connection with financial records? In both cases, **liability** really has the same meaning—it represents an obligation to pay money to someone else.

One important type of liability, for example, is an insurer's **loss reserves**. Remember from Chapter 5 that Clarence Atwood set up a loss reserve as soon as he had information on Ruth Manning's accident. This loss reserve was a best current estimate of the future amounts that would be paid out on this accident that had already happened. Loss reserves are calculated for every claim, and the insurance company must have enough assets to pay all claims when they are settled. Although it is important that loss reserves be accurate, the information is based on estimates.

Another type of insurance company reserve is the **unearned premium reserve**. At any time, an insurance company's **unearned premium** is the amount of premium dollars the insurance company would have to give back if all policyholders immediately canceled their insurance. Although that is highly unlikely, it shows that the insurance company has not really earned all its premium dollars until the end of the period for which the premium was paid.

> The **unearned premium** on a policy is the money an insurer would have to give back if the policy were canceled.

Only certain kinds of assets, referred to as "admitted assets," are counted

An **unearned premium reserve** is a liability that represents the premium dollars the insurance company would have to give back if all policyholders immediately canceled their insurance.

Surplus is the difference between an insurer's admitted assets and its liabilities.

when determining an insurance company's financial condition. Insurance regulations are specific about how these assets are measured.

The difference between an insurance company's assets and its liabilities is its **surplus**. "Surplus" often refers to something that is left over and therefore unnecessary. Although "surplus" funds are "left over" after subtracting liabilities from assets, "surplus" funds are quite necessary. An insurance company's surplus provides it with the financial backing to write new business, and it provides a cushion against losses that were not anticipated when the reserves were set up. A major hurricane, for example, might cause an insurer to spend part of its surplus to pay claims.

Insurance regulators do more than review insurance companies' Annual Statements. They also visit insurance company offices and audit the records to be sure that they are accurate and complete and that the company is operating in accordance with all applicable regulations.

When an insurance company's records show that it has financial problems, insurance regulators might take steps to keep the company from becoming insolvent. If necessary, insurance regulators can take control of the company. If all else fails, insurance regulators might liquidate the failed insurance company. Whatever the procedure, regulators try to resolve the problem so that policyholders receive as much protection as possible. However, when an insurance company fails, claimants might not receive payment in full.

Insurance guaranty funds provide a system to pay the claims of insolvent property and liability insurers. Generally, the money in these guaranty funds is provided by charges assessed against all insurers in the state.

All states have established **insurance guaranty funds** for property and liability insurance that provide a system to pay the claims of insolvent insurers. Generally, the money in these guaranty funds is provided by charges assessed against all insurers in the state.

Although policyholders want low insurance rates, they also want to deal with insurers that are financially sound. A number of organizations, such as A.M. Best, Standard & Poor, and others, publish insurance company ratings that provide some idea of each insurer's financial stability. Each rating organization uses its own system for assigning ratings. Insurance regulators also have their own rating systems. Although insurance company ratings are important, no rating system is perfect. One major problem is that most data involve things that have already taken place, but the policyholder must be concerned about the future.

Effects of Financial Regulation.   Financial regulation requires insurers to maintain detailed and accurate records in a certain format and to provide them periodically to regulators. Many of these records come from the codes that must be used on many different insurance company forms. Every change in reporting requirements creates changes in the accounting and coding system used by insurers.

Every insurance company tries to remain financially solvent. Every insurance company also tries to qualify for a good financial rating by regulators and rating organizations. A good financial rating is important because people and businesses are more willing to buy insurance from a company with a good rating, and stockholders are more willing to invest in a stock insurance company with a good rating.

Financial rating systems change because measuring the financial soundness of any insurance company is difficult. When rating systems change, insurance companies might also change certain practices to continue to qualify for a good rating.

COST CONTAINMENT

Loss costs reflect the costs of the goods and services purchased with money paid by insurers. Efforts to control the costs of insurance claims, without reducing service, have led to many changes.

Insurance premium levels are high when loss costs are high. *Property insurance* pays for the replacement or repair of the insured's damaged property. *Property damage liability insurance* pays the costs to replace or repair property damaged by an insured who is legally responsible for the damages. Both property and liability insurance loss costs increase when property values go up. Loss costs also increase when labor costs rise because it costs more to pay workers to repair damaged property. For example, both cars and car repairs cost much more now than they did a few years ago. Therefore, auto insurance loss costs are higher and auto insurance costs more. Insurance companies have an interest in encouraging manufacturers to design autos that are less damageable and easier to repair, and they work closely with auto repair shops to keep their repair bills down.

Bodily injury liability insurance is affected by medical cost levels. Medical loss costs have been even more difficult to control than property loss costs. Various steps have been taken to limit the amounts health insurers will pay to health care providers for each kind of medical treatment. However, controlling medical costs paid by liability insurance has been difficult. Under our legal system, an injured party has the legal right to recover reasonable expenses from the party responsible for the injury and it often can be difficult to prove that particular medical expense was not reasonable.

Both bodily injury and property damage costs are affected when a claim involves extensive legal proceedings. Insurance companies have been working with government agencies, health care providers, and members of the legal profession to find ways to control both property repair and health care costs as well as costs associated with the legal system. As new cost containment approaches evolve, insurance claims work will also change.

AUTOMATION

Insurance companies strive to be as efficient as possible. The more they can streamline their operations, the more insurers can lower administrative costs. As expenses are reduced, the opportunity for profit increases. Lower expenses also enable insurers to provide insurance at lower premiums. But premiums are not the only basis for competition; insurers also compete on the basis of service.

Computers have been partly responsible for both increased efficiency and improved service. Insurance offices have changed dramatically as computer terminals displaced manuals and paper files on an increasing number of desks. Changes that used to be manually coded and rated before being processed and filed are now completely handled in seconds by a person who has access to a computer.

This rapid processing reduces expenses by cutting down the number of steps that a series of clerks would otherwise take. There are also many service-related advantages of rapid processing. For example, since the information stored in the computer's memory is up-to-the-minute, a claims adjuster who can determine coverage by means of a computer inquiry obtains information that includes a policy change processed in another office just minutes earlier. Before computers were so widely used, current coverage information might not have been so readily available.

Insurance company home, regional, and branch offices are not the only places where computers are found. Most producers have acquired computer equipment to handle billing and accounting needs, among other things. All insurance organizations are steadily adding computers, improving computer programs, or increasing the use of existing computer systems.

Today, terminals in many insurance agencies communicate directly with the large computer systems in an insurance company home, regional, or branch office. By eliminating the need to rely on the postal service, this obviously makes for more rapid processing. Interfacing also eliminates some duplication of effort. For example, when a producer can use a computer terminal to get current information from an insurance company's customer file immediately, it is not as important for the producer to maintain a duplicate paper file. Computers also greatly reduce the number of times a given item of information must be processed. Instead of separately setting up customer files for accounting, underwriting, and claims purposes, a single entry into the computer can do it all.

Many insurance jobs have changed as a result of the expanding use of computers. Although automation has eliminated some jobs, other jobs have been added since people are needed to operate and maintain computer systems. Those who are willing to work with new technology have had many opportunities to take on new responsibilities.

REORGANIZATION

Shifting insurance regulation, the need for greater efficiency, the need to control costs, and the expanding use of automation are among the changes that lead insurance organizations to reorganize. Every reorganization leads to a reassignment of insurance people who must face new challenges.

"Surely there must be a better way to keep track of his claim cases."

Reprinted with the permission of Bituminous Casualty Corporation.

Mergers and Acquisitions

It is not unusual to hear that one insurance organization has merged with or acquired another. This causes changes for many people working for the combined organization, as attitudes, reporting relationships, and jobs change. Similar changes take place when an insurance organization is purchased by another corporation engaged in an unrelated business. Producers are affected by changes in the companies they represent, and vice versa.

One noticeable trend in insurance marketing has led to the growth of national insurance brokers. A number of national firms have expanded their operations by merging with many other insurance agencies throughout the country (and throughout the world), as well as expanding their clientele through other means.

Independent agencies have also been expanding by acquiring or merging or affiliating with other regional or national agencies.

In general, whether one is concerned with insurance companies, national brokerages, or local agencies, the trend, at the moment, is towards fewer organizations each handling more business.

Centralization and Decentralization

Centralization is the process of moving activities to a central location. For example, an insurance company that formerly prepared policies in field offices might decide to issue all insurance policies at a single processing center. Another insurer might decide to underwrite all homeowners policies in one processing center rather than in many field offices. Generally speaking, insurance company centralization moves some processes farther away from the insured.

Decentralization takes place when activities are moved away from a central location. With insurance organizations, decentralization usually means processes and decision-making authority are moved geographically closer to the insured. As examples of decentralization, the underwriting authority of field office underwriters or the claims draft authority of producers might be increased.

Redeployment of Human Resources

Nearly every merger, acquisition, reorganization, or automation is intended to make insurance organizations more efficient. Many also have the effect of eliminating obsolete jobs or creating new jobs. Others eliminate jobs in one location but create different jobs at a new location. Whenever jobs move, some people might move, some might be laid off, and others might be hired. Many might need to be trained to handle new responsibilities.

UNBUNDLING OF INSURANCE SERVICES

Traditionally, insurance companies have offered one type of product—

insurance policies. As illustrated throughout this book, an insurance policy might actually be accompanied by several services, including:

- payment for losses,
- claims adjusting services,
- loss control advice and services, and
- risk management advice and services.

Unbundling happens when insurance claims adjusting, loss control, risk management, or other services are sold separately rather than being "bundled" together with an insurance policy, for which a single insurance premium is charged.

These and other insurance company and producer services have traditionally been "bundled" together. For the payment of a single insurance premium, policyholders could receive all the services in the bundle, and the only way to purchase any insurance service was to buy the entire bundle.

The traditional approach is still common. However, especially for large accounts, there is a trend towards "unbundling"—offering the various services separately or in any combination desired by the buyer. A separate charge is associated with each service that is used. Some risk managers might not buy every service from the same supplier. They might furnish some services themselves rather than purchasing them from outsiders. This concept will become clearer after reading the examples in the following paragraphs.

Payment for Losses

The most obvious "service" provided by insurance is the insurer's promise to pay for losses. However, some businesses have the financial resources to pay for many losses themselves. They do not need the loss-financing service provided by insurers. Instead, they "self-insure."

With "**self-insurance**," or "**retention**," a business does not transfer its risks to an insurance company or anyone else. It pays for all losses with its own resources.

With "**self-insurance**," a business does not transfer its risks to an insurance company or anyone else. It does not share losses with anyone else. Rather, it pays for all losses with its own funds. It keeps, or "retains," the losses, rather than having some other party bear them. Sometimes the term "**retention**" is used instead of "self-insurance" to reflect the fact that the business "retains" its own losses and does not actually insure them.

Many of the largest corporations have taken a special approach to "self-insurance." They have set up **captive insurance companies**. A captive insurance company is an insurance company owned and operated by the corporation or corporations it insures. Some captive insurance companies

A **captive insurance company**, or **captive**, is an insurance company owned and operated by the corporation it insures. Some captives are owned by more than one corporation, in which case the owners, to some extent, share each other's losses.

sell insurance policies only to a parent firm (a corporation owning the captive), but others engage in insurance transactions with other corporations as well. Captive insurance companies can purchase reinsurance, from other insurance companies, to protect themselves and their parent firms against unbearably large losses. The many other reasons large corporations form captive insurance companies would require more extensive discussion than this chapter permits.

The increased use of "self-insurance" and the formation of captive insurance companies have had significant effects on the insurance business. First, a new type of competition (captives) has resulted. Second, insurance companies have realized that corporations that do not purchase insurance still need loss control and claims administration services, and they might still need some expert risk management service. Although some corporations are able to establish a claims administration department and loss control department using the corporation's own employees, most large self-insured businesses find it desirable to purchase at least some services from an insurer that has experts available in different locations. Therefore, insurance companies, producers, and consultants have begun to sell these services separately.

Loss Control Services

Insurers who choose to "unbundle" their loss control services sell loss control services for a fee to businesses that have a "self-insurance" program. The loss control service is usually provided by the same loss control representatives who deal with the insurer's policyholders.

Insurers are not the only parties that provide loss control services. *Independent outside organizations*, which have no direct relationship with any insurance company, also operate in many areas. Insurers and independent loss control services compete for the same buyers of "unbundled" loss control service.

Claims Administration

Claims administration involves investigating and settling claims, as well as handling claims files and monitoring the progress of every claim that has not yet been settled. Sophisticated use of computer capabilities is a key to efficient claims administration because the volume of records is often enormous.

As with loss control services, "unbundled" claims administration service is provided on a fee basis by some insurance companies or producers, often using the same claim adjusters used by the insurers. In addition, independent adjusters also sell their claims administration services in direct competition with insurers.

Risk Management Consulting Service

This book has illustrated some types of risk management service provided by insurers and insurance producers. You have seen, for example, how Paul Proctor helped All-Sports identify its loss exposures and decide how to deal with them. Insurance was not the only "tool in Paul's toolbox." In some cases, he recommended that certain loss control measures—such as not leaving the truck unattended when it was loaded—would eliminate loss possibilities or at least reduce the likelihood of loss to the point where All-Sports could safely "self-insure."

Any corporation that has decided to "self-insure" most of its risks needs a great deal of expertise. It needs to make certain that its exposures have been identified and dealt with in a way that provides adequate safeguards to prevent financial catastrophe. This expertise is often available from a **risk management consultant**. A risk management consultant provides expert advice to corporations regarding how their risks should be treated. A risk management consultant can also aid in the many details of purchasing appropriate insurance, setting up a captive insurer, administering a "self-insurance" program, or selecting and monitoring organizations that will provide loss control and claims services.

A **risk management consultant** provides expert advice to corporations regarding how their risks should be treated.

The Effect of Unbundling of Insurance Services

The nature of the insurance product is changing. Insurers have traditionally sold insurance in the form of payment for losses, but much closer attention is now being paid to the services that accompany insurance. Obviously, this trend affects insurance buyers who carefully consider each item in the "bundle" when purchasing traditional insurance. It also affects insurance producers, who have a much broader spectrum of unbundled risk management services to sell than when they were concerned only with traditional insurance.

If you are working in claims or loss control or in some aspect of the insurance business that relates to risk management service, you might sometimes provide service to a self-insured client. Even though many of the same types of claims or loss control activities are required, you will find that the relationship is different. For example, when service is provided for a fee, the buyer might have a greater say in deciding how the service is provided. Services are also evaluated more carefully when they are "unbundled" and paid for individually. Corporations that buy unbundled services will expect to find that they are dealing with highly qualified people—or they will find another service provider that has people who can provide the service they expect.

YOUR FUTURE IN THIS CHANGING WORLD

The changing world of insurance offers many opportunities for people who are flexible enough to accept them. The people best able to perform well, as insurance practices change, are generally those who have studied how insurance works. Having acquired a good understanding of their job and the business skills surrounding it, they are able to apply their knowledge and skills to meeting new challenges. In contrast, people who do not prepare themselves for the opportunities that usually accompany change might find their careers at a standstill.

How can you prepare for a successful future in insurance? You can begin, of course, by performing well in your present job. Every insurance job is important in making insurance work in order to provide its many benefits to the public. While you master your present responsibilities, you might want to ask some questions about your future—questions like "Where do I want to go?" and "How do I get there?"

The Path to Your Career Goals

The path to your career goals will inevitably involve two elements—experience and education. Experience is what you are gaining day by day as you perform your present job. Education is what you are doing now, as you read this book—which helps you understand not only your own job, but also other things about insurance.

Although you have learned much about insurance by reading this book, you might still feel that you know so much less than others in the business that you can never catch up. Actually, you are not at all alone—most insurance people did not know much about insurance until after they entered the business. Few people learn much about insurance in high school or college.

Organizations in the insurance business have always found it necessary to develop employees like you through on-the-job training programs, seminars, and continuing education courses. A variety of learning opportunities are available to employees in any insurance organization.

In a larger insurance organization, the **training director** or **training department** is usually responsible for matching employees with the various educational programs that will help them develop their knowledge and ability. Many organizations have developed a **career path program** that helps employees see what combination of experience and education will help them advance toward their career goals.

Insurance training departments have developed their own training programs, on a variety of topics, for their employees. Insurance employers spend a great deal of money developing schools or seminars, conducting them, paying for employees' transportation and housing as they attend the schools, and providing regular paychecks to those who attend on company time.

Although many insurance schools or seminars deal with such topics as insurance coverages, underwriting practices, or claims procedures, many others do not involve the technical aspects of insurance. Some address areas such as sales skills, communications skills, math, and accounting.

Independent study courses are available from several commercial vendors covering many technical topics, including risk management, production, underwriting, rating, and claims handling. Correspondence courses, which might include a grading service on the quiz for each assignment, are also available. Various study programs and seminars are provided by various local, state, and national producer trade associations, many dealing with current developments and serving to keep experienced insurance people up-to-date.

The National Association of Insurance Women, the CPCU Society, and other insurance associations encourage continuing educational opportunities through their national organizations and their local chapters.

The Insurance Institute of America (IIA) and its companion organization the American Institute for Chartered Property Casualty Underwriters (AICPCU), which are nonprofit educational organizations, provide a major source of formal educational programs in insurance and risk management. **INTRO**, the **Introduction to Property and Liability Insurance** course for which this book was written, is one of IIA's courses. Most states require insurance producers to meet certain "continuing education" requirements to keep their licenses to sell insurance. Institute courses and many others have qualified under the various state continuing education programs.

These opportunities for additional learning should suggest some paths you will probably take if you have decided to move ahead in your insurance career. Insurance is a dynamic business in a highly competitive setting. As you become more involved in the insurance business, you will see how your continued growth, your development on the job, and your opportunities for advancement will be improved by participation in educational programs. You can advance in the competitive world of insurance if you equip yourself to become a candidate for advancement.

You have learned much about insurance by reading this book. Perhaps doing so has whetted your appetite to learn even more. Perhaps it has also helped you to see how exciting your future in insurance can be. **You** are among the people who make insurance work!

Glossary

A

AAI®

Accredited Adviser in Insurance, a designation awarded by the Insurance Institute of America (IIA) to those who have completed a three-semester educational program designed for insurance producers.

Accident report form

A form used to record key information about an accident.

Account

A person, business, or organization that has purchased insurance.

Account analyst

See customer service representative.

Account current

The billing statement an insurance company sends to its producer.

Account selling

Trying to handle all of a client's insurance needs rather than providing for only a portion of those needs.

Accounts receivable insurance

Covers the cost of reconstructing accounts receivable records that have been damaged or destroyed by a covered peril. Also covers any payments that cannot be collected because records cannot be reconstructed.

Acquisition cost

The price for which property was originally purchased, built, or otherwise acquired.

Actual cash value

The value of property as figured by determining what it would cost to replace the property and then adjusting this replacement cost by subtracting an amount that reflects depreciation.

Actuary

A person who uses complex mathematical methods, usually with the aid of computers, to analyze loss data and other statistics and develop systems for determining future premiums.

Administrative assistant

See customer service representative.

Adverse selection

The increasing likelihood that consumers will purchase insurance when the premium is low relative to the risk.

Agency billing

See producer billing.

Agency underwriter

See customer service representative.

Agent

A producer who represents one or more insurance companies. *See* exclusive agent, independent agent, producer.

"All-risks"

"All-risks" property policies, also called "special" or "open-perils" policies, cover any loss unless it is caused by an excluded peril described in the policy. In an "all-risks" policy the burden of proof is on the insurer. All losses are covered unless the insurance company can prove that the loss was caused by an excluded peril. Compare specified perils.

American Institute for Chartered Property Casualty Underwriters, AICPCU

The nonprofit organization that provides study materials, conducts national examinations, and awards the professional designation CPCU® to candidates who meet the necessary education, experience, and ethics requirements. A companion organization to the Insurance Institute of America (IIA).

App, application, application form

An application form, or app, gathers information about an applicant that will be used by underwriters.

Assets

Items of value, such as stocks, bonds, and buildings.

Assigned risk plans

See automobile insurance plans.

Audit

During an audit members of the home office staff underwriting department examine files to see whether the underwriting guidelines are being followed.

Audited premium

See premium auditor.

Auto medical payments coverage

See medical payments coverage (auto).

Auto physical damage coverage

See physical damage coverage (auto).

Automobile insurance plans

Residual market plans providing auto insurance for those that cannot obtain coverage in the voluntary market. Sometimes called assigned risk plans.

Bailee

A person or business that has in its care, custody, or control property belonging to someone else. Dry cleaners are a common example.

Bailees customers insurance

Covers losses to customers' property in the custody of a bailee. Most policies provide coverage regardless of whether the insured bailee is liable for the loss. Bailees customers insurance is a type of inland marine insurance.

Bind, bind coverage, binder

An insurance agent is usually authorized by the insurance company to bind coverage, stating that certain specified coverage is in force with a specific insurance company as of a particular date and time (or immediately). A binder is a statement that coverage is in force. Its purpose is to provide temporary coverage until an actual insurance policy can be issued. A binder need not be in writing.

Boiler and machinery inspectors

Specialists who periodically inspect objects insured by boiler and machinery insurance to detect problems that could lead to an explosion or breakdown. Inspections by boiler and machinery inspectors prevent many boiler and machinery losses.

Boiler and machinery insurance

Insurance covering explosions of boilers and other pressure vessels, both fired and unfired, as well as breakdown of various types of machinery.

Branch office

A local insurance company office, usually located away from the home office, providing service to accounts in a limited geographical area.

Broad form homeowners policy

A personal insurance policy providing residential property coverage on buildings, personal property, and loss of use against loss by sixteen named perils, as well as medical payments and personal liability coverage.

Broker

Brokers are insurance producers. They resemble agents except that, in the legal sense, they represent the party seeking insurance.

Building and contents insurance

Property insurance providing coverage for buildings, personal property, or both at the location or locations described in the policy.

Burden of proof

The challenge of proving a loss is covered or not covered. *See* "all-risks," specified perils. The burden of proof can be important in cases in which a loss is obvious but its cause is not obvious.

Burglary

A type of theft committed by someone who breaks into something (such as a building) and illegally removes money or other property.

Business income insurance

Coverage designed to help a business survive an interruption in its earnings. Indemnifies a business for its loss in profits caused by the interruption and also pays the business expenses that continue during the interruption. Makes up for what would have been earned during the period when a business is temporarily inactive because business property has been damaged by a covered peril.

Cancel, cancellation

Stopping coverage during the policy period is cancellation. A policyholder can cancel most policies at any time; state laws often prohibit insurers from canceling policies that have been in force for a certain period of time.

Captive, captive insurance company

An insurance company owned and operated by the corporation or corporations it insures. (Note: Direct writers and exclusive agents are sometimes called captive agents; that terminology is not used in this book.)

Chartered Property Casualty Underwriter, CPCU®

A professional designation awarded by the American Institute for CPCU to candidates who have met the educational, experience, and ethics requirements. *See* American Institute for Chartered Property Casualty Underwriters.

Claim

A demand by a person or business that is seeking to recover for a loss. A claim may be made against an individual or against an insurance company.

Claim file

A folder or computer record that is created ("opened") when a claim is made.

Claimant

Anyone who presents a claim that might be covered by insurance. For a liability insurance loss, the claimant is a person or business that has suffered a loss and seeks to collect for that loss from an insured. For a property insurance loss, the claimant is the insured who wants the insurance company to pay for repairing or replacing his or her damaged property.

Claims adjuster

The person directly responsible for investigating and settling claims that might be covered by insurance.

Claims clerk

A person who has the job of taking claims reports over the telephone and doing other things that help in the process of adjusting claims.

Class rating

An insurance rating system that places similar insureds into categories or classes and applies the same rate to all insureds in the same class.

Coinsurance clause

A provision in many property insurance policies reducing the amount that will be paid for a loss occurring when property is underinsured.

Collision

One vehicle running into or being struck by another vehicle or object.

Combined loss and expense ratio, combined ratio

The sum of the loss ratio and the expense ratio. When the combined ratio is less than 100 (percent), an underwriting profit is earned.

Commensurate

Showing an appropriate relationship. A premium is "commensurate" with the exposure when there is a close relationship between the size of the premium and the risk assumed by the insurer.

Commercial insurance

Commercial insurance covers businesses or institutions such as schools, hospitals, and governments.

Commercial umbrella policy

Provides "excess" coverage in the event of a liability claim that is big enough to exhaust the limits of a business's general liability or auto liability policy.

Commercial underwriter

A person who analyzes insurance requests from businesses and other organizations. *See* underwriter.

Commission

A portion of insurance premiums paid to a producer for his or her sales and service activities.

Completed operations liability coverage

Pays when the insured is liable for bodily injury or property damage caused by work that the insured has completed—such as repair work to customers' property.

Comprehensive (an auto insurance coverage)

Also called "other than collision," covers auto physical damage losses by nonexcluded perils other than collision. Comprehensive coverage is not truly comprehensive in scope; to cover all insurable auto physical damage perils, one must purchase both comprehensive and collision coverages.

Conditions

In an insurance policy, provisions that explain the duties, rights, and options of the insured and the insurance company.

Contents

See personal property.

Contingencies

Contingencies involve unpredictable or extraordinary events that might draw on an insurance company's assets. Insurers generally try to retain a portion of their profits to build a surplus that provides a cushion for contingencies.

Corporation

Technically an artificial person, a corporation is a distinct legal being that is owned by stockholders.

CPCU®

See Chartered Property Casualty Underwriter.

Customer

A person, business, or organization that has purchased insurance.

Customer service representative

A person who supports the sales efforts of a producer. Other titles for a customer service representative include agency underwriter, insurance placer, administrative assistant, marketing specialist, account analyst, and office manager.

Damage

Loss or harm resulting from injury to a person, to property, or to someone's reputation. Compare damages.

Damage to your auto coverage

Damage to your auto coverage, also known as auto physical damage coverage, insures against loss resulting from damage to an auto owned or operated by the insured, and it also provides coverage if the car is stolen.

Damages

Money that the law requires one party to pay to another because of loss or injury suffered by the other party. Compare damage.

D&B, Dun & Bradstreet

Dun and Bradstreet (D&B) is the world's largest credit reporting information on business applicants for insurance. Underwriters use D&B's services as a source of underwriting information. A "D&B" reports on the history of the company and the background of its owners and managers, describes its operations, outlines its paying record, analyzes its financial condition, and assigns a credit rating.

Dba

Doing business as, used to refer to the name under which a sole proprietor or partner operates a business.

Declarations, declarations page

The page or pages of an insurance policy containing information, such as the insured's name and address, that the policyholder declared (stated as facts) on the application for insurance.

Deductible

A portion of a covered loss that is not paid by insurance. The deductible is subtracted from the amount the insurer would otherwise be obligated to pay.

Definitions

In an insurance policy, provisions that define the words and phrases that have a special meaning when they are used elsewhere in that policy. Words defined in some policies are printed in boldface or enclosed by quotation marks.

Depreciation

Loss in value of property that develops as items age, wear out, or become obsolete. In a sense, depreciation reflects value that has already been used up.

Diary, diary system

A manual or computer system that calls a file to somebody's attention on a specified date.

Direct billing

A process through which the insurance company sends bills directly to the policyholder and the policyholder makes payments directly to the insurance company. The insurance company pays to the producer commissions or other compensation for producing new business and servicing renewal business.

Direct losses

Almost instantaneous reduction in value of property resulting directly from damage to that property. Compare indirect losses.

Direct mail
See direct response marketing system.

Direct response marketing system
An insurance marketing system that has no local producers making face-to-face sales but handles sales by mail or telephone.

Direct writer
A producer who sells insurance as an employee of one insurance company. The term direct writer is also used to refer to an insurance company that sells insurance directly to insurance buyers through employees.

Dividends
Profits shared with stockholders (of a stock insurance company) or policyholders (of a mutual insurance company).

Draft
Essentially the same as a check written on the insurance company's checking account. Drafts are used to pay claims and may be written by a claims representative or by a producer with draft authority.

Draft authority
A producer with draft authority has permission to handle small claims and issue drafts (similar to checks) to pay certain types of covered claims that are within the dollar limit of the draft authority.

Drive-in claims service
A facility for providing repair estimates on damaged cars that are still driveable.

Dun & Bradstreet
See D&B.

E

Employee dishonesty coverage
Insurance against loss of money and other property through theft by one or more employees. Also called fidelity coverage and fidelity bond.

Endorsement
A document used to amend the coverage in an otherwise complete policy.

Estimate
An evaluation of the cost to repair a damaged car. The estimate may be made by a body shop or a physical damage appraiser, also called a material damage appraiser.

Exclusions
Insurance policy provisions that restrict the broad terms of the insuring agreement by stating some exceptions to coverage—certain activities, loss causes, property, persons, and places—for which the insurer does not provide coverage.

Exclusive agent
A self-employed producer who has a contract to sell insurance exclusively for one insurance company (or several related companies).

Expense ratio
The percent of premiums that goes to pay the insurance company's operating expenses.

Experience modification, mod
A workers compensation premium adjustment factor based on the loss experience of the insured employer.

Experience rating
A process by which the insurance premiums of larger businesses can be modified, to some degree, based on their own past loss records.

Expiration, expiration date, expire
An insurance policy's coverage ceases, or expires, at the end of the policy term or policy period (typically one year). The expiration date is also known as the x-date

Exposure units

The standard units used in insurance rating.

Exposures

Exposures, or loss exposures, are situations that could lead to an accidental loss.

FAIR plans

Fair Access to Insurance Requirements residual market plans providing property insurance for those that cannot obtain coverage in the voluntary market.

Fidelity bond, fidelity coverage

See employee dishonesty coverage.

File (noun)

A file is a paper or computer record that includes most of the information concerning a particular prospect, applicant, or policyholder.

File (verb)

To provide information, such as revised insurance rates, to state insurance regulators.

File and use law

A type of rate regulation under which insurance companies are permitted to use new rates as soon as they have been filed with the state insurance department

Flex rating, flex-rating law

A type of rate regulation under which insurers may raise and lower rates within a certain range ("band") without specific approval from state regulators.

Form

A preprinted document, often several pages long, containing standard wording that makes up the bulk of an insurance policy.

General liability insurance

Covers some of the major liability exposures of a business, including liability related to the premises, operations in progress, products, and completed operations.

Guaranty fund

A system to pay the claims of insolvent property and liability insurers. Generally, the money in guaranty funds is provided by charges assessed against all insurers in the state.

Hard market

The time period during an insurance cycle during which insurers become more selective, making it more difficult to get insurance, even at higher prices.

Hazard

Anything that increases the chance of an accident or increases the chance that any accident that happens will be severe.

Health insurance

A category of insurance that provides two major types of benefits: payment of medical costs (hospital bills, doctors' fees, etc.) and disability income (monthly income to disabled workers during their disability).

Historical loss costs

Data reflecting the dollar losses relating to each exposure unit in the past.

Home office

An insurance company's headquarters.

Homogeneity, homogeneous

Similarity among insureds in the same rating class. All insureds in the same class of a sound classification and rating system should be fairly homogeneous. *See* perfect homogeneity, workable homogeneity.

IIA Insurance Company

Not the name of a real insurance company, IIA Insurance Company is a fictional insurer, created for purposes of this book. IIA might market insurance through almost any insurance marketing system.

Indemnify

To restore the party that has had a loss to the same financial position it occupied before the loss.

Independent adjuster

Independent contractor that provides claims adjusting services to various insurance companies and charges a fee for each claim handled.

Independent agency, independent agent

An independent agent sells insurance as a representative of several unrelated insurance companies. The independent agent's business is an independent agency.

Indirect loss

Loss of earnings or extra expenses taking place over a period of days, weeks, or months following a direct loss. Increases with the passage of time.

Individual rating

A rating system used when every insured is unique. Each insured is assigned an insurance rate that reflects its own unique characteristics.

Inland marine insurance

A group of coverages, described in the Nation-Wide Marine Definition, which generally have something to do with transportation or communication. Evolved from ocean marine insurance.

Inside adjuster

Also known as a telephone adjuster, a claims adjuster who settles claims without conducting any outside investigation. An inside adjuster is generally used when the claim is clearly covered and there is no question about the circumstances of the accident or the validity of the claim.

Inspection

A loss control representative, sometimes called a safety engineer, performs loss control surveys (also called inspections) and prepares written loss control reports. (*See* loss control report.)

Insurance

A system by which a risk is transferred by a person, business, or organization to an insurance company (insurer), which reimburses the insured for covered losses and provides for sharing the costs of losses among all insureds.

Insurance agent

A producer who represents one or more insurance companies. Compare broker.

Insurance commissioner

See insurance regulation.

Insurance company

Also known as an insurer, an organization that sells insurance policies that protect insureds against financial hardship caused by financial loss.

Insurance cycle

See hard market, soft market.

Insurance department

See insurance regulation.

Insurance guaranty fund

A system to pay the claims of insolvent property and liability insurers. Generally, the money in guaranty funds is provided by charges assessed against all insurers in the state.

Insurance Institute of America, IIA

The nonprofit educational organization that publishes this book, for use in the INTRO program, and provides many other educational programs for people who work in the area of property and liability insurance. The IIA also awards the AAI designation and other associate designations to those who complete its associate programs.

Insurance placer

See customer service representative.

Insurance policy

A contract that states the rights and duties of the insurance company and the insured.

Insurance premium

A periodic payment by the insured to the insurance company in exchange for insurance coverage. A periodic payment is one that must be made at certain time intervals. Also, the price of insurance for each unit of exposure. The rate is multiplied by the number of exposure units to arrive at a premium.

Insurance proposal

A booklet that highlights the important features of the proposed coverage and related services and states the premium.

Insurance rate

The price of insurance for each unit of exposure. The rate is multiplied by the number of exposure units to arrive at a premium.

Insurance rating system

An orderly method for arriving at an appropriate premium.

Insurance regulation

Insurance is regulated by the states. Each state has an insurance department headed by an insurance commissioner. All insurance commissioners are members of the National Association of Insurance Commissioners.

Insurance Services Office, ISO

The largest insurance service office in the country, ISO performs a variety of services such as developing statistical classification systems and collecting statistical data on insured claims from a large number of insurance companies, analyzing this information, and using it to develop cost data. Insurance companies that subscribe to ISO's services may use this loss cost information in setting their own insurance rates.

Insured

A person, business, or organization that is covered by an insurance policy.

Insurer

Also known as an insurance company, an organization that sells insurance policies that protect insureds against financial hardship caused by financial loss.

Insuring agreement

A provision in an insurance policy stating, in broad terms, the promises made by the insurance company. An insurance policy provides coverage only if the claim is within the scope of the promise expressed in an insuring agreement.

Inventory

Stock; merchandise a store intends to sell. May also refer to materials or products on hand.

ISO

See Insurance Services Office.

Judgment rating

A type of individual rating used to develop a premium for exposures for which there is no established premium-determining system. The underwriter relies heavily on his or her experience in setting the premium.

Liability (accounting concept)

As an accounting concept, liabilities are financial obligations, such as unpaid debts, bills that come due in the future, loss reserves, and unearned premium reserves.

Liability (legal concept)

As a legal concept, liability means that a person, organization, or group of people is legally responsible, or liable, for the injury or damage suffered by another person, organization, or group of people.

Liability coverage (auto)

Auto liability coverage will apply if an insured person or business is responsible for hurting someone else or damaging someone else's auto or other property as a result of an auto accident. This is an example of liability insurance.

Liability insurance

Liability insurance covers accidental losses resulting from injury to the body or damage to the property of someone else for which the insured is legally responsible (legally liable). If the loss is covered by the insurance policy, the payment is made directly to the party that suffered the loss.

Life insurance

A type of insurance designed to pay funds to ease the financial problems that arise from uncertainty regarding the timing of death.

Limits, limits of insurance, limits of liability

Limits, also called limits of insurance, limits of liability, or policy limits, indicate in an application how much insurance is requested. Once the policy is issued, the limits in the policy set the maximum dollar amount the insurance company will pay.

Line underwriting activities

Underwriting activities involving decisions on individual applicants or insureds, based on underwriting guidelines published by staff underwriters.

Litigation

The process of carrying on a lawsuit.

Loss control report

Written by a loss control representative, a loss control report provides a firsthand picture of the applicant for the underwriter, describing the operations and hazards of the applicant's business as they relate to the type of insurance the applicant is requesting. The report also describes safety programs and other measures to control the hazards. The report not only describes strengths and weaknesses but also makes recommendations for improvement. The content of the loss control report varies according to the type of insurance.

Loss control representative

Sometimes called a safety engineer, a person who performs loss control surveys (also called inspections) and writes loss control reports. *See* loss control report.

Loss control survey

See loss control report.

Loss costs

See historical loss costs, prospective loss costs.

Loss exposures

Loss exposures, or exposures, are situations that could lead to an accidental loss.

Loss ratio

The percent of premiums that goes to pay claims.

Loss reserve

An insurance company's best current estimate of the total dollar amount that will be paid in the future for an accident that has already occurred.

Mandatory rates

A type of rate regulation under which the state insurance department or a state-approved service organization develops insurance rates that must be used by all insurers.

Manual premium

The premium determined from the rating manual, not including discounts or surcharges.

Manual of underwriting policy

See underwriting guide.

Market value

The price at which a particular property item could be sold.

Marketing specialist

See customer service representative.

Material damage appraiser

Also called physical damage appraiser, a person who estimates auto repair costs based on auto parts prices and labor costs.

Medical payments coverage (auto insurance)

Covers the medical expenses of a covered person injured in an auto accident. The coverage applies regardless of fault.

Medical payments coverage (general liability policy)

Pays for injuries to customers and other members of the public who are injured on the business premises, regardless of whether the business is legally responsible for the injury.

Medical payments to others coverage (homeowners policy)

Provides coverage for the medical expenses of others (not insureds) who are injured because of the insured's premises, activities, or pets.

Miscellaneous provisions

The provisions in an insurance policy that do not qualify as declarations, insuring agreements, exclusions, conditions, or definitions.

Mod

See experience modification.

Motor vehicle record, motor vehicle report

Also known as an MVR, lists the moving violations (such as speeding) and serious accidents that a driver has had in the past several years.

Mutual insurance companies

Insurance companies owned by their policyholders. Profits earned by a mutual insurance company might be returned to policyholders in the form of dividends.

MVR

See motor vehicle record.

National Association of Insurance Commissioners (NAIC)

State insurance regulators belong to this organization, which coordinates insurance regulation among the states.

National Council on Compensation Insurance (NCCI)

The service organization responsible for developing workers compensation insurance loss cost data in most states.

National flood insurance policy
Flood insurance, which may be sold by any licensed insurance agent, is available through a program developed by the federal government but often sold through private insurers.

No-fault auto insurance
Loosely, no-fault insurance means that each policyholder has a right to recover financial losses from his or her own insurance company, regardless of whose fault caused the accident. Strictly, no-fault auto insurance applies only to accidents under a state no-fault law that (1) requires insurance companies to pay policyholders regardless of fault and (2) restricts the ability of accident victims to sue others for their injuries.

No-filing law
Also known as open competition, a form of rate regulation (actually the absence of rate regulation) under which no rate filing is required because insurance regulators neither approve nor disapprove insurance rates.

Nonrenew, nonrenewal
When an insurer decides not to renew a policy at the end of a policy period, this is not a cancellation but a nonrenewal. The insurer "nonrenews" the policy.

Ocean marine insurance
Insurance on ships and their cargoes.

Office manager
See customer service representative.

Open competition
Also known as a no-filing law, a form of rate regulation (actually the absence of rate regulation) under which no rate filing is

required because insurance regulators neither approve nor disapprove insurance rates.

Open-perils
See "all-risks."

Oral evidence
Statements from people—often people who were at the scene of an accident—to help clarify the events surrounding the accident.

Other than collision coverage
Also called comprehensive, covers auto physical damage losses by nonexcluded perils other than collision.

Out-of-court settlement
An out-of-court settlement is arrived at when people negotiate and reach agreement without having a court handle the case. Out-of-court settlements can save everyone time and money.

Package discount
See package policy.

Package policy
An insurance policy combining coverages from two or more individual property and liability policies into a single insurance policy. The premium for a package policy might be lower than the premium for the same coverages purchased separately. This premium reduction is considered a package discount.

PAP
See personal auto policy.

Partnership
An association of two or more persons joined to carry on a business.

Peak season coverage
Property insurance providing different lim-

its of insurance during different periods of the year, to reflect expected seasonal changes in property values.

Perfect homogeneity

Completely identical loss characteristics of all members of a rating class, perfect homogeneity is a theoretical concept that is impossible in practice. *See* homogeneity, workable homogeneity.

Peril

A cause of property losses. Fire is one example of a peril.

Personal articles floater, personal articles floater policy

Also available as a scheduled personal property endorsement to homeowners policies, provides broad coverage for specified items such as jewelry, furs, silverware, and guns.

Personal auto policy, PAP

A specific standard auto policy designed to meet the auto insurance needs of a typical person or family.

Personal injury protection

No-fault coverage that applies to auto-related injuries.

Personal insurance

Insurance coverages purchased by individuals and families to cover nonbusiness exposures.

Personal insurance underwriter

An underwriter who specializes in personal insurance. *See* underwriter.

Personal liability

The general (non-auto-related) liability exposures that accompany a person's non-business activities.

Personal property

Everything except land and buildings and other structures attached to the land. Examples include merchandise, furniture, supplies, stock, and inventory. Sometimes called contents, although most insurance policies covering personal property cover not only property contained in a building but also property near the building.

Physical damage appraiser

Also called material damage appraiser, a person who estimates auto repair costs based on auto parts prices and labor costs.

Physical damage coverage (auto)

Auto physical damage coverage, also known as "damage to your auto" coverage, insures against loss resulting from damage to an auto owned or operated by the insured, and it also provides coverage if the car is stolen. Auto physical damage coverage is property insurance.

Physical evidence

Any tangible thing that is relevant in determining the facts concerning an accident.

Policy

A contract that states the rights and duties of the insurance company and the insured.

Policy limits

Limits, also called limits of insurance, limits of liability, or policy limits, indicate in an application how much insurance is requested. Once the policy is issued, the limits in the policy set the maximum dollar amount the insurance company will pay.

Policy period

The dates during which an insurance policy is in force.

Policy provision

Any statement in an insurance policy.

Policyholder

A person, business, or organization that has purchased insurance.

Premium

See insurance premium.

Premium auditor

A person who examines policyholders' records at the end of the policy period to determine the final, audited premium.

Premium discount

A workers compensation insurance discount applied to the policies on larger businesses to recognize the fact that some of the expenses of selling and servicing workers compensation insurance do not vary in proportion to the premium.

Premium financing
A payment plan that may allow the insured to pay part of the premium when coverage takes effect and pay the rest during the policy period.

Prior approval law
A type of rate regulation under which the state insurance department must approve rate changes before they can be put into effect.

Producer
Anyone who "produces" insurance business by selling insurance. *See* agent, independent agent, exclusive agent, direct writer, and broker.

Producer billing
Also called agency billing, a process through which a bill for the insured is prepared in the producer's office and the premium is paid directly to the producer's office. Meanwhile, the insurance company bills the producer for premiums due on all policies the producer has sold. The producer collects premiums and remits them to the insurance company after deducting the producer's commission.

Products and completed operations liability coverage
Pays for loss resulting from liability (legal responsibility) for bodily injury or property damage that takes place away from the insured's premises and is caused by a product sold by the insured or a service completed by the insured.

Profits
Income that exceeds expenses. All or part of an insurer's profits may be paid to stockholders or policyholders as dividends.

Property insurance
Covers accidental losses resulting from damage to property of the insured. If the loss is covered by the insurance policy, the payment is made directly to the insured.

Proposal
A booklet that highlights the important features of the proposed coverage and related services and states the premium.

Prospect
A person, business, or organization to which a producer hopes to sell insurance. After the sale is completed, the prospect becomes a customer, client, policyholder, or account.

Prospective loss costs
Data indicating the dollar losses, relating to each exposure unit, that can be expected in the future. Prospective loss costs are based on historical loss costs plus some adjustments.

Protection class
Used in pricing property insurance at a particular location, protection class is the rating of the local fire department's capabilities and the availability of fire hydrants and other water supply sources. Protection classes are usually numbered 1 through 10, with 1 being best and 10 having essentially no fire protection.

Provision
Any statement in an insurance policy.

Provisional premium
The premium paid at the beginning of a policy year on a reporting policy, subject to adjustment at the end of the policy year. *See* reporting policy.

Quotation, quote
A statement regarding the premium that will be charged for certain coverage.

R

Rate

The price of insurance for each unit of exposure. The rate is multiplied by the number of exposure units to arrive at a premium.

Rate filings

Documents submitted ("filed") with a state insurance department that contain the proposed rates and also, when necessary, the statistics on which the rates are based.

Rate regulation

The control by state insurance regulators over the rates and classification and rating systems used by insurers.

Rate suppression

When government regulators hold insurance rates at a level below their true economic cost.

Rater, rating clerk

A person who calculates insurance premiums with the aid of a computer, and possibly also using a calculator and a rating manual.

Rating manual

A book or computer program used in determining premiums.

Real property

Land and buildings and other structures attached to the land.

Regional office

A local insurance company office, usually located away from the home office, providing service in a specified geographical area.

Regulation

See insurance regulation and rate regulation.

Reinsurance, reinsurer

An agreement by one insurer (the primary insurer) with another insurer (the reinsurer) with which a risk is shared.

Renewal questionnaire

A form that asks questions about changes during the past coverage period.

Rental reimbursement coverage (auto)

Pays the cost of renting a substitute for a car disabled in an accident.

Replacement cost, replacement cost value

The current replacement cost of a building is the amount it would cost to construct the building today using materials of the same kind and quality, with no deduction for depreciation. The replacement cost of a house does not include the value of the land because the land itself will not be damaged by most perils.

Reporting coverage, reporting policy

Property insurance that requires monthly (or other period) reports to the insurance company stating the current values of insured property. Premiums are based on the values reported. A provisional premium is collected at the beginning of the year; the final premium is computed based on the average of the monthly values reported.

Residual market

Applicants rejected by underwriters in the voluntary market might find insurance available through residual market programs such as auto insurance plans and FAIR plans. Some residual market programs have been formed by government bodies to provide insurance for those who could not otherwise get it. Also called shared market.

Retention

Retention, also called self-insurance, involves paying losses with one's own funds rather than purchasing insurance.

Retirement plans

Retirement plans, including employer-sponsored pension plans and individual annuities, provide income for people who retire. Plans that guarantee income for life, no matter how long the person may live, are provided through life insurance companies.

Risk
The possibility of financial loss.

Risk management consultant
A person or organization providing expert advice to corporations regarding how their risks should be treated.

Risk manager, risk management department
A risk manager is responsible for preserving a firm's assets against accidental losses of various kinds. Risk managers buy insurance, promote sound loss control, and manage retention (self-insurance) programs for their employer's organization. Large firms might have a risk management department involving many employees, and small organizations might have just one person who performs both risk management duties and other responsibilities.

Robbery
A type of theft committed by someone who threatens a person and forces him or her to give money or other property to the thief.

Safety engineer
See loss control representative.

Sales representative
See producer.

Schedule rating
Underwriters may use schedule rating if they are permitted to "schedule" or assign credits (discounts) or debits (surcharges) when they can identify some characteristics that are not considered in the established rating system but that affect the loss potential of a particular insured.

Scheduled personal property endorsement
See personal articles floater.

Self-insurance
Rather than transferring its risks to an insurance company or anyone else, a business pays for all losses with its own resources.

Self-insured retention, SIR
In a personal or commercial umbrella policy, a deductible that applies to liability losses not covered by other policies.

Shared market
See residual market.

SIR
See self-insured retention.

Social Security
A federal insurance program that provides (1) monthly income to retired people, (2) monthly income to the dependent survivors of workers who die before retirement, (3) monthly income to disabled workers, and (4) Medicare health care benefits to people age sixty-five and older.

Soft market
The time period during an insurance cycle during which insurance prices are lower and insurance is readily available.

Sole proprietorship
A business owned and operated by an individual.

Special homeowners policy
A homeowners policy that covers loss to the building from all perils except for those specifically excluded. Personal property coverage is for specified perils, the same as in the broad form homeowners policy.

Special property policy
See "all-risks."

Specified perils
Specified perils property policies cover any loss that is caused by one or more of the covered perils that is named (specified) in

the policy. The burden of proof is on the insured. To prove that a loss is covered, the insured must prove that it was caused by one of the perils described (specified). Compare "all-risks" and burden of proof.

Staff underwriting activities

Underwriting activities involving decisions on an insurance company's entire set of accounts. Staff underwriters' decisions are published in underwriting guidelines used by line underwriters.

Stock

See inventory.

Stock insurance companies

Insurance companies owned by stockholders, also called shareholders, who have invested in the insurance company by purchasing shares of stock. Stockholders hope the value of their stock will increase. They also might receive a share of the insurance company's profits in the form of dividends.

Submission

The package of materials that will go to the underwriter as part of a request for a quote (or a request for insurance). An app (application) is usually the most important part of the submission.

Subrogate, subrogation

When the insurer pays the insured for a loss, the insurer takes over the insured's right to collect damages from the other party responsible for the loss through a process called subrogation. The insurance company may subrogate against the party directly responsible for the loss.

Surplus

The difference between an insurer's admitted assets (assets that may be counted when determining financial condition) and its liabilities. *See* assets and liability (accounting concept).

Survey, survey questionnaire

A survey questionnaire, or survey, is a form that lists a large number of loss exposures often found in businesses. The producer and the insurance buyer use the survey form as a list of possibilities. The business being surveyed is evaluated according to the list to find the actual exposures of the business.

Tape or CD coverage (auto)

Pays for loss to stereo tapes or compact discs in a car.

Tax appraisal value

A dollar figure assigned to property by tax appraisers solely for use in determining property taxes.

Telephone adjuster

Also known as a inside adjuster, a person who settles claims without conducting any outside investigation. An inside adjuster is generally used when the claim is clearly covered and there is no question about the circumstances of the accident or the validity of the claim.

Term

Policy period, the period during which a policy provides coverage.

Theft

Any act of stealing. Burglary, robbery, and employee dishonesty are types of theft.

Time element insurance

Covers loss of business income and other indirect losses resulting from direct damage to property.

Towing and labor coverage (auto)

Pays for road service or towing.

U

Umbrella policy
A liability insurance policy that takes over where basic liability policies leave off. Personal umbrella policies typically provide $1 million or more of coverage on top of auto or homeowners policies. A commercial umbrella policy provides similar coverage for businesses. Umbrella policies usually include a self-insured retention that operates like a deductible. *See* self-insured retention.

Unbundling
When insurance claims adjusting, loss control, risk management, or other services are sold separately rather than being "bundled" together with an insurance policy for which a single premium is charged.

Underwriter
An underwriter evaluates requests for insurance, determining which applicants are accepted and which are rejected, as well as how much coverage the insurer is willing to provide and at what price. A commercial underwriter handles commercial insurance; a personal insurance underwriter handles personal insurance.

Underwriting authority
The limit on decisions an underwriter can make without receiving approval from someone at a higher level.

Underwriting gain, underwriting profit
An underwriting gain, or underwriting profit, occurs when the combined loss and expense ratio is less than 100 (percent). The insurance company, in effect, has money left over after paying losses and meeting expenses.

Underwriting guide, underwriting guidelines, underwriting manual
A book or computer database that communicates staff underwriters' guidelines to the line underwriters who must follow them. It details the underwriting practices of the insurance company and provides specific guidance about how underwriters should analyze all of the various types of applicants they might encounter.

Underwriting loss
When the combined loss and expense ratio is greater than 100 percent. The opposite of an underwriting profit. *See* underwriting gain.

Unearned premium
The money an insurer would have to give back under each policy if it were canceled.

Unearned premium reserve
A liability (in accounting records) that reflects the premium dollars the insurance company would have to give back if all policyholders immediately canceled their insurance.

Unfired pressure vessel
An air pressure tank or other pressurized device with no flame or burner.

Uninsured motorists coverage
A coverage in personal or commercial auto policies that provides protection against bodily injury loss (also property damage in some states) when the insured is injured in an accident with a hit-and-run motorist or a motorist who has no insurance.

Unisex rating
An auto insurance classification and rating

system that provides the same rates for both males and females.

Unit
See exposure units.

Valuation clause
A provision in a property insurance policy stating the method that is used to place a value on damaged property covered by the policy.

Vehicle identification number, VIN
The serial number of a car, usually located on top of the dashboard.

Voluntary market
Applications accepted or rejected voluntarily (without regulatory constraint) by insurance companies are considered to be in the voluntary market.

Workable homogeneity
All insureds in the same class of an insurance classification system are fairly homogeneous. *See* homogeneity.

Workers compensation insurance
Protects employers against financial loss by paying certain benefits required by law to employees who are injured in the course of their employment.

X-date
See expiration date.

Index

D

E

M

N

R